Reflections on the Holocaust

Reflections on the Holocaust

Festschrift
for
Raul Hilberg
on His Seventy-Fifth Birthday

Edited by
Wolfgang Mieder
and
David Scrase

The Center for Holocaust Studies
at the University of Vermont

Burlington, Vermont
2001

The publication of this *Festschrift* has been made possible by various generous contributions. We wish to express particular appreciation to Jerold D. Jacobson, Esq., a former student of Professor Raul Hilberg and 1962 graduate of the University of Vermont, and his wife Gertraude Holle-Suppa who have provided financial support in memory of their recently deceased fathers, Sidney Jacobson and Robert Suppa.

ISBN 0-9707237-4-1

Published by the Center for Holocaust Studies
Old Mill, Room 301
University of Vermont
Burlington, Vermont 05405

Manufactured in the United States of America
by Queen City Printers Inc.
Burlington, Vermont 05401

Raul Hilberg

Table of Contents

Preface

Ever since Professor Raul Hilberg arrived on campus in 1956, he has had a lasting and inspiring influence on the faculty and students of the University of Vermont. For forty-five years his lectures and writings have touched and influenced thousands of listeners and readers not only in Vermont but also throughout the United States and in many countries of the world. Raul Hilberg is without doubt the dean of Holocaust studies in their widest scope, and it is indeed appropriate that his immediate colleagues honor him with a *Festschrift* on the occasion of his seventy-fifth birthday on 2 June 2001.

Professor Hilberg has been honored previously on numerous occasions. There is no need to list all of his richly deserved honors here, but let us at least mention that here at the University of Vermont he occupied the John G. McCullough Chair in Political Science from 1978 until his retirement from active teaching in 1991, that he was honored with the coveted George V. Kidder Outstanding Faculty Award in 1988, and that he received an honorary doctorate degree from his home institution in 1991. This was also the year that members of his university expressed their collective appreciation of his accomplishments by organizing a most memorable symposium on the Holocaust. The proceedings of this special event were subsequently edited by James S. Pacy and Alan P. Wertheimer, long-time colleagues and friends of Raul Hilberg, in a significant volume entitled *Perspectives on the Holocaust: Essays in Honor of Raul Hilberg* (1995).

In order to continue and foster the legacy of Holocaust studies begun by Professor Raul Hilberg, the Center for Holocaust Studies at the University of Vermont was established in 1992 under the directorship of Professor David Scrase of the Department of German and Russian. Professor Howard Ball from the Political Science Department, then Dean of the College of Arts and Sciences, was instrumental in establishing the Center as an administrative unit. David Scrase as its director is assisted in his duties by both the Holocaust Studies Faculty Steering Committee and the Holocaust Studies Advisory Board. It is from these two groups that twelve colleagues and friends have answered our call for contributing an essay to this *Festschrift* honoring Raul Hilberg.

As can be imagined, all contributions are at least to a degree informed by the magisterial writings of Raul Hilberg. Indeed, publications on the Holocaust are impossible without some dependence on the work of this great scholar. His *magnum opus* on *The Destruction of the European Jews* (1961), expanded in 1985 to three volumes, continues to be the standard work on the Holocaust. Of much importance are also his books *Documents of Destruction* (1971), *Sonderzüge nach Auschwitz* (1981), *Perpetrators, Victims, and Bystanders: The Jewish Catastrophe, 1933-1945* (1992), and his autobiography *Politics of Memory: The Journey of a Holocaust Historian* (1996). But this is not the place to refer to and to comment upon the many publications (and their translations in numerous languages) that Raul Hilberg has penned during a period of about forty-five years since earning his Ph.D. degree in 1955 from Columbia University in New York City. Suffice it to say that Raul Hilberg is an eminent scholar and superb mentor of peers and students alike, a colleague and a friend who deserves our deepest respect and sincerest admiration.

We will also refrain from commenting on the twelve essays included in this celebratory volume. Their titles speak for themselves as their contents continue the pioneering work of Professor Raul Hilberg. As is the case with every *Festschrift*, the individual articles cover a wide variety of subject matters by scholars from various fields of interest. While the Holocaust is a common theme to all of them, they concern themselves with different aspects of this dark period during the twentieth century. It is for this reason that we as editors have decided to arrange the essays in alphabetical order according to their authors. The papers stand as individual studies on the Holocaust, but as a group of articles they pay honor and respect to Professor Raul Hilberg as he celebrates his seventy-fifth birthday and a life dedicated to the study of the Holocaust.

Summer 2001   Wolfgang Mieder
                                                                               David Scrase

Essays

Nazi *Justiz*

The Destruction of Individual Rights in Germany, 1933-1945

Howard Ball

On 13 July 1934, Adolf Hitler declared in the *Reichstag*: "Whenever someone reproaches me with not having used the ordinary court for their sentencing, I can only say: 'In this hour I am responsible for the fate of the German nation and hence [I am] the supreme law lord of the German people'" (quoted in Friedman 1972, II, 1220). The primary task of Germany's *Führer*, Hitler said, was to preserve, promote, and protect the racial purity of the German people (Lippman 1993, 260). In carrying out this primary task, Hitler quickly transmuted the machinery of justice that existed in Germany when he assumed power. German law, lawyers, prosecutors, and judges were enveloped by the Nazi Party; most became willing accomplices in the destruction of the European Jews

Nazis were Germans who fervently believed in and accepted without constraint the ideology of National Socialism. It had five essential features: Racial supremacy; a homogeneous *Volk* social community; obedience to a charismatic *Führer*; the need to conquer "living space" for the *Volk* state; and the creation of a Third Reich that would last for a thousand years (Fischer 1998, 131). The 1920 platform of the Nazi Party contained the core of the anti-Jewish policy implemented when Hitler became Chancellor in late January 1933. Points 4-6, and 8 dealt directly with the "Jewish Problem." Citizenship in the *Volk* state was "only for those of German blood. Accordingly no Jew may be a member of the nation." (Point 4) Non-citizens, i.e., Jews, could live in Germany but only as "guests" of the nation. (Point 5) The right to vote was a right of citizenship. (Point 6) All non-German immigration must be prevented (Point 8) (Friedländer 1997, 26).

For the Nazi, the "Jew was considered an outward manifestation of [an] inherent biological deficiency" (Miller 1995, 4). Only by destroying this mortal enemy, the germ carrying parasitic Jew, could the German *Volk* State be preserved. "In Hitler's eyes, the Jews were Germany's principal adversary" and had to be destroyed (Hilberg 1985, 10). The destruction of the Jews, Raul Hilberg taught us, "was an administrative process, . . . a series of administrative measures, begun in February 1933, aimed at a definite group" (Hilberg 1985, 27).

1. The Destruction Process

Hilberg's research showed that the "destruction process has an inherent [three-step] pattern" (Hilberg 1985, 267-269). The first step was the *definition* of the group that had to be destroyed for the State to survive. The "Jew" was defined, with two exceptions (Klemperer 1998), by decree and in the law as a person "descending from two Jewish grandparents belonging to the Jewish religion or married to a Jewish person on 15 September 1935, and persons descended from three or four Jewish grandparents" (Hilberg 1985, 38). The exceptions involved the two categories of Mischlinge: second degree, that is, a person descended from one Jewish grandparent, and first degree, a person descended from two Jewish grandparents who were not religious Jews, and not married to a Jewish person on 15 September 1935 (Hilberg 1985, 38).

Accompanying that definition of "Jew" was Hitler's "insistence not to exempt any segment of Jewry from the application of anti-Jewish measures. No Jew was to be overlooked in the dragnet." There was the imperative need to ostracize the Jew in Germany; to separate Jew from German. "The complex relationships between Jews and non-Jews [had] to be severed with least harm to individual Germans and to the economy as a whole." (Hilberg 1992, 20) That meant, for example, that restrictive edicts aimed at Jewish physicians had to be postponed – briefly – because of the adverse impact on German patients. "Thousands of Jewish doctors meant tens of thousands of German patients. Disrupting the ties between these physicians and a vast number of patients could have caused unnecessary discontent. Hitler preferred to wait." (Friedländer 1997, 32)

The second step in the destruction of the Jews was the need to *concentrate* the Jews (for ease in managing them) in ghettos. "Ghettoization" had a double purpose in the occupied countries, especially Poland and Eastern Europe: "To isolate disease and to kill Jews." Concentrating Polish Jews in ghettos led to the death of between 35% to 40% of Polish Jewry.

"Ghettoization killed as effectively, if not as efficiently, as the death camps" (Glass 1997, XVI).

The third step in this planned destruction process was the "final solution:" *annihilation* of the Jews – first civil, i.e., legal death, and then the planned physical annihilation in the death camps. Murder of group members based on race, color, religion, etc., occurred throughout history. What made the Nazi destruction of the Jews "unprecedented" was their "subjection of Jews to a degrading regimen of shame, humiliation, and loss of identity, before actually killing them" (Bauer 2001, 27). This "systematic humiliation" of the German Jews took place through the implementation of decrees and laws that peeled away all rights enjoyed by citizens.

At the September 1935 Nazi Party Conference, held in Nuremberg, Hitler promulgated two significant decrees. They marked, in practical and symbolic ways, the civil death of Jews in the Third Reich. The first was the Citizenship Law, which deprived all "not of German blood" of their rights as citizens in the Third Reich. There was also the Law for the Protection of German Blood and German Honor. The first paragraph stated: "Marriage between Jews and citizens of German or related kinds of blood is forbidden. Marriages contracted in violation of this rule are null and void." This "blood law" provided prison sentences for both partners; either prison or the concentration camp because the race was dishonored. While there was no death penalty attached to violators of the law, those dishonoring the race, always the Jewish defendant, were often sentenced to death.

This was done, according to detailed instructions from the Ministry of Justice, by combining the 1935 blood law with two 1933 decrees: The Law on Dangerous Habitual Criminals and the Decree on Asocial Elements. If a person was convicted of a premeditated crime, including racial sexual offenses, he could receive a sentence of *death "if the protection of society and the need for just atonement require it"* (my emphasis) (quoted in Muller 1991, 112).

After these 1935 decrees, discrimination and isolation of the Jews in Nazi Germany grew in intensity and ferocity (Muller 1991,116). And, in 1941, came the "final solution," the physical extermination of the Jews. The killings, Hilberg recorded, "had to be conducted in a manner that would limit psychological repercussions in the ranks of the perpetrators, prevent unrest among the victims, and preclude anxiety or protest in the non-Jewish population" (Hilberg 1992, 21).

Hilberg also taught us that the participants in the destruction process came from all strata of society, from all walks of life, from all occupations. "Functionaries were needed in the destruction process across the entire *Volk,* including doctors and lawyers" (Hilberg 1992, 21). This essay examines the role of the German legal community in the destruction of European Jewry.

2. February-March 1933: The End of Constitutional Government in Germany

Constitutional systems place a premium on the inalienable rights of persons in society. The hallmarks of constitutional governments such as Germany's Weimar Republic, 1918-1933, included the subjection of state authority to the Rule of Law, the equality of all citizens before the law, as well as certain inviolable rights such as speech, assembly, personal privacy, and religion. That western concept was buried when the Nazis came to power at the end of January 1933.

Hitler "despised lawyers." He perceived them "as pencil pushers who filled whole volumes with tangled commands" (quoted in Muller 1991, 295). He "viewed the law as a pragmatic mechanism to advance the Nazi cause. It was Hitler's anti-democratic, nationalist, racist, and revolutionary principles which formed the foundation of the National Socialist legal system" (Lippman 2000b, 104.). The legal profession was to serve as the "guardian of the law;" its sole function was to safeguard the interests of the *Volk* state.

Like their *Führer*, Nazis were "legal atheists: They did not believe in [traditional] law" (Miller 1995, 2). They disdained the fundamental principles of Roman Law, long followed in Germany and in the rest of Europe. The 1920 Nazi Party platform stated that "Roman law, which serves the individualistic, materialistic world order, must be replaced by a mystical German Common Law," one limited to those of "German blood." (Lippman 1997, 202) Hitler repeatedly dismissed the Roman code as "Romano-Jewish-Byzantine law" (quoted in Lippman 1993, 261).

The decline in respect for the Rule of Law, however, began before Hitler came to power. German courts and judges were notoriously conservative and nationalistic. They were "reluctant participants" in the Weimar Republic (Lippman 1997, 239). The death of the Rule of Law actually began when these conservative German judges, who expressed sympathy for the Nazis in the 1920s, and who had no love of democracy, gave preferential treatment to accused criminals who acted from "nationalistic" motives against the Weimar government. Such gentle judicial treatment from the bench "had disastrous consequences, for they encouraged the radical right and undermined the confidence of the supporters of democracy" (Hilberg 1992, 21).

The end of constitutional government in Germany came about one day after the *Reichstag* fire of 27 February 1933: Hitler issued the *Reichstag* Fire

Decree for the Protection of the People and the State. It was the first of many thousands of decrees issued by the Nazis between 1933 and 1945. It annulled almost all the basic rights of citizens guaranteed by the German Constitution.

5 March 1933 was the last democratic election in Germany until the Second World War's end in Europe. The Nazi Party polled over 17 million votes (44% of the total cast) and, combined with the votes of the ultra-nationalistic Nationalist Party, Hitler had a majority of sixteen votes in the *Reichstag*. The legislature, however, was to cease functioning as an independently elected power in German politics by the end of that same month.

On 24 March 1933, the Law for the Solution of the Emergency of People and Reich, the Enabling Act, was promulgated. It freed Hitler from the written constraints of the Weimar Constitution. The Enabling Act abrogated the traditional separation of powers between the executive (the *Führer*) and the legislature (*Reichstag*); it concentrated all government emergency powers in the Reich Chancellor, totally circumventing the *Reichstag*. The Act deprived Germans of all personal rights: Individual freedom, the right to privacy, speech and assembly, the right to form organizations, the right to own property was suspended. All federal and state limitations on police measures against undesirables were lifted by the Enabling Act (Muller 1991, 47).

The Enabling Act was both the foundation of Nazi rule and "the end of Germany as a constitutional state" (Muller 1991, 34). It gave the cabinet power to promulgate laws and treaties without parliamentary approval for four years. Finally, the Chancellor could deviate from any of the requirements of the Constitution if the public order required such action (Lippman 1997, 202-204).

On 31 March 1933, the Decree for the Protection of the National Socialist Movement against Malicious Attacks on the Government was issued, effectively closing down all political opposition to the Nazis. On 14 July 1933, the Law against a New Formation of Parties was promulgated. This ended political democracy in Germany because the Nazi party by law became the only legal political party in Germany. With this rapid collapse of constitutional democracy in Germany, the role of law, lawyers, and judges took on a new form.

3. From Roman Law to Nazi Law and Jurisprudence

"The original tool for anchoring the destruction process [of the Jews] in a legal framework was the law or decree, i.e., a measure drafted in an agency, coordinated with other agencies insofar as their jurisdiction was touched by the proposed contents, and then published in a legal gazette" (Hilberg 1992,

71). These decrees, statutes, and ordinances, over four thousand of them published in the two first years of the Nazi regime alone, reflected the will of the *Führer*.

As early as April 1933, for the first time since their emancipation in 1871, German Jews experienced the painful reality of formal *governmental* discrimination (Gay 1992, 161-163). After the 1935 Nuremberg decrees, the Jewish community in Germany (*both* secular and religious Jews) was devastated spiritually, civilly, and economically. After 1935, the Nazi version of America's "Jim Crow" system of segregation and separation of black Americans from white Americans was in place. Across the broad spectrum of social interactions, Germans administered to Germans; German Jews administered to German Jews (Glass 1997, xvii) .

In April 1933, the Law for the Restoration of the Professional Civil Service mandated the "retirement" of all "non-Aryan" civil servants, which meant the removal of all Jewish judges, public prosecutors, and lawyers (Lippman 1997, 226-229). Jewish professors were forced out of all German law schools; 120 of a total of 378 faculty. Tenure was abolished for all remaining law professors; they could be removed if they were "politically undesirable." Jewish lawyers were purged from the German bar. (Jews constituted 16% of all lawyers in 1933. Twenty-five per cent of Germany's defense attorneys were Jewish. Sixty per cent of the Berlin bar was Jewish. In Prussia alone, 643 Jewish judges were dismissed.) Throughout the German states (*Länder*), gangs of bullies literally dragged Jewish lawyers, prosecutors, and judges from their courtrooms. Once outside, they were beaten unmercifully (Friedländer 1997, 29).

After March 1933, lawyers in Nazi Germany took a Nazi oath: "I swear to remain loyal to Adolf Hitler, the leader of the German nation and people. And conscientiously to fulfil the duties of a German attorney" (Muller 1991, 64-67). In April 1933, the Association of Prussian Judges proclaimed that its members would "enter the front line of Adolf Hitler's ranks for unconditional solidarity is necessary for the success of the struggle." The Saxony Association of Judges and Public Prosecutors placed itself "jubilantly and dutifully under the leadership of the people's Chancellor, Adolf Hitler" (quoted in Lippman 1997, 233-236).

Interior Minister Wilhelm Frick said that "everything which is useful for the nation is lawful; everything which harms it is unlawful" (Quoted in Lippman 2000b, 116). This totally flexible demarcation between lawful and unlawful conduct was quite ambiguous and thoroughly unsettling for citizens and judges alike (Brecht 1999). As an invidious consequence, usual in a dictatorship that rejects the Rule of Law, "individuals were placed in the perplexing position of being unable to predict when their actions might result in criminal liability" (Lippman 2000b, 114). So too were the prosecutors and judges in Nazi Germany. They regularly needed instructions from the Reich Ministry of Justice as to when a particular type of conduct became unlawful and what the punishment was to be for such unlawful actions.

4. Nazification of the German Judicial System

The German legal system before 1933 had a uniform code of civil and criminal law. The major responsibility for implementing the law was vested in courts located in every federated German State (*Länder*). State leaders selected judges and public prosecutors to administer justice. There were over 2,000 local courts (*Amtsgerichte*) in Germany in 1933. These courts had original jurisdiction to hear minor civil cases and criminal offenses that arose in each of the states and that were punishable by a jail sentence of a year or less. Each court had a single presiding judge who heard evidence and issued rulings – with the assistance of a lay advisor. Original jurisdiction over more important civil and criminal cases was handled by almost 200 district courts (*Landsgerichte*).

The first level of appellate courts was the district court of appeal (*Oberlandsgerichte*). The president of each district court of appeal also served as the administrative head of all the courts within the district. The *Reichsgericht*, the Supreme Court of the Reich, located in Leipzig, was the "final arbiter of the law." It heard appeals from the lower appellate courts as well as criminal appeals from the trial courts. It also had original jurisdiction over treason cases (Lippman 1993, 280). In less than a year after Hitler gained power in Germany, the Nazification of the German judicial system was completed.

a. The Third Reich's Ministry of Justice

The administration of justice in Nazi Germany was concentrated in the Ministry of Justice. On 16 February 1934, the First Law for the Transfer of the Administration of Justice was promulgated. The Ministry of Justice was given the authority to assume the administration of justice in all the German federated states. The Ministry's major task was to make sure that lawyers, prosecutors, and judges throughout Nazi Germany hewed to the *Führer's* policies and pronouncements. The Roman Law concept of a trial as a clash between opposing views was replaced by the "new legal order," one in which these three participants in the administration of justice in Germany had a unanimity of aim. The Ministry's pronouncement: judges, prosecutors, and defense attorneys must join "as mutually supportive comrades in the fight to preserve law" (Lippman 1997, 217).

Otto Thiereck, the Minister of Justice after 1941, because of his distrust of the judges, regularly issued confidential guidelines for them, called "Judge's Letters" (*Richterbriefe*). These confidential letters, first distributed in September 1942, were "filled with exhortations to the utmost ruthfulness in the imposition of sentences" (Miller 1995, 51). Thiereck's letters usually consisted of examples of cases where the prosecutor or the judge failed to follow the Nazi policy position; the letters were intended to instruct all prosecutors and judges how to act in these cases.

Nevertheless, the Justice Ministry bureaucracy also routinely issued instructions to prosecutors concerning the appropriate punishment in all major criminal trials taking place across Germany. The prosecutor, in turn, informed the judge of the Ministry's view *prior to the trial*. Additionally, Hitler declared that he would directly intervene in the judicial process "when the judges do not understand the demand of the hour" (quoted in Lippman 1997, 235). The Nazi judges handling criminal cases quickly learned the "demand of the hour." Acquittals in the regular criminal courts declined from 13% in 1932 to less than 7% in 1940.

b. Nazi "Justiz"

The main task of the lawyers, prosecutors, and judges in Nazi Germany was to act in concert to protect the racial purity of the German people. They had to insure that there was an absolute separation of the Aryan from the Jewish race in order to prevent the "betrayal of the race" (quoted in Muller 1991, 90). To that end, the meaning of decrees and laws was continually expanded, interpreted broadly, by the judges (with guidance from the Ministry of Justice).

For example, in a series of court decisions construing the 1935 Law for the Protection of German Blood and Honor, "a measure that prohibited entry into marriage as well as extramarital relations between Jews and Germans," criminal conduct changed regularly. Sexual intercourse did not have to be consummated to trigger the criminal provisions of the law; sexual gratification of one of the persons in the presence of another was sufficient. Touching or even looking might be enough. Even having coffee together in a public café became a criminal offense. The reasoning: "the law covered not only blood but also honor, and a German, specifically a German woman, was dishonored if a Jew made advances toward her or exploited her sexually in any way" (Hilberg 1992, 72).

A legal provision, if it "plainly fell short of covering a problem," could be applicable by the judge using the "analogy principle" (Hilberg 1992, 72-73).

Nazi judges "also arbitrarily presumed facts and broadly interpreted statutes in order to convict defendants of crimes carrying the death penalty" (Lippman 1993, 296).

c. Some Significant Nazi Judicial Decrees and Laws

As already noted, the Nazi regime promulgated thousands of decrees and laws between 1933 and 1945 to maintain total control over every aspect of German life. In 1933, the death sentence was authorized in the Law for the Protection against Violent Political Acts. It was authorized for a number of crimes to replace existing laws that did not allow capital punishment. Judges were authorized to sentence a defendant to death "whenever milder penalty has been prescribed hitherto." On 24 April 1934, the meaning of "high treason" against the German *Volk* was greatly expanded and the death sentence was authorized in many instances. It gave immense discretionary power to the sentencing judge. Section 83 of the revised Law defining High Treason stated, in part, that the death penalty shall be inflicted "if the act was directed toward influencing the masses by making or distributing writings, recordings, or pictures, or by the installation of wireless telegraph or telehone" (Friedman 1972, II, 1215).

After 1934, existing sections of the German Penal Code were amended to provide for the death penalty. For example, Section 90 (f) said that "whoever publicly, or as a German abroad, causes serious danger to the reputation of the German nation by an untrue or grossly inaccurate statement, shall be punished by confinement in a penitentiary." In September 1934 it was amended: "In especially serious cases a German may be punished by death."

A final example: On 28 June 1935, the Law to Change the Penal Code was enacted. It was a total "repudiation of the rule that criminal statutes should be definite and certain. [It] vested in the judge a wide discretion in which Party political ideology and influence were substituted for the control of law as the guide to judicial decision." Article 2 said, in part, that "if no specific penal law can be directly applied to this act, then it shall be punished according to the law whose underlying principle can be most readily applied to the act" (Friedman 1972, II, 1216).

d. Creation of the Special Courts (Sondergerichte)

In March 1933, the Ministry of Justice created Special Courts with jurisdiction over most of the ordinary criminal cases, including (after 1939) offenses against the war economy and acts which threatened public welfare during wartime. In addition, these courts had exclusive authority to hear cases involving the "opponents of the new Regime."

They consisted of a president and two associates, all jurists. The courts were located in the territory covered by each regular district court in Germany. With the creation of these courts, public prosecutors had the option of taking their case into either the regular court or the Special court. Most chose to move their cases into the Special courts that sprang up during the Third Reich's existence.

These courts were not constrained by conventional procedures or legal doctrines, however perverted these became after Hitler took power. There was no provision for legal appeal of their rulings. Punishment generally took place within 24 hours of conviction and sentencing. After 1940, this Special court's jurisdiction was extended to all crimes that were "severe, notorious, or a threat to public safety" (Lippman 2000b, 111).

In July 1933, the Nazis issued a Law for the Prevention of Progeny with Hereditary Diseases, essentially a decree that provided for the sterilization of mentally retarded Germans. Almost 200 special Hereditary Health (Eugenics) Courts were created by the Ministry to implement the provisions of the 1933 law.

In April 1934, the People's Court decree created the special People's Court, which replaced the German Supreme Court as the tribunal of first and the last resort in all treason trials. It was a five-person panel: two Nazi judges and three lay members (who were Nazi Party members or military loyalists). Dressed in red robes, until then worn only by the *Reichsgericht* judges, they were guided solely by politics, not law. Its objective was not to dispense impartial justice "but to annihilate the enemies of National Socialism." Between 1937 and 1944, this Court heard over 14,000 important cases; over 5,200 defendants were sentenced to death during this time.

Between 1942 and 1944, more than half of the defendants brought before the People's Court were sentenced to death (Lippman 1997, 251-254). These defendants were sentenced to death under paragraph five of the Decree on Martial Law. That decree imposed the sentence of death on anyone who "publicly attempts to paralyze or undermine the will of the German Nation to defend itself."

As the war continued, the Nazis found ordinary crimes dramatically increasing. Crime had become, by 1942, a severe problem in the Third Reich. In 1937, there were little more than 18,000 criminal cases; by 1942, there were 288,000 criminal cases. Juvenile crimes in 1940 totaled about 21,000; by 1942, they had increased to almost 53, 000 cases.

Another major decree led to a dramatic increase in the number of death sentences meted out by German judges. The defendants were foreign nationals accused of criminal acts in the nations occupied by the Nazi military forces. In December 1941, the infamous *Nacht und Nebel* (NN), Night and Fog, Decree was proclaimed by the Nazi regime "in order to deter resistance to the Nazi regime and to instill fear among the population" (Lippman 1997, 288-289). It called for the death sentence for all criminal acts committed by non-Aryans against the Third Reich or its occupation forces in Europe. The People's Court heard these cases in a totally secretive manner; there were no public hearings.

Implementation of the NN decree led to the deportation and execution of thousands of Poles, Jews, and other civilians. Arrested by the State Police, the Gestapo, they were brought to Germany, prosecuted, imprisoned in cruel and inhuman conditions and sentenced to death. "They were held incommunicado and denied due process of law, denied the right to introduce evidence, to be represented by counsel and to be informed of the charges against them. Records were not maintained of the defendants' trials, imprisonment, or fates" (Lippman 2000b, 178). More than half of them were sentenced to death.

5. The Post-War Trials of Nazi War Criminals

In Moscow, November 1943, the allied powers (America, Great Britain, and Russia) agreed to punish the leading political and military leaders of the Nazi regime when the war ended. Initially, the thought was to summarily execute thousands of them. However, by the winter of 1944-1945, President Franklin D. Roosevelt, Prime Minister Winston Churchill, and Chairman Josef Stalin, agreed on the creation of an international war crimes tribunal to try the major Nazi leaders (Ball 1999, 44-53 passim).

Almost two dozen major Nazi war criminals were prosecuted before the International Military Tribunal, held in Nuremberg, Germany, in 1945 (Ball 1999, 54-68 passim). Lower-level Nazi criminals "were prosecuted before courts [both civil and military] in the countries in which they committed their catastrophic acts" (Lippman 2000a, 3-5). These trials took place in the four zones of Germany occupied by the allied powers, as well as in Great Britain, France, Russia, Canada, Poland, Norway, and the Netherlands.

The United States conducted 12 multi-defendant trials of lower level Nazi Party and military officials in the American-occupied zone in Germany: The Medical case; the Milch case; the Justice case; the Flick case; the Farben case; the Hostage case; the RuSHA case, the *Einsatzgruppen* case, the High Command case; the Ministries case; the Krupp case, and the Southeast or Hostages case (Avalon Project 1996). In the end, 177 men and women were brought to trial, 142 were convicted, and 25 executed after trial (Ball 1999, 56). One of the trials involved charges brought against sixteen

Nazi judges, prosecutors, and judicial administrators. It was referred to as the "Justice" case; one of the defendants was *Landgerichtsdirektor* Oswald Rothaug.

a. The "Justice" Case: U.S. v. Josef Altstoetter, et al. (1947)

The Americans' jurisdiction to arrest, indict, try and punish those Nazis found guilty was based on the Allies' creation of the Allied Control Council (ACC) after the unconditional surrender of Nazi Germany in May 1945. The ACC was the international authority charged with reconstructing Germany and with punishing Nazi war criminals. To these ends, the ACC promulgated Control Council Law 10, which defined the jurisdictional, procedural and substantive powers of all tribunals created by the allied nations to try accused Nazi war criminals.

Control Council Law No. 10, dated and signed by the four allied powers in Berlin on 20 December 1945, was formally called "Punishment of Persons Guilty of War Crimes, Crimes Against Peace, and Against Humanity" (Avalon Project 1996-2000). It was created "in order to provide a uniform set of laws and procedures for prosecuting the remaining German war criminals" (Lippman 2000b, 281).

Law No. 10 contained five Articles. Article II enumerated the actions "recognized as a crime" by the ACC. These included:

crimes against the peace: the "Initiation of invasions of other countries and wars of aggression in violation of international laws and treaties,"

war crimes: "Atrocities or offenses against persons or property constituting violations of the laws or customs of war, including but not limited to, murder, ill treatment or deportation to slave labor or for any other purpose," and

crimes against humanity: "Atrocities and offences, including but not limited to murder, extermination, enslavement, deportation, imprisonment, torture, rape, or other inhumane acts committed against any civilian population, or persecutions on political, racial, or religious grounds whether or not in violation of the domestic laws of the country where perpetrated."

Penalties included jail terms and capital punishment. Article III gave the four occupying powers (the United States, Great Britain, Russia, and France) the right to arrest and bring to trial all persons "suspected of having committed a crime" described in Article II. Article IV outlined the legal processes due those arrested and indicted, including opportunities to present witnesses in the defendant's favor.

The "Justice" case was heard by the three-judge Military Tribunal III, established on 14 February 1947 by order of the U.S. Military Governor for

Germany. On 4 January 1947 nine high ranking officials in the Nazi Ministry of Justice and seven judges and prosecutors were indicted by the American prosecutorial team, led by Brigadier General Telford Taylor. The prosecution's task was to demonstrate a pattern of consensual, willing judicial and prosecutorial support for the Nazi programs of persecution, sterilization, extermination and "other gross violations of human rights." Taylor and his staff had to present evidence that the defendants "*consciously furthered*" the implementation of crimes against humanity (Taylor 1992).

The indictment contained four counts:

(1) *conspiracy* to commit war crimes and crimes against humanity, from January 1933 to April 1945 (subsequently dropped by the tribunal because it "was beyond the jurisdiction of this court.")

(2) war crimes,

(3) crimes against humanity,

(4) membership in a criminal organization (Friedman 1972, II, 1196-1199).

At the opening of the trial in March 1947, Taylor observed the "unusual" nature of the prosecution: The defendants were charged with crimes "committed in the name of the law. [They] were the embodiment of what passed for Justice in the Third Reich." The sixteen defendants were charged with "judicial murder and other atrocities which they committed by destroying law and justice in Germany and utilizing emptied forms of legal process for persecution, enslavement, and extermination on a vast scale:"

> The dagger of the assassin was concealed beneath the robe of the jurist. . . .
> The defendants distorted and perverted legal equity and justice in Germany.
> [They transformed the legal system into a[n] integral part of the dictatorship.
> . . . Defendants were bullied, brow-beat and denied elemental rights. [Their trials were] horrible farces, with vestigial remnants of legal procedure which only served to mock the hapless victims (Friedman 1972, II, 1196-1198).

On 15 January 1947, President Harry S. Truman appointed three civilian lawyers to serve as judges of American Military Tribunal III in Nuremberg. They took leaves of absence from their judicial responsibilities and returned to America after the trial concluded in December 1947. The presiding judge was Justin W. Harding, the Assistant Attorney General of Ohio. He was joined by James T. Brand, a Justice of the Oregon Supreme Court, and Malloy Blair, a judge who sat on the Court of Civil Appeals for the Third District of Texas.

The trial took nine months. One hundred thirty-eight witnesses presented oral testimony. The prosecution presented 641 documentary exhibits while the defense presented 1, 452 pieces of evidence. And, as one observer wrote, the evidence was "damning" (Muller 1991, 271). On 4 December 1947, Military Tribunal III rendered its judgment in the "Justice" case. (In December only fourteen defendants remained in the dock. One had committed suicide and a second was dropped from the proceedings because of ill health.) Ten of the fourteen were found guilty on one or two counts (counts two and three); four were sentenced to life in prison and the other six received prison terms of between 5 to 10 years. One of those receiving life imprisonment was Oswald Rothaug. He was found guilty of crimes against humanity while serving as the Presiding Judge of the Special Court in Nuremberg.

b. Defendant Oswald Rothaug

Oswald Rothaug was born on 17 May 1897. He served in the German army during World War I. After the war, he continued his legal education. He passed his final law exam in 1922 and in 1925 passed the State examination for the higher administration of justice. He began his legal career as an assistant judge in a number of courts in his state. In 1927, Rothaug was appointed public prosecutor in Hof in charge of criminal cases.

In 1929, he officiated as prosecutor in the district court in Nuremberg where, in 1933, he became the senior public prosecutor in that court. Later that year, after the Nazi Party gained control of Germany, he was appointed public prosecutor of the district court in Schweinfurt. After he joined the Nazi Party, effective May 1937, he was appointed presiding judge (President) of the Special Court in Nuremberg. From May 1943 until the end of the war, he served as senior prosecutor in the People's Court in Berlin. There he handled major cases of high treason as well as cases involving the undermining of public morale in the *Reich* territories.

From the beginning of the Third Reich, Rothaug was "well-connected in Nazi Party circles" (Lippman 2000b, 186). He also served as a prosecutorial advisor with the Security Police (SD) on legal matters (Friedman 1972, II, 1244). By all accounts, Rothaug was a "tough fanatic who inspired fear even in his prosecutors" (Hilberg 1985, 46).

As the testimony at his trial revealed, Rothaug "enthusiastically embraced National Socialist ideology." The tribunal noted that Rothaug "exhibited an attitude of virulent hostility toward Poles and Jews." He hated them and "this antagonism was illustrated by his advocacy of discriminatory measures against [them], the substance of which," noted the tribunal, "was incorporated into the 1942 Decree Against Poles and Jews" (Friedman 1972, II, 1246-1247).

He was charged under counts two, three, and four (Rothaug was a member of a criminal organization – the Nazi Leadership Corps). The tribunal noted that "the questions to be determined [in Rothaug's case] are: first, whether he had *knowledge* of any crime so established by the evidence in this case; and second, whether he was a *willing participant* in or took a *consenting part* in the Nazi plan for the persecution, oppression, and extermination of Poles and Jews" (my emphasis) (Friedman 1972, II, 1244).

The prosecution presented their case against Rothaug. It was one that included specific cases presided over by him while he was the presiding judge of the Special Court in Nuremberg. Taylor argued that Rothaug's actions in three cases involving Poles and Jews rose to the level of crimes against humanity. In the first case, two female Polish teenagers were arrested in the vicinity of a small, harmless fire in an armaments plant. They were accused, indicted, and prosecuted in Rothaug's Special court in Nuremberg. Rothaug sternly rejected the suggestion of the prosecutor that the two girls, Ms's Durka and Struss, be tried in juvenile court.

They were tried before Rothaug and, in a trial that lasted less than an hour, without effective legal representation, were found guilty by him. Both were sentenced to death, which occurred four days later. The American tribunal concluded that the two youngsters had received a "grossly and fundamentally unfair trial" and were executed simply because they were Poles.

A second case presented, as evidence of Rothaug's criminality, was a trial that involved a Polish farmhand, Mr. Lopata. He was accused of making "indecent advances" to his German employer's wife. He was sentenced to death by Rothaug. In his death sentence ruling, Rothaug stated that Lopata "gives the impression of a thoroughly degenerate personality whose inferiority is based on his being a part of Polish sub-humanity." The Polish man's "insubordination and attack against German Blood and Honor must be met with the death penalty in order to preserve security within the *Reich.*"

A third, and, for the tribunal, a most shocking case Rothaug presided over involved a 68 year old Jewish man and a young, thirty-year-old, German woman. The "record in this case," wrote the tribunal, "shows that Lehmann (Leo) Katzenberger, a merchant and the head of the Jewish community in Nuremberg, was sentenced to death for violating Paragraph 2 of the Decree Against Public Enemies and violating Article 2 of the Law for the Protection of German Blood and Honor."

(The Decree Against Public Enemies stated that "whoever commits a crime or offense against the body, life, or property, taking advantage of air raid protection measures, is punishable by hard labor of up to 15 years or for life, and in particularly severe cases, punishable by death." Article 2 of the Law for the Protection of German Blood and Honor, prohibited Germans and Jews from having sexual intercourse.)

During the Spring 1941 an arrest warrant was issued for Katzenberger. He was accused of having intimate sexual relations with Irene Seiler. "According to the results of the police inquiry, actual intercourse had not been proved, and Katzenberger denied the charge." Seiler told the police that her family had known the defendant for many years before she came to Nuremberg and that "his relationship to her was a friendly and fatherly one; [she] denied the charge of sexual intercourse." He once gave her a bouquet of flowers, and once took her for coffee. They smoked the same brand of cigarettes, but there was nothing sinister or sexual about their relationship. It was, she told the investigating judge, a "friendly, fatherly relationship." After examining all this information, the investigating judge, Hans Groben, told Katzenberger's lawyer that it was "the right time to move against the warrant of arrest."

Rothaug, however, immediately "ordered that the Katzenberger case be transferred from the criminal division [district] court to [his] Special Court." Rothaug was going to send the "syphilitic Jew" to his death, a witness recounted during Rothaug's 1947 trial. According to another witness, even though there were two Associate judges sitting on the case (Dr.'s Ferber and Hoffmann), Rothaug ran the show. He "dominated the prosecution, especially through his close association with the senior Public Prosecutor, Dr. Schroeder."

Rothaug told the assistant prosecutor, Hermann Markl, that, in Rothaug's eyes, "there was sufficient proof of sexual intercourse to convince him, and that he was prepared to condemn Katzenberger to death." Katzenberger was then charged with race defilement and with an additional count under the Decree against Public Enemies, which made the death sentence permissible.

Prior to the start of the trial, Rothaug spoke with the medical Counsellor for the court, the prosecution's medical expert, Dr. Armin Baur. The judge told the doctor that he wanted to sentence Katzenberger to death and that the doctor had to examine the defendant with that in mind. The exam was, said Rothaug, a "mere formality since the Jew would be beheaded anyhow." When Baur protested, pointing to the defendant's age and that "it seemed questionable whether he could be charged with race defilement, Rothaug stated: 'It is sufficient for me that the swine said that a German girl sat on his lap and that he kissed her on the cheek.' "

The trial itself, held in March 1942, was a circus. The tribunal noted that it "was in the nature of a political demonstration. High Party officials attended, including Reich Inspector Oexle." Rothaug "encouraged" witnesses to incriminate the defendant and, on one occasion, the judge gave the audience "a lecture on the subject of the Jewish question." After the evidence was presented, Rothaug spoke to the prosecutor again. From evidence and testimony presented in 1947, Rothaug "made it clear that he expected the prosecution to ask for a death sentence." Rothaug gave the prosecutor "written suggestions as to what he should include in his arguments." The prosecutor asked for death for Katzenberger and Rothaug sentenced the man to death. The sentence was carried out three months later. In his order, Rothaug said:

> The Jew's racial pollution amounts to a grave attack on the purity of German blood, the object of the attack being the body of a German woman. [He is] a people's parasite. [His action constituted] an attack on the security of the national community during an emergency. The only response to the defendant's frivolity is the imposition of the death penalty.

The tribunal's judgment noted that "the evidence establishes beyond a reasonable doubt that Katzenberger was condemned and executed because he was a Jew; and Durka, Struss, and Lopata met the same fate because they were Poles. The defendant Rothaug was *the knowing and willing instrument* in the Nazi regime's program of persecution and extermination. . . . Rothaug's trials lacked the essential elements of legality." Rothaug, concluded the tribunal, was "the personification of the secret Nazi intrigue and cruelty." He was "a sadistic and evil man" and his Court was an "instrumentality of terror which won the fear and the hatred of the population" (my emphasis).

The judges concluded that Rothaug was not guilty of violating counts two and four, but found him guilty of committing crimes against humanity (count three). "The evidence as to the character and activities of the defendant is voluminous." There were *absolutely* no "mitigating circumstances" in his case, the Tribunal concluded. The defendant Rothaug

> took a consenting part in the plan for the prosecution, oppression, and extermination of Poles and Jews. His attitude of virulent hostility toward those races is proved from many sources and is in no wise shaken by the affidavits he has submitted on his own behalf. . . . He identified himself with the Nazi's national program and gave himself utterly to its accomplishment. He participated in the crime of genocide (Friedman 1972, II, 1245-1246).

Rothaug was unrepentant. In his closing statement to the tribunal he claimed that he acted "with a pure heart and without malice. I applied the laws of my country in the manner in which they were intended, to the best of my conscience and belief. We were no specialists in crimes against humanity, and no proof has been furnished in any single case that, in any connection, we had applied an illegal method" (Friedman 1972, II, 1265).

He was sentenced to life imprisonment for crimes against humanity in December 1947. However, less than a decade later (1956), Rothaug was released from prison. And he was the *last* of the ten convicted jurists to be released.

6. Conclusion

Dr. Lothar Kreyssig, a judge on the Court of Guardianship in the town of Brandenburg *an der* Havel, evidently was the only judge known to have openly resisted Nazi control of the judiciary. (Two other judges resisted the Reich but involved themselves in the German resistance to Hitler. Both of them, Dr. Karl Sack, a member of the Military Court Panel for Treason and High Treason, and Dr. Johann von Dohnanyi, a Supreme Court judge, were caught and executed by the Nazis.) *No other judge* resigned in protest or pled ill-health to avoid serving on the Nazi bench between 1933 and 1945.

Kreyssig, a member of the Confessional Church, publicly protested the arrest of German theologian Martin Niemoller (who was subsequently executed for high treason). He publicly stated that the Nazi regime's religious policies were "injustice masquerading in the form of law." He had the audacity to send a letter to the President of the Prussian Supreme Court protesting the continued execution of inmates at mental hospitals and German concentration camps. He issued injunctions against mental hospitals prohibiting them from relinquishing custody over their resident wards without his permission. In addition, he filed criminal charges against the Nazi party leader responsible for the regime's euthanasia program. All his actions were fruitless. However, he was not executed by the *Gestapo*. He was forced to resign his position. However, he received his full pension rights (Lippman 1997, 244-247).

Kreyssig was the exception that proved the rule, as Hilberg noted in his penultimate book: Professional jurists in Germany during National Socialism believed they were doing justice by obeying the Nazi decrees and laws and that, if they had not, Germany would have evolved into a totally lawless society (Hilberg 1985, 74). The judges, prosecutors, and judicial administrators on trial at Nuremberg refused to acknowledge that their actions were criminal. They insisted, to the end, that they were professionals who had "mechanically" applied legal principle in cases before them (Lippman 1997, 301-304 passim).

Richard A. Posner, a highly respected U.S. Court of Appeals judge, recently accounted for the failure of German justice from 1933 through 1945.

The story of the German judges can help us to see that judges should not be eager enlisters in popular movements of the day, or allow themselves to become so immersed in a professional culture that they are oblivious to the human consequences of their decisions.

Literature Cited

Avalon Project at Yale Law School. 1996-2000. *The Nuremberg War Crimes Trials.* http://www. Yale. edu/lawweb/avalon/imt/imt.htm.

Ball, Howard. 1999. *Prosecuting War Crimes and Genocide: The Twentieth Century Experience.* Laurence, Kansas: University Press of Kansas.

Bauer, Yehuda. 2001. *Rethinking the Holocaust.* New Haven, Connecticut: Yale University Press.

Brecht, Bertolt. 1939. *Fear and Misery of the Third Reich.* London: Methuen.

Fischer, Klaus P. 1998. *The History of An Obsession: German Judeophobia and the Holocaust.* New York: Continuum Press.

Friedländer, Saul. 1997. *Nazi Germany and the Jews, Volume One: The Years of Persecution.* New York: HarperCollins.

Friedman, Leon, ed. 1972. *The Law of War, A Documentary History – Volume II.* New York: Random House.

Gay, Ruth. 1994. *The Jews of Germany: A Historical Portrait.* New Haven, Connecticut: Yale University Press.

Glass, James M. 1997. *"Life Unworthy of Life": Racial Phobia and Mass Murder in Hitler's Germany.* New York: HarperCollins.

Hilberg, Raul. 1985. *The Destruction of European Jewry.* New York: Holmes and Meier.

Hilberg, Raul. 1992. *Perpetrators, Victims, Bystanders:The Jewish Catastrophe, 1933-1945.* New York: HarperCollins.

Klemperer, Victor. 1998. *I Will Bear Witness: A Diary of the Nazi Years, Volume I: 1933-1941.* New York: Random House.

Lippman, Matthew. 1993. "They Shoot Lawyers, Don't They?: Law in the Third *Reich* and the Global Threat to the Independence of the Judiciary." *California Western International Law Journal* 23: 135-272.

Lippman, Matthew. 1997. "Law, Lawyers, and Legality in the Third Reich." *Temple International and Comparative Law Journal* 11: 1999-2137.

Lippman, Matthew. 2000a. "Prosecutions of Nazi War Criminals before Post-World War II Domestic Trials. *Yearbook of International Law* 8: 1-97.

Lippman, Matthew. 2000b. "The White Rose: Judges and Justice in the Third Reich." *Connecticut Journal of International Law* 15: 1-135.

Miller, Richard L. 1995. *Nazi Justiz: Law of the Holocaust.* Westport, Connecticut: Praeger Publishing Co.

Muller, Ingo. 1991. *Hitler's Justice: The Courts of the Third Reich.* Cambridge, Massachusetts: Harvard University Press.

Taylor, Telford. 1992. *The Anatomy of the Nuremberg Trials: A Personal Memoir.* New York: A.A. Knopf.

The Treatment of Ukrainian Jews
by Forces of the
Seventeenth German Army Command:

22 June - 31 July 1941

Robert Bernheim

The womb of dawn exploded with a deafening barrage. At precisely 03:15 on 22 June 1941, thousands of German guns and artillery pieces commenced a massive fusillade by targeting established border fortifications, roads, communication junctions, and areas of high Red Army troop concentrations (*BA-MA*, RH 20-17/23). With *Luftwaffe* bombers streaking overhead, and the curtain of heavy shelling shifting to the rear, the men and combat engineers of the Seventeenth German Army Command (*AOK 17*) swept through the Galician border region of Poland, and into the territory of the Soviet Union behind rapidly advancing columns of armor. "Operation Barbarossa" was underway in western Ukraine (*BA-MA*, RH 20-17/38).

Within a month, the Seventeenth Army Command, under the direction of General Karl Heinrich von Stülpnagel, slashed southeast and captured Lemberg (L'viv), Tarnopol (Ternopil'), Proskurov (Khmel'nits'kiy – Proskuriv), and Vinnica (Vinnytsia), while successfully breaching the entrenched fortifications of the Stalin Line. During this time, at least 540,000 Jews in the *shtetlekh* and cities along the front came under the authority of *AOK 17* (Altshuler 1998, 226-227, 329-330). By the spring of 1942, a majority of these Jews were dead, murdered, in large part, by the security forces of the *SS*, the Police, and their eastern European collaborators in the wake of the advancing *Wehrmacht*. (see Hilberg 1985, 273-335; Krausnick and Wilhelm 1985; Arad, Krakowski, and Spector 1989; Headland 1992; Gitelman 1997; and Pohl 1997).

Leading scholars and historians have noted that these mobile killing actions against Jews could only have occurred with the logistical and tactical support, and oftentimes collaborative, effort of the German armed forces. As Raul Hilberg states: "This cooperation was all the more remarkable because the Security police had expected little more than grudging acquiescence in the killing operations" (Hilberg 1985, 301). However, in the hundreds of pages of official war diaries (*Kriegstagebücher, KTB*) produced by the nine forward German infantry divisions of von Stülpnagel's army through July 1941, there is virtually no mention of collaboration with the *SS*, nor any description of actions against the thousands of Jews whose villages and towns they fought through and captured. The envelope of silence in the official war diaries extends through the chain of command to the corps and army levels as well.

We may know where, when, and how Jews were murdered, but we have rather limited knowledge of what proceeded the destruction of the Jewish communities in western Ukraine. Were the motives of the *Wehrmacht* different from the *Einsatzgruppen*? What role did the German army play in preparing the way for the killing operations? Did the *Wehrmacht* participate only in occasional random acts of violence and terror? Were they killing Jews as reprisal for alleged *NKVD* (People's Commissariat of Internal Affairs – Soviet Secret Police) and Red Army killings of German POWs, or were the activities of the military units in keeping with the full scope of a declared ideological and racial war to eliminate Bolshevism and exterminate Soviet Jewry (*BA-MA*, RW-4, v.578)?

The focus of this paper will be to investigate these questions using a combination of primary source documents and eyewitness accounts. By triangulating data from the war diaries about troop movement and location, and other military records with personal manuscripts and testimonies by Ukrainian Jewish survivors, a comprehensive portrait of the first month of the German invasion unfolds.

The first section of this paper examines the content of the war diaries. Simply because the official reports omit *Wehrmacht* responses toward Jews does not mean that they lack value to the historian. On the contrary, even without direct mention of actions against Jews, they provide key dates, locations, combat intelligence information, and a paper trail of orders from above, which are essential in corroborating other sources. What the historical record doesn't show, though, is a more nuanced and textured picture of what occurred in these Jewish communities when the German troops arrived.

The second section of the paper will examine and explore this perspective through the collective testimony of eyewitnesses to the initial phase of the invasion. It is only through these eyewitness accounts that the treatment of local Jewish populations by front line units of the Seventeenth Army prior to the mass killings can come to light. If the voices of the perpetrators, through the operational situation reports in the war diaries or other summary accounts, maintain a silence, then it is left to the voices of the victims who survived to fill in the gaps. This is a story that has yet to be told in its entirety.

The foundation of our understanding of the daily events in the military campaign along what the Germans referred to as the Eastern Front is the *Kriegstagebuch*. As the infantry divisions of *AOK 17* fought eastward in the largest land invasion to date, detailed records of their operational activities were filed and passed along the chain of command at least twice a day by Intelligence officers (*Ic*), Operations Staff officers (*Ia*) and Quartermaster Staff officers (*Ib*). Typically, these war diary entries included such diverse subjects as unit locations, POW tallies and interrogation of prisoners, lists of captured goods and equipment, combat conditions and results, weather, reconnaissance, supply line requests, and occasionally the number of Red Army Political Commissars executed "in accordance with instructions" (*BA-MA*, RH 26-24/71). Orders and directives from Army Group South or higher to the Army Command, Corps, and division levels were also exchanged through this same infrastructure.

While the war diaries are silent on the treatment of Jews by *Wehrmacht* units, they are not lacking in detail on the perceived power and role of Jews in Soviet military and economic life. In an expanding definition, Jews came to represent all forms of opposition and ideological evil. As the *Ic* for the 295th Infantry Division recorded in the summary of POW testimony for I July 1941, 3% of Red Army troops supposedly are Communist party members, but of those 3%, 50% are Jews (*BA-MA*, RH 26-295-16).

As the attack progressed east, the rhetoric increased. Images of the Jew as an unlawful irregular soldier and *NKVD* agent (NARA, RG 242, T-315, Roll 2316, FN 293), political Commissar (*BA-MA*, RH 26-24/72), and partisan (*BA-MA*, RH 26-125/27) all developed prominence.

The inclusion of the perceptions of Jews in the war diaries is noteworthy. Wherever and whenever the *Wehrmacht* encountered military resistance and social unrest, the label "Jew" was affixed and a scapegoat created. Reflecting central components of National Socialist ideology and worldview, Intelligence officers in each of the forward divisions of *AOK 17* ascribe powers to the Jews that far exceed reality. Whether written to please superior officers and maintain the official party line, or simply out of a blind belief that Jews commanded such power, antisemitism fermented the logic of front line military intelligence.

The inclusion of the perception of Jews in the war diaries also makes the omission of any direct contact with the Jewish communities that much more problematic. There were over a quarter of a million Jews concentrated in the areas around L'viv, and another 134,000 within the Tarnopol region (Altshuler 1998, 329-330). In the Soviet areas, 35% of the Jewish *shtetlekh* in all of Ukraine fell under *AOK 17* control during the first month. These include communities within the Vinnitsa and Kamenets-Podol'sk *oblast'* (Altshuler 1998, 17, 45).

So to what can we attribute the silence of the war diaries in the face of such large numbers of Jews? First, the invasion of the Soviet Union was designed to be a ten-week *Blitzkrieg* against a colossal, but weak and unorganized enemy (*BA-MA*, RW-4, v.578). The rapid thrust of von Stülpnagel's troops into the heart of Ukraine underscored this belief. Since the military administration of the occupied territories was intended to be transitory in such a quick, and decisive campaign, the *SS, SD, Gestapo* and police, and not the *Wehrmacht*, would handle issues pertaining to Jews (NARA, RG 242, T-312, R 669, FN 8303632-938). Thus, before a single shot was fired, the relationship between the army and the security forces was defined and delineated, and *Ia* and *Ic* officers may not have wanted to deal with areas not within their jurisdiction.

Second, with the exception of the 19 May 1941 order on "The Conduct of the Troops in Russia," a directive that warned: "this struggle requires ruthless and energetic action against Bolshevik agitators, guerillas, saboteurs, and Jews, and the total elimination of all active or passive resistance" (*BA-MA*, RW-4, v. 578 and RH 26-97/4), very few pre-invasion regulations addressed the relationship of the *Wehrmacht* and the Jews. Clearly, this was to be a war of annihilation and destruction, but it lacked specific regulations for implementation. In the absence of such guidelines, it is understandable that comments about the treatment of Jews might appear misplaced in the war diaries.

Third, the accounts in the war diaries could very well be sanitized versions of events. Since the treatment of Jews was primarily to be a matter for security forces, omitting any incidents involving the *Wehrmacht* would not be out of keeping with regulations, even if it was clearly an error of commission.

Given the restricted evidence about the treatment of Jews by the front line soldiers of the Seventeenth Army in the war diaries, we need to consult other primary source documents to provide details. It might appear that the *Einsatzgruppen* Reports would offer an excellent comparative source, and indicate types of collaboration and cooperation between *Wehrmacht* and the mobile killing units. While these Operational Situation Reports (OSR) do provide examples of an Army-*SS* partnership in the destruction of Ukrainian

Jewry by enhancing our understanding about how the army and the mobile killing units functioned together, the details are often lacking.

Within days of the attack on the Soviet Union, *SS* mobile killing units of *Einsatzgruppe C* followed in the wake of *AOK 17*. Armed with orders to pacify and secure the territories captured by the German military, *Einsatz-kommandos IV a, IV b, V,* and *VI* unleashed a campaign of murder and terror against local Jewish populations (Center Moscow 500-1-25 in USHMM, RG 11.001M, R 183). A report filed by *Einsatzgruppe C* to Berlin in the first week of July 1941 documents the number of Jews and others killed by *EK IV b* (the *EK* eventually subordinated to *AOK 17*), and emphasizes the spirit of cooperation by the army units in Tarnopol and surrounding areas (OSR 14, OSR 19, OSR 24, and OSR 28 in NARA, RG 242, T-175, R 233, FN 2721432-33, 2721474, 2721536-43, and 2721585-87):

> [. . .] 20 more Jews slain in the streets by Ukrainians and soldiers as retaliation for the murder of 3 (German) soldiers who were found in prison, tied, their tongues sliced and eyes gouged out. The German Army demonstrates a gratifyingly good attitude towards Jews. Zlochev was searched for agents and archives (OSR 14).

At this time, regiments of the 295th and 125th Infantry Division were moving through Zlochev and Tarnopol. The *Ia* and *Ic* war diaries for the 295 I.D. and 125th I.D. record only the combat reports, some POW testimony, and marching orders. There is nothing on Jews or cooperation with the *Einsatzgruppen* (*BA-MA*, RH 26-295-1940-41 Ia, RH 26-295-16 1940-41 Ic, RH 26-125-27 Ic, and NARA, RG 242, R 1950, FN 097-123).

OSR 24 from 16 July 1941 also re-enforces negative stereotypes that leadership positions in the Communist party or police were often held by Jews, and that they abused this power at the expense of German army or air force prisoners. Regardless of the veracity of the reports, the perception that Jews wielded both immense political and economic power became a justifiable excuse for murder, and, in this case, additional grounds for reprisal killings. In "The General Situation on Arrival" summary section, it states:

> In many cases, the (German) prisoners must have been tortured terribly: Bones were broken [...]. In Sambor, the (German) prisoners were gagged and thus prevented from screaming during torture and murder. The Jews, some of whom held official positions, in addition to their economic supremacy, and who served in the Bolshevik police force, were always partners in these atrocities (OSR 24).

The report goes on to note that: "The investigation at Zlochev proved that the Russians, prior to their withdrawal, arrested and murdered indiscriminately a total of 700 Ukrainians, including the entire local Intelligentsia. By order of the *Wehrmacht*, the militia retaliated by arresting and shooting several hundred Jews. The number of Jews liquidated may run to about 300-500" (OSR 24).

In a summary account, OSR 28 explains that 127 executions were carried out in the city Tarnopol by *EK IV b*, allegedly in response to the grisly scenes of murder and torture discovered by German forces as they captured Soviet positions in the pre-1939 Polish provinces. According to the Operational Situation Report: "Before their retreat, as in L'viv and Dubno, the Russians there went on a rampage. Disinterments showed ten bodies of German soldiers (POWs). Almost all of them had their hands tied behind their backs with wire. The bodies showed traces of severely cruel mutilations such as gouged eyes, severed tongues, and limbs" (OSR 28). Although the identity of the 127 victims is not specified in the report, the response is swift and direct for those allegedly responsible: "The troops passing by who saw these horrors, in part, the bodies of the murdered German soldiers, killed approximately 600 Jews, and burned down their houses" (OSR 28).

Such killings of male Jews by mobile killing squads and divisions of *AOK 17* clearly reflect a sanctioned policy of reprisal. According to the 13 May 1941 directive on "The Decree for the Application of Military Law in the Area of Barbarossa and Special Measures to be adopted by the Troops," soldiers could take retribution against the civilian population without fear of court-martial, even if their actions would normally be considered a crime. They could also employ such tactics as summary execution or collective measures for acts of sabotage. Warfare in the Russian campaign would, therefore, be free of conventional restraints. Specifically, the order stated in part:

1. Criminal acts by hostile civilians are withdrawn from the jurisdiction of courts-martial and summary courts-martial until further notice.

2. The troops are to kill irregulars (*Freischälerei*) mercilessly in battle or while escaping.

3. All other attacks by hostile civilians against the *Wehrmacht*, its personnel and entourage are to be repressed by the troops on the spot with the most extreme measures, including annihilation of the attacker. Wherever the application of such measures was neglected or was not immediately possible, suspicious elements are to be brought before an officer as soon as possible. The officer will decide whether they are to be shot. If conditions do not permit a rapid identification of individual perpetrators, collective reprisal measures are to be carried out summarily against towns from which the *Wehrmacht* was attacked insidiously or treacherously, by order of an officer with the rank of battalion commander or higher (Broszat 1972, 181-183, 518).

From the *Einsatzgruppen* reports it is clear that the *Wehrmacht* and security forces applied this directive on a number of occasions in the first four weeks of the invasion. Incidents of Soviet atrocities and German reprisals in L'viv, Tarnopol, Sambor, Zlochev, and other communities within the pre-1939 Polish border region are also represented in the *AOK 17* divisional war diaries, and are often characterized by a sense of righteous indignation (*BA-MA*, RH 26-97-100, 9 July 1941 near Czarny-Ostrow, for example).

Using the discoveries of alleged *NKVD* and Red Army atrocities against German POWs as thinly veiled excuses for justifiable retaliation (Musial 2000, 200-249) subsumes the murder of Jews into the larger context of war. In doing so, the execution of Jewish non-combatants ceases to be a criminal act, and simply gets filed with reports to commanding officers and the *Wehrmacht* War Crimes Bureau as a response to additional cases of Judeo-Bolshevik cruelty and aggression.

Furthermore, it appears that units of the Higher *SS* and Police Leader South and the Order Police may have been more involved in the killing of Jews during the first month of the campaign in Ukraine than the mobile killing units of *Einsatzgruppe C* (Pohl 1997, 73). According to the surviving records of the Order Police, the 1st SS Brigade and battalions of the *Ordnungspolizei* operated near the advancing front in Ukraine (Breitman 1998) between the Sixth Army under von Reichenau to the north, and the Seventeenth Army to the south. Their participation in atrocities is noted in the British decodes of German police reports, yet very little attention is given to the role and support of the *Wehrmacht* during this time (PRO, HW 16/32 and PRO, HW 16/45).

 While they are chilling in scope and depth, the summary reports of *EK IV b* as well as the material found in the Police Decodes never indicate which divisions of *AOK 17* are operating in the area. The operational situation reports also describe cooperation with the military in broad strokes, and do not always distinguish between rear area and forward units of the *Wehrmacht*, or even between *Waffen SS* and *Wehrmacht* units operating in the same general region (OSR 19 and OSR 28 in relation to actions in the town of Zborow, for example). Only when using dates and troop locations from the war diaries is it possible to place a division in the area of *EK IV b*.

In spite of fragmented documentation, located in the *AOK 17* war diaries, *Einsatzgruppen* reports, and Police Decodes, we still know very little about the details of German actions against Jews in eastern Galicia (Gross 2001, 20, footnote 6, 210) and western Ukraine. How and when were Jews gathered and selected? What degree of collaboration did the non-Jewish neighbors offer in the round up and execution of Jewish men and communist functionaries? Where did these killings take place? What events proceeded the shootings? What happened to the bodies of the victims? What events followed the killings? What impact did this have on the rest of the community?

In the absence of documentary evidence to address these questions, eyewitness accounts are necessary to fill in the gap, whether reprisals took place or not, and provide the details of how the soldiers in von Stülpnagel's army treated local Jewish populations upon arrival in their communities. Documents still play a central role, however, in the corroboration of these testimonies. Divisional records in the war diaries verify eyewitness accounts by establishing precise dates, times, and unit locations as troops moved through a town or region. Even if *Ia* and *Ic* officers purposefully omitted material from the war diaries on the treatment of Jews, they had no apparent reason to falsify information on troop location. Such data inextricably links German infantry divisions to Jews in Ukrainian cities, towns and villages, and to the stories told of events that took place there.

Eyewitness testimony, however, can be problematic for historians. If testimonies are not given contemporaneously to the event, the subjects may encounter lapses in memory over the years resulting in gaps in the historical accuracy of the account. Memory can fail or fade with time, and make it much more difficult to recall, for instance, specific dates or the order of events during the German occupation. Yet, as Lawrence Langer notes in discussing the reliability of memory:

> How credible can a reawakened memory be that tries to revive events so many decades after they occurred? [...] There is no need to revive what has never died. Moreover, though slumbering memories may crave reawakening, nothing is clearer in these narratives than that Holocaust memory is an insomniac faculty whose mental eyes have never slept (Langer 1991, xv).

If we accept the fact that documentary evidence often omits data or information, as in the case of the war diaries and the treatment of Jews, and yet, we still rely upon it to build a body of historical evidence, than we should also accept that, while survivor testimony may contain flaws, it is eminently useful in offering acumen into events we have few details about. Lawrence Langer adds that "testimonies resting unseen in archives are like books locked in vaults: they might as well not exist" (Langer 1991, 36). Recognizing this, Christopher Browning states:

> It is no offense to survivor memory to accept their fallibility as witness; they often openly admit to failing memory themselves. [...] It is no act of disrespect to subject survivor testimonies to the same critical analysis that we would the conflicting and powerful testimony of other historical witnesses [...]. (Browning 2000, 91).

In spite of the potential frailty of memory, these testimonies may be the only sources we have to access the events not covered by documentary evidence. As Yehuda Bauer states:

> Because the documentation is largely one-sided, that is German, survivors' testimonies are crucial to understanding the events of the period. They become extremely useful and reliable when cross-checked with and borne out by many other testimonies. They are then, I would argue, at least as reliable as a written document of the time.
>
> All of this has to be stated explicitly because it strengthens the argument for the explicability of the Holocaust: the more testimonies we have, as well as documentation, the greater our chances of explaining and understanding what happened (Bauer 2001, 25).

Not only should testimonies be critically analyzed and referenced with other testimonies, they should be cross-checked, when at all possible, with documents as well. In this case, all testimonies can be referenced back to material found in divisional war diaries of the Seventeenth German Army Command. The collection of eyewitness accounts for this study came from both printed and oral testimony by Jewish Holocaust survivors. All were present in Ukrainian towns when forces of *AOK 17* arrived during the first month of the invasion, and their collective testimony provides insights into the actions of front line German divisions that simply cannot be found in any other sources.

The body of this testimony can be divided into two geographic sections:

1. The Medzhibozh-Letichev region in northern Podolia along the main route from Proskurov to Vinnitsa taken by the 97th Light Infantry Division and 4th Mountain Division from 8-17 July 1941. According to the 1939 census, there were 2,347 Jews living in Medzhibozh who comprised 51.6 percent of the total population. Letichev had a total population of 5,346, of whom 1,946 were Jewish (36.4%) (Altshuler 1998, 227).

2. The parallel path to the south from Zinkov, through Bar and on to Zhmerinka and Nemirov taken by the 100th Light Infantry Division, 125th Infantry Division, and 1st Mountain Division 10-22 July 1941. 1939 census records indicate that Zinkov had a Jewish community of 2,248, or 35.6% of the total population. Out of 9,413 people in Bar, 3,869 (41%) were Jewish. Zhmerinka had 4,630 Jews, or 17.8% of the population, and Nemirov had 3,001 Jews out of a total population of 8,176 (36.7%) (Altshuler 1998, 227-228).

Uniformly, testimony by survivors in both regions on the chronology of events parallels the war diaries for the divisions involved. Those within both groups also remark immediately on the physical appearance of the German troops, as well as the variety and vast numbers of their equipment. Rivka A.

observed that when German troops entered her town of Nemirov on 22 July 1941, "These were young, well-fed Aryans. There was a major highway, Vinnitsa-Uman, going through Nemirov. Soon these roads were used to transport heavy machinery: motorcycles, tanks, loaded trucks." Through the eyes of a fifteen-year old, they seemed invincible (Rivka A., questionnaire). Although Pavel S. was younger, he came away with a similar impression looking to the skies covered by an umbrella of low-flying aircraft in support of ground forces (Pavel S., questionnaire). In Zinkov, Ilya Abramovich noted:

> [...] My brother moved the blankets from the window to see just a little. He said, "Germans!" I looked too. I saw lots of bicycles left near the fence outside our house. I also saw huge, covered trucks moving down the road. I could hear sharp commands shouted out. I saw men in unfamiliar uniforms. They were young and tanned. A few had their sleeves rolled up above their elbows. This is how the Germans entered Zinkov (Abramovich 1991, 12).

Survivors in both groups, however, differ on several issues. Those whose towns were captured by the 100th Light Infantry Division and 125th Infantry Division speak of horrific rumors about what the Germans will do once they arrive, while those in the Medzhibozh-Letichev region describe a sense of false hope about the nature of the pending German occupation. Rivka A. and her family were extremely leery as the German forces approached. Her community of Nemirov was the farthest east of all the survivors noted in this study, and the Germans did not arrive until four weeks after the invasion began. She notes:

> We heard many rumors, and they were invariably very disturbing. When the Germans occupied Poland in 1939, Polish Jews escaped to Ukraine. Some of them were in Nemirov. They told us what they witnessed. Before the war we also saw a film "Professor Matlok." This Matlok was a professor of Medicine, a famous expert, but he was killed because he was Jewish. We thought the same thing (Rivka A., questionnaire).

Pavel S. also reports on rumors. "We heard about killings of Jews by Germans in Braidov, about 4-5 miles toward Vinnitsa. It was very unsettling for us" (Pavel S., questionnaire). Ruth D. in Bar stated: "The uncertainty. Not knowing what would happen. You hear things about the Germans, and of course, you are afraid. There was no way we could really know" (Ruth D., personal interview).

While rumors probably were just as prevalent in Medzhibozh and Letichev, it was a sense of false hope, not pending doom, which led to inaction and a dramatic underestimation of German intentions. Leonid Rapoport, in a recently published manuscript, observed that Jews in the *shtetl* of Letichev simply did not know what to do. Since they did not know what the ultimate plans of the German occupiers would be, and remembering the relatively benign occupation of Ukraine during the First World War, many Jews chose not to evacuate when the fighting drew closer in early July. According to Rapoport, all the others viewed those who did leave as foolish, especially if some of the more prominent families or influential leaders decided to remain behind (cited from Chapin and Weinstock 2000, 668).

In addition, evacuation was not an easy task. With Red Army forces either pulling back, or being rushed to the front, the situation on the roads was chaotic. Khaya Burshteyn Malkiman notes: "Dad, Mom, and we three sisters got out of Letichev and into Vinnitsa with great difficulties. The evacuation was very troubled. Letichev did not have a railroad, and we got into Vinnitsa on passing cars, buggies, and by walking" (cited from Chapin and Weinstock 2000, 669).

German dive bombers attacked these routes, and distinctions between civilian and soldiers were not made. Jews from Medzhibozh were among those killed on an evacuation train in the days shortly before the arrival of German troops. When word reached town that a prominent dentist, Oigenzight, was among the dead, it simply re-enforced the idea that it would be safer to stay (Chapin and Weinstock 2000, 669).

However, both groups of survivors are quite clear on one key point: German front line troops entering their communities for the first time initiated terror tactics, enthusiastically pursued humiliating and dehumanizing activities as forms of "entertainment," and were responsible for murdering small groups of, mainly, Jewish men for no apparent reason. Ilya Abramovich recalls the first two days the Germans came to Zinkov:

> During the day (10 July), German soldiers kept coming in and out of our house. It was the first time I heard the word "*Jude*" (Jew). We heard the sound of shootings. Children were screaming, and women were crying while dogs in the town barked constantly. Above the wailing I could hear Germans yelling. That first night, none of us closed our eyes.

Abramovich described events of the second day:

> That same day (the 11th), Germans moved from house-to-house looking for gray-bearded Jewish elders. The soldiers laughed and entertained themselves playing a game of pulling the beards of an old Jewish man and yanking him like a ball from one to another. The weak elders were forced to crawl, and the Germans kicked them. After torturing them enough, the Germans decided to arrange a public barbershop. They cut the hair on the faces of the Jewish elders with a meat cleaver. Sometimes they took a piece a skin along with the beards. When they finished cutting, they continued to torture and beat up the Jewish elders using whatever they had available, like sticks or boots (Abramovich 1991, 13).

In Medzhibozh, German troops carried out similar activities. Moishe Eyngorn described a work detail as follows:

> They (German troops) put a mentally retarded person (Ioske-Haim Bers) into a puddle, made him hold two bricks and took a picture of him. They also took the eldest people in town, including my father, Shloime Teper-Eyngorn, Meer Gurtnberg, Pinhes Fun Dem Honick (it is a nickname "Pinhes made of honey" – translator's note), Bunim-Motl Avrom Bereshes, Itshok Shoihet and others, put them face down to a puddle and a German gendarme walked over their old backs. When the poor old men got up from the puddle, their faces and beards were dirty, they were forced to sing, then to graze on grass, then to dance – the Germans took pictures of every pose. Before letting them go, they cut their white beards using knives. This was the first day of our acquaintance with the Germans (Dimshitz 1994, 171).

In Bar, the arriving Germans also treated Jews with disdain, torturing and beating them without explanation. Forced to carry out tedious tasks, Jews could not walk on the sidewalks. Whenever a German soldier or officer approached, the Jews working had to take off their caps or face severe punishments (Schlomo G. questionnaire). Celia Michelson, in a testimony at Yad Vashem, noted that on the first day German troops arrived in Letichev, they rounded up Jewish children in a church, and forced them (her brother Mutty Burshteyn among them) to take hot asphalt into their bare hands (Chapin and Weinstock 2000, 671).

However, German soldiers went beyond such sadistic acts of humiliation. In Letichev, Pinchas Michelson and Froim Burshteyn reported that the Germans ordered the chief rabbi of Letichev and twenty-five of the most prominent young Jewish males to go to the outskirts of Letichev. There the Germans summarily shot these men, and dumped them in a mass grave in Zavolk. Following the war, the Volk River flooded the area of the grave, and the bones were washed into the streets of Letichev. Several survivors reburied the bones in a mass grave site in Zaletichevka (Chapin and Weinstock 2000, 671).

Similar incidents occurred in Nemirov and Bar. Rivka A. reports: "When the Germans arrived, everyone was very nervous, because they remembered the non-belligerency pact we had with Germany. As soon as Germans entered our town, they seized 30 young and strong Jews and took them to be shot nearby. They made people work, beat them" (Rivka A., questionnaire). Moishe A. of Bar recalls that: "the Germans got rid of all potential opposition right away. They ordered a group of young Jewish men to arrange a transport of horses. These boys never returned (Moishe A., questionnaire). And in Zinkov, Ilya Abramovich recalls:

In the afternoon a neighbor accidentally found the crippled Shlomie and his wife, who had been hacked to death in their house. The room where they had been killed was flooded with blood; there were splashes of blood even on the ceiling. Everything was turned upside down, although there was nothing to rob in his house. What happened to their children? Nobody ever saw them again. Zinkov, scared to death, buries two more victims. We also found out that two old Jewish female peddlers who sold seeds, lollipops, and fruit at the market square had been killed on that first day by the Germans. Why were these people killed? For what reason?

That night, we again heard shootings, and bullets ricocheting. The Germans took valuables, including our horse and chickens. All dogs in our village had been killed. On the morning of July 12th, drunken German soldiers shot an eighteen year-old Jew named Schwarz. They also shot a Jewish man, and left him bleeding in a basement where other Jews had been hiding. They put heavy stones over the opening to the basement. For three days we heard screams, but couldn't go to help. Then it became quiet (Abramovich 1991, 13).

According to a testimony given by Yehudis Vaynblat-Laufer, several Jews from Zinkov actually greeted the arriving Germans on 10 July 1941 with traditional gifts of salt and bread as expressions of their gratitude for being "liberated" from the yoke of Soviet oppression. For such gratitude, they were shot on the spot (Chapin and Weinstock 2000, 668). In Zinkov, there was a German troop presence for three days. Ilya Abramovich recorded the events of the third day:

On the 12th of July, a German officer killed a Jew named Elya. The officer came up to the house of this man, and ordered him to clean his boots. Elya said, "I will not clean fascist boots!" For this reply he was shot on the spot. His body was left in the dust in front of his house. The Germans would not allow the body to be moved, and soon it swelled up in the heat.

The Germans left Zinkov soon after. They departed unexpectedly, without noise, shootings, and screams. They just took off and left. The next morning, boys around the town confirmed that no German soldier was left in our town. Not a single German soldier could be found. Overcoming fear, residents started to come out of hiding. Everyone wanted to make certain that the Germans had really left Zinkov. At the crossroads in the center of town, everybody began to express an opinion of what had just happened. A man who loved politics and was a hat maker in town declared with a great deal of authority, "Our troops have made peace with the Germans, and the Germans have left for the old border."

We didn't believe him (Abramovich 1991, 13).

How do we evaluate this collective body of testimony? If the killings of Jews in these communities over a two-week period were in response to alleged *NKVD* or Red Army atrocities, there would be comments in the war diaries, or more references in the OSR of the *Einsatzgruppen*. With the exception of an incident mentioned by the 100th Light Infantry Division the day after arrival in Zinkov when engineers of an artillery reconnaissance patrol were found "murdered and mutilated" south of Adamowka, the war diaries make no connections or references (*BA-MA*, RH 26-100/36).

In juxtaposing the accounts of 8-22 July 1941 found in the war diaries of the 97th and 100th Light Infantry, 125th Infantry, and 4th Mountain Divisions with those of the survivors above, the lack of any mention of Jews is striking. For example, when a bicycle reconnaissance patrol of the Advanced Detachment of the 100th Light Infantry Division entered the northern Podolian town of Zinkov on the morning of 10 July 1941, they encountered weak enemy resistance. Motorized units of the division quickly followed. In the evening report to the LII Army Corps, officers of the *Ic* Intelligence Branch wrote the following summary of the day's activities:

> 9:20 A.M. Rear guard forces thrown back eastwards toward Adamowka. Effective fire on enemy battery positions south of Strychowce and on small retreating columns.

> 11:30 A.M. Enemy routed (ejected) from Zinkov (*BA-MA*, RH 26-100-36).

The reports from the *Ia* – Operations Branch were somewhat more descriptive. In the division orders for the 10 July, the Advanced Detachment under Colonel Recknagel was to kickstart the day in Zinkov and proceed to Wonjkowce (NARA, RG 242, T-315, R 1214, FN 882, 885). The evening report to the LII Army Corps noted:

> Weather: Rain at night, sunny throughout the day.

> [...] 11:30 A.M. Zinkov won (captured). Enemy flees in several directions. Enemy command in disarray. The progress of the Advanced Detachment along the road was slowed due to the results of last night's rain. At 4:45 P.M. the Advanced Detachment captured Wonjkowce [...]. (NARA, RG 242, T-315, R 1214, FN 881).

Such details in the *Ia* and *Ic* war diaries, however, do not take away from the testimonies through what they omit. Rather they re-enforce and corroborate eyewitness accounts through their precise tracking of troop movement and daily location reports. Both sources are essential components for understanding the events of late June and early July 1941.

Yehuda Bauer has said that the job of a historian is "to do two things, especially when dealing with a subject such as this: one research and analyze; and two, remember that there is a story to be told, a story that relates to people's lives. So a real historian is also a person who tells (true) stories (Bauer

2001, ix-x). In this case, the true stories relate to the time when German troops first entered Ukrainian towns and villages in the summer of 1941. Yet, this is a story that is not often told. A paucity of direct documentation in German military sources, such as war diaries, has limited our access to these events. In addition, Jewish survivors' eyewitness testimonies often do not go into detail in describing the first days of the German occupation because they were either never asked, or the horror of what followed may have seemed so much greater. In concert with one another, however, war diaries and eyewitness testimonies offer the most comprehensive story of how the *Wehrmacht* units acted when they first contacted Ukrainian Jews.

Manifold evidence in the collective testimony of Jewish eyewitness accounts documents that at least three divisions (100th Light I.D., 97th Light I.D., and the 4th Mountain Division) of the nine deployed in forward areas of the Seventeenth German Army Command at the end of the first week in July 1941 took part in excesses against local Ukrainian Jewish populations. Two others (the 295th I.D. and the 125th I.D.) may have done so in the former Polish provinces of western Ukraine. These excesses range from dehumanizing and abusing Jewish men for purposes of sadistic entertainment, to criminal acts of murder and summary executions. When compared to the numbers of Jews murdered by the security forces of the *SS* and police, these killings seem rather small and insignificant. Such statistics, however, often create a superficial point of comparison by implying that the merits of historical attention are directly proportional to the highest body counts. A few dead Jews can mask the role played by front line troops in preparing the way for killing actions to take place at all.

In addition, post war investigative reports and trials focused less on the role of the *Wehrmacht* and more on the *SS* or local collaborators. The trials before the International Military Tribunal in Nuremberg directed little attention to the army, and thereby set the stage for the rise of the "Myth of the *Wehrmacht*" as an honorable institution amidst the ideologically perverse Nazi regime. The Soviet Extraordinary Commission also concerned itself more with the extent of *SS* and *Gestapo* massacres and the location of local collaborators and witnesses than the behavior of German troops at the outset of the occupation. Furthermore, West German war crimes investigations have given little attention to soldiers, and more to police and *SS* personnel.

Should these facts diminish or relegate the treatment of Ukrainian Jews by front line German soldiers to a secondary historical tier of critical inquiry? Since the invasion of the Soviet Union was designed as an institutionalized war of destruction, both strategic objectives and ideological aims helped shape the vision for military planners. From the pre-invasion directives ironing out jurisdiction between Army units and security forces over the "special tasks" (Krausnick and Wilhelm 1985, 115-117, and Breitman 1998, 36) to the details of daily operational situation reports, the *Wehrmacht* cooperated with the *SS* and police. Without the military success of the army, the security forces, however, would not be able to carry out their own objectives. Where testimonies can be corroborated, it is clear that the arrival of the army in Jewish towns and villages fractured most hopes for evacuation. The majority of those caught were murdered within the year, and the vibrancy of *shtetl* life in western Ukraine perished with them.

Moreover, in the documented cases, the German army initiated a policy of dehumanization and a campaign of terror and intimidation that often resulted in the murder of innocent civilian Jews, many of whom were prominent leaders in the religious and civic community. Using the pre-invasion directives as possible justification, the army units also targeted Jews for reprisals for the alleged mistreatment of German POWs. Since the nature of warfare on the Eastern Front involved a mutual escalation of violence, such killings could possibly be overlooked as part of the daily realities of war. As Christopher Browning notes: "Nothing helped the Germans wage a race war as much as the war itself" (Browning 1992, 186).

Do these excesses and crimes make the entire Seventeenth Army Command a criminal organization? Not necessarily. We must rely on available evidence. It is a fact that orders were not coming from above, as seen in the *Ia* war diaries, which encouraged genocidal acts against Jews. The atmosphere and tone for such activities were already set in the orders issued prior to the invasion. However, it does become clear two months later that army units were taking excessive liberties against Jews, and that the Army High Command viewed these actions as interfering with the military objectives of the *Wehrmacht*. The fact that a directive was issued to counter excesses is evidence enough (NARA, RG 242, T-315, R 2316, FN 336-337).

In summary, we have only begun to examine this component of the German occupation of Ukraine. Ruth D. recalls: "The day the Germans came to my town (Bar) was the beginning of my sorrows. I will not talk about it. It is too painful. I (later) lost forty-two members of my family in one day. I don't even want to remember what started it all" (Ruth D., personal interview). Her story and that of many others are yet to be told. In order to achieve a comprehensive portrait of the events that took place when German troops first entered Ukrainian towns and villages, all voices must be heard. We have the voice of the perpetrators through the reams of military documents and war diaries; we have only begun to hear the voices of the victims through testimonies and written sources; and we have hardly heard the voices of the bystanders, the Ukrainian townspeople who also witnessed the arrival of the *Wehrmacht*. Until we can hear all the voices and read the sources about the events that "started it all," the story of the Holocaust in Ukraine is still a fragmented mosaic.

Archival Sources

Bundesarchiv-Militärarchiv, Freiburg, Germany (BA-MA).

National Archives and Records Administration, College Park, Maryland (NARA).

Public Record Office, London, England (PRO).

United States Holocaust Memorial Museum Archives (USHMM).

Personal Interviews and Questionnaire Responses

Moishe A., questionnaire response. English translation provided by Sardar Shokatayev, Middlebury College.

Pavel S., questionnaire response.

Rivka A., questionnaire response. English translation provided by Katya Levitan, Middlebury College.

Ruth D., personal interview. 4 April 2001.

Schlomo G., questionnaire response. English translation provided by Sardar Shokatayev, Middlebury College.

Literature Cited

Abramovich, Ilya. 1991. *Ne Zabyt*. New York: Effect Publishing. English translation provided by Vadim Altskan, United States Holocaust Memorial Museum and Andrei Takhteyev, Middlebury College.

Altshuler, Mordechai. 1998. *Soviet Jewry on the Eve of the Holocaust: A Social and Demographic Profile*. Jerusalem: The Centre for Research for East European Jewry.

Arad, Yitzhack, Shmuel Krakowski, and Shmuel Spector, eds. 1989. *The Einsatzgruppen Reports: Selections From Dispatches of the Nazi Death Squads' Campaign Against Jews July 1941-January 1943*. New York: Holocaust Library.

Bauer, Yehuda. 2001. *Rethinking the Holocaust*. New Haven: Yale University Press.

Breitman, Richard. 1998. *Official Secrets: What the Nazis Planned, What the British and Americans Knew*. New York: Hill and Wang.

Browning, Christopher. 1992. *Ordinary Men: Reserve Police Battalion 101 and the Final Solution in Poland*. New York: Harper Collins.

Browning, Christopher. 2000. *Nazi Policy, Jewish Workers, German Killers*. Cambridge: Cambridge University Press.

Broszat, Martin et al., eds. 1972. *Anatomy of the SS State*. New York: Walker and Company.

Chapin, David A., and Ben Weinstock. 2000. *The Road from Letichev: The History and Culture of a Forgotten Jewish Community in Eastern Europe*. Manuscript.

Dimshitz, Vladimir. 1994. *Istoriya Evreev Na Ukraine I v Belorussii*. Saint Petersburg: Petersburg Jewish University. English translation provided by Sardar Shokatayev, Middlebury College.

Gitelman, Zvi. 1997. *Bitter Legacy: Confronting the Holocaust in the USSR* Bloomington: Indiana University Press.

Gross, Jan T. 2001. *Neighbors. The Destruction of the Jewish Community in Jedwabne, Poland*. Princeton: Princeton University Press.

Headland, Ronald. 1992. *Messages of Murder: A Study of the Reports of the Einsatzgruppen of the Security Police and the Security Service, 1941*. London: Fairleigh Dickinson University Press.

Hilberg, Raul. 1985. *The Destruction of the European Jews*. New York: Holmes and Meier.

Krausnick, Helmut, and Hans-Heinrich Wilhelm. 1985. *Die Truppe des Weltanschauungskrieges: Die Einsatzgruppen der Sicherheitspolizei und des SD, 1938-42*. Frankfurt: Fischer.

Langer, Lawrence. 1991. *Holocaust Testimonies: The Ruins of Memory*. New Haven: Yale University Press.

Musial, Bogdan. 2000. *"Konterrevolutionäre Elemente sind zu erschießen": Die Brutalisierung des deutsch-sowjetischen Krieges im Sommer 1941*. Berlin: Propyläen.

Pohl, Dieter. 1997. Die Einsatzgruppe C. In *Die Einsatzgruppen in der besetzten Sowjetunion 1941/42*, ed. Peter Klein, pp. 71-87. Berlin: Hentrich.

Pain, Prejudice, and the Legacy of the Shoah

On the Vexing Issue of Polish-Jewish Relations

Jonathan Huener

To some readers, the topic of this essay may appear rather tangential to our study of the Holocaust and of only seconday importance to the process and mechanics of destruction that has traditionally been the focus of our inquiries. A tremendous debt is owed to scholars such as Raul Hilberg, for it is only on the basis of their research over recent decades that we can begin to evaluate with objectivity and empiricism some of the intractable issues connected with the Holocaust that are so laden with the burdens of national identity and historical memory.

Relations between Poles and Jews before, during, and after the Second World War is one such problem. On the one hand, this relationship has, over the centuries, been a history of coexistence and cooperation, of common purpose and common defense of the shared goals of mutual tolerance and emancipation from foreign domination. But it is also a history of conflict, discrimination, violence and, during the German occupation of Poland, of indifference to and even complicity in the crimes of the Shoah. In the aftermath of the war, debates over the issue of Polish-Jewish relations have often been rife with accusations and reflex defenses that have done little, if anything, to bring these two groups that suffered so tragically at the hands of the Nazis closer to any form of meaningful discourse or mutual understanding. The issue of Polish-Jewish relations is also a subject that is crucial to our study and understanding of the Holocaust and its legacy, not only in contemporary Poland, but also in Israel and in the United States, where Jewish and Polish Americans often find themselves embroiled in a fruitless exchange of stereotypes and accusations.

This essay[1] will focus on the issue of Polish-Jewish relations since the German invasion of Poland in 1939, with special attention to the ways in which the German occupation, the crimes perpetrated in Poland, and relations between Poles and Jews during this period have been understood and disputed throughout the years since the end of the Second World War. On the most basic level, to address Polish-Jewish relations since the Second World War is to confront and revisit, if somewhat indirectly, the history of the Shoah in Polish lands, the region that was home to more than half of Nazism's Jewish victims. Considerations of the level of interaction between Poles and Jews during the occupation, or how Polish anti-Semitism affected this interaction, or the motivations behind Polish aid or indifference to Jews – all of these highly charged issues should encourage us to examine more closely the goals, means, policies, and crimes of German rule on Polish lands in the years 1939-1945. In a field so fraught with polemics, an empirical approach should, ideally, forestall reflex accusation.

The problem of Polish-Jewish relations also encourages us to consider somewhat more broadly how non-German peoples reacted to and recall the destruction of Jews in their homeland. This is not an attempt to shift responsibility away from the perpetrators, nor should it encourage reckless generalizations about "Polish," or for that matter "Dutch" or "Ukranian" behavior in the face of genocide. The questions, nonetheless, remain. What *was* the response of the non-Jewish bystander, or the bystander people that witnessed, resisted, or cooperated in the crimes of the Shoah? Is it even appropriate to designate a particular people, such as the Poles, as "bystanders" to the Shoah? As useful as such categorizations may be, it is worth noting that when they are cast too broadly they can diminish both the specificity of historical experience and the nuance so crucial to legitimate scholarship. Moreover, the label of "bystander" presents methodological problems, particularly in this context. As Antony Polonsky has observed: "Discussing the actions of the 'bystander,' we are principally arguing not about what they did, [...] but about 'sins of omission' – what they did not do. Yet 'counterfactual' history is highly problematic, and attempts to speculate on what might have been are open to serious question" (Polonsky 1997, 193).

In addition, the subject of Polish-Jewish relations encourages us to examine how the instrumentalization of history can, over time, lead to misapprehensions and a misguided historical understanding of the realities and meaning of the German occupation of Poland and the crimes perpetrated there. The issue of Polish-Jewish relations has been exploited as both a weapon of accusation and as defensive shield, and has even been put to political use, especially in postwar Polish society.

Finally, as noted above, relations between Poles and Jews have been the focus of controversy and debate, no less so today than fifty years ago. Relations between Poles and Jews and the differing ways that scholars and students, Poles and Americans, Jews and Roman Catholics have understood those relations is anything but neutral. This history and the collective memories of it have been embattled, and remain so to this day.

It seems somehow inappropriate that the terrorization and subjection of one people, and the annihilation of another, would be a subject of such contention. But the legacy of Jewish-Polish relations during the occupation, and more specifically, the degree of Polish complicity, accomodation, or resistance, is bound to be bitter. Its legacy is bitter because so much of the genocide took place on Polish soil (the extermination centers were all located in occupied or annexed Poland), and the majority of Jewish victims of the Shoah had been Polish citizens prior to the war. Its legacy is bitter because although more than 90% of Polish Jews were killed, many of those who did survive chronicled or testified about their experiences – experiences that often included criticisms of Poles for their indifference towards the massacre unfolding before their eyes. Its legacy is bitter because Poles, although not targeted for systematic extermination, were nonetheless subjected to a level of brutality unknown in West European regions of the Nazi imperium, and they have justifyably remembered and commemorated the occupation as a period of both tremendous suffering and valiant resistance against the Nazis. In short, the Poles were most certainly victims – victims not only of the German occupation, but also of the Soviet occupation from 1939-1941 and, in the eyes of the majority of the population after the liberation from Nazism, victims of the postwar, Soviet-installed communist regime as well (Polonsky 1997, 194). It is therefore not surprising that many Poles, with the memory of their own persecution so vivid, have traditionally reacted to accusations of indifference to or complicity in the crimes of the Shoah with defensiveness and even hostility. Finally, the legacy is bitter because Poles, faced with a memory of the occupation that includes both compassion and complicity, both resistance and acquiescence, are often accused of an inveterate anti-Semitism, while Poles have often responded with claims of a reflex Jewish "anti-Polonism."

As Alexander Smolar has noted, "what is at stake in the continuing controversy between Poles and Jews, at least in respect to the war, is not the ultimate fate of the Jewish nation. At stake is a moral judgement on Polish attitudes toward the destruction of the Jews" (Smolar 1987, 34). To elaborate on Smolar's point: at issue is not whether the annihilation of Jews took place on Polish soil, for this is beyond question. The debate centers instead on the extent to which Poles resisted, assisted, or did their best to ignore the genocide perpetrated in their midst. Categorizations can certainly further polemicize this debate, but it is nonetheless possible to detect in the literature two dominant interpretations of the issue. One is based on the premise of "historic discontinuity"[2] – that the brutality of occupation and war ameliorated relations between Jews and Poles, that traditional animosity between the two groups was diminished in the face of the German threat and, more importantly, that Poles did as much for Jews as could have been expected, given the dangers involved in assistance or rescue. The other interpretation has traditionally emphasized "historic continuity," postulating anti-Semitism as a constant in Polish culture that manifested itself in the Poles' indifference towards and even culpability for genocide.

Interestingly, both interpretations use historical arguments to bolster their positions. For centuries Poland was a haven for Jews, who, in the early middle ages, were invited into Polish lands to help develop the economy and infrastructure. Jews in Poland generally enjoyed greater autonomy than in other European countries, and although subjected to discrimination, to the anti-Jewish traditions of the Roman Catholic Church, and to violence from time to time, they were not expelled. By the middle of the 18th century fully one-third of all Jews in the world lived in the Polish-Lithuanian Commonwealth. Like other minorities in the Commonwealth, Jews remained, to a great extent, outsiders. Yet despite (or perhaps because of) this status, their community prospered, as Jews were allowed to work various trades, were important craftsmen of the rural economy, and developed a vibrant and respected intellectual and religious culture.

With the partitions of the late 18th century, Poland existed only as a nation. It was a living and noble entity in the minds of its loyal patriots, but Poland no longer existed as a state on the political map of Europe. The preservation of national traditions remained, however, crucial to the identity and national aspirations of Poles, as they actively and at times covertly cultivated what were regarded as the essential components of their national identity: the Roman Catholic faith, the Polish language and literature, or the tendency to revolt against their overlords, to name only a few. Some Poles were eager to assimilate Jews into the national community. Most Polish nationalists, however, considered the salient elements of Polish identity inaccessible to Jews, who did not speak their language or speak it well, who rejected the Catholic faith, and who by and large lived in separate communities, whether as a result of discrimination or by choice. In other words –

and this is particularly significant for the fate of the Jews during the German occupation – for most Poles, Jews were not considered part of what Helen Fein has called "the universe of obligation [...] that circle of persons towards whom obligations are owed, to whom rules apply and whose injuries call for expiation by the community" (Fein 1984, 33).

In the late 19th century anti-Jewish sentiment assumed in Poland, as elsewhere, a particularly venomous tone, especially with the advent of the nationalist *Endecja* movement, which placed the struggle against Jews at the center of its political agenda. When Poland once again received its independence after the First World War, hopes were high for a new era of tolerance and coexistence. Political and economic conditions in interwar Poland were not, however, conducive to toleration of Poland's substantial and varied ethnic minorities, and the liberal ideal became increasingly lost in the efforts to construct a strong nation-state, especially after the death of Marshall Jozef Pilsudski in 1935. At best, the Jews were regarded by the majority of Poles as a separate minority group; at worst, they were the targets of anti-Semitic agitation, violence, and even demands from the nationalist, xenophobic right for their emigration (Polonsky 1997, 198).

With the outbreak of war in September 1939 and subsequent occupation of Poland by both the Germans and Soviets, relations between Jews and Poles worsened. This was, in the first place, the result of Nazi efforts to exacerbate Polish animosity towards Jews by rewarding denunciations, encouraging expropriation of Jewish property, and inciting and encouraging violence against Jews. Moreover, common among Poles during the first two years of the occupation was the perception that they were suffering more than were the Jews: whereas Jews remained in Poland, Poles were deported by the hundreds of thousands to Germany for labor; whereas Jews had their own governmental institutions or councils, subject as they were to the Nazis, Poles had no political or cultural representation; whereas Jews were clearly the victims of Nazi violence and murder, Poles were both randomly and systematically rounded up, incarcerated, and tortured as political prisoners (Hilberg 1992, 204). Evidence for this was the notorious Auschwitz camp, which was originally developed to detain Polish political prisoners. 147,000 Polish political prisoners were deported to Auschwitz, approximately half of whom perished there.

The tremendous suffering of the Poles during the war is not open to debate. The country lost approximately 20% of its citizens (half of whom were Jews who perished in the Shoah), and 2 million were sent to the *Reich* for labor. Between September 1939 and February 1940, more than 200,000 Poles were forcibly expelled from the annexed Warthegau region, and already in the first months of the occupation more than 50,000 Poles were killed. It was obvious that the Nazis were not interested in gaining the assistance of a collaborationist government, as in France, or a collaborationist administration, as in the Netherlands. Instead, they aimed to colonize and enslave the Polish lands, and therefore undertook a ferocious effort to decimate the infrastructure and human resources of Poland In this they succeeded. More than 38% of physicians, 28% of university and college professors, 56% of lawyers, and 27% of Catholic priests did not survive the occupation (Symonowicz 1960, 83). Despite this level of destruction, the Germans were met with fierce resistance. Poland had the most extensive underground network and army in Nazi-occupied Europe – something about which Poles continue to be proud – and the Germans were quick to undertake collective reprisals for acts of resistance. For good reason, Poles have commemorated and mourned these darkest years in the history of their country.

The annihilation of Jews in Poland is more familiar to most of us. The first month of the war saw the death of approximately 5,000 Polish Jews, and once the occupation regime was established, Jews were subsequently confined to ghettos, subjected to forced labor, and deported to concentration camps. The advent of the so-called "final solution" accompanied the euphoric victories of the campaign against the Soviet Union. Mobile killing units were deployed behind the advancing lines of the German army, resulting in the deaths of at least one million Jews. Mobile units were also subsequently deployed in occupied Poland in actions familiar to us from the work of Christopher Browning and others. Open air shootings continued, but this form of mass killing gave way to a technology and process more efficient and less damaging to the morale of the perpetrators: annihilation by poison gas. By the end of 1942, the vast majority of Polish Jews were dead, but the extermination centers erected on Polish territory remained the destinations for Jews from all over Europe. The killing continued, especially at Auschwitz, where the destruction process reached its apex with the gassing of some 400,000 Hungarian Jews in the spring and summer of 1944.

The suffering of Jews in occupied Poland can be compared to that of the Poles, but should never be equated, as was common in the historiosophy of communist Poland, especially in the years of the so-called "anti-Zionist" campaign of the late 1960s. Polish nationalists and communist propagandists were often eager to cite a quantitative parity in losses, but more importantly, were also intent on postulating a *qualitative* parity in the treatment of the two groups at the hands of the Germans. Although widely accepted, this distortion of the historical record did not go entirely unchallenged in

Poland. To quote Andrzej Szczypiorski, the celebrated Polish novelist and ardent advocate of Polish-Jewish dialogue:

> This issue cannot be presented as a question of statistics, the percentages of losses. It is a question of the completely different way the Nazis treated Jews and Poles. The conditions under which these two groups lived were wholly different [...]. On account of his Jewishness a Jew was condemned to death. On account of his Polishness a Pole was condemned to life under the rule of force, to a life of poverty, humiliation, repressive measures, terror, and also random murder. However, the planned, industrialized murder on a mass scale in the gas chambers of Treblinka, Auschwitz, Chelmno or Belzec did not embrace Poles. Whoever says otherwise engages in the falsification of history. The planned murder swept only the so-called elite sections of the Polish people. The overwhelming majority of Poles, however, remained outside its range" (cited from Krakowski 1988, 323-324).

The fate of Poland's Jews, and Jews from across the European continent, was certainly not unknown, and was rather ineffectively concealed from the Polish population. As Raul Hilberg has succinctly noted: "Almost everywhere in Poland, Jewish death was proximate" (Hilberg 1992, 203). It is therefore not surprising that the greatest burden on the relationship between Poles and Jews centers on the issue of Polish responses to the persecution of Jews in their midst. How could a civilized country witness the process of genocide and fail to stop it? Any knowledgable student of the era would agree that different behavior on the part of some Poles would have saved some Jews, but that the overwhelming majority of the Jews residing in or deported to occupied Poland were doomed. The problem, however, of Polish aid to Jews, or the absence of such aid, remains. This is the crux of the debates over Polish-Jewish relations during the occupation.

Poles have frequently been condemned as willing accomplices or at least indifferent to the suffering of Jews. In, for example, the oft-cited memoirs of Mordekhai Tenenbaum, commander of the Jewish Fighting Organization in the Bialystok Ghetto, we read: "Had it not been for the Poles, for their aid – passive and active – in the 'solution of the Jewish problem in Poland,' the Germans would never have been as succcessful as they were. It was the Poles who called out 'Yid' at every Jew who escaped from the train transporting him to the gas chambers, it was they who caught these unfortunate wretches and who rejoiced at every Jewish misfortune. They were vile and contemptible" (cited from Polonsky 1997, 194).

Is one justified in condemning the Poles as eager spectators, or as a "nation of extortioners"? Indeed, some Poles profited from the Nazi seizure of Jewish property, and some made brief careers of the practice of blackmailing or betraying Jews to the German authorities. It is, however, impossible to determine the percentage of Poles who behaved in such a manner, and is inappropriate to characterize as such the Polish population as a whole. Defenders of Polish behavior note that these extortionists or *szmalzownicy* were subject to the death sentence from the Polish underground. They note the activities of the Council for Aid to the Jews, or Zegota, which helped find refuge for persecuted Jews, supplied them with food and false documents, and provided medical care. Zegota had thousands of Jews under its charge in Warsaw alone, and its efforts, while succeeding in saving only a small percentage of Jews, were nothing short of heroic. Furthermore, apologists cite the aid offered the Jews by the underground military of the Armia Krajowa, or Home Army, linked to the London exile government, and the communist Armia Ludowa, or People's Army. The Armia Krajowa served as a conduit to London and elsewhere for information regarding the persecution and extermination of Jews on Polish territory, and both organizations provided small quantities of weapons and ammunition to the Jews during the Warsaw Ghetto Uprising.

Was such assistance minimal? Inadequate? Insufficient? Rare? Widespread? Assistance was not the norm, but was the exception, and in occupied Poland the penalty for assisting a Jew was death – a sentence often carried out on one's family as well. In short, to offer aid to the Jews was extremely difficult and undertaken at tremendous risk. This is the factor most frequently cited by those attempting to explain or justify the behavior of Poles. In the words of Jan Jozef Lipski, a former soldier in the Armia Krajowa and, it should be noted, a vocal critic of Polish indifference towards the Jews: "It is true that it took an act of heroism to save Jews. I know of people who were armed when they were captured by the Germans and who managed to survive the concentration camps, but I know of no person who hid a Jew and survived being discovered, nor have I heard of such a person" (Lipski 1990, 66).

Critics of Polish behavior, while not denying this grave personal threat, cite the presence of a pervasive and deep prewar and wartime anti-Semitism as the basis of Polish indifference and greatest barrier to assistance (Lipski 1990; Gutman and Krakowski 1986). The Polish-Jewish emigré Jan Tomasz Gross has recently made this argument more forcefully and has also highlighted the inconsistency of the traditional exculpative argument, stating: "[...] there were other kinds of activities prohibited by the Nazis under penalty of death that the Poles massively engaged in. Simply: if we adopt a certain framework for the explanation of people's behavior it must be consistently applicable across the whole range of comparable choices in a given situation." In short, according to Gross, "the 'cost' difference between joining an anti-Nazi conspiracy and helping out the Jews was frequently marginal" (Gross, 2000b, 78; also Gross 1998, 33-37).

We know that between 20,000 and 40,000 Jews survived on the so-called "aryan side" in occupied Poland, but how are these numbers to be interpreted, and how do they detract from, or fortify, the moral judgements that are so frequently made? The complexity and passions of the debate are well illustrated by the ways in which statistics are often used at cross purposes, either as evidence that Poles did all that could be expected of them, or that Poles did far too little to assist their Jewish neighbors. Five and a half thousand Poles have now been recognized as "Righteous Gentiles" by Yad Vashem. Their heroism as individuals is not at issue here; at issue is whether this number should be understood in the broader sense as evidence of Polish valor and selflessness, or as evidence of Polish complicity and indifference.

One particular act of resistance and support for the Jews vividly illustrates the complexity of the question posed here. In August 1942 a noted Roman Catholic author, Zofia Kossak-Szczucka, published an underground appeal to Polish Catholics to protest the destruction of Jews. The text is both anti-Semitic and, at the same time, a clarion call for Polish Catholics to speak out in condemnation of German policies. To quote from the document's concluding sentences: "We, Catholic-Poles, do speak out. Our feelings toward Jews have not changed. We continue seeing them as political, economic, and ideological enemies of Poland. Moreover, we are aware that they hate us more than they hate Germans, that they blame us for their misfortune [...]. Our awareness of these feelings, however, does not release us from the duty to condemn the crime" (cited from Blonski 1996, 183). Some have claimed that this is evidence of Polish willingness to aid even those whom they mistrust or despise; for others, this is evidence that even those Poles who did aid the Jews did so grudgingly and in spite of themselves (Blonski 1996, 184, 189). A conclusive explanation eludes us, making any categorical assessment of Polish behavior all the more difficult.

The gravity of these issues makes it even more regrettable that for nearly forty years there was little open discussion over the realities and complexities of the Jewish-Polish relationship. Such a conversation was silenced by state authority, was avoided out of a desire to avoid the painful memories of a tragic past, or was simply absent because of the lack of a "Jewish voice" in postwar Poland. Ironically, the first years after the liberation offered perhaps the best opportunity for research and writing on the history of the occupation and Jewish-Polish relations. In fact, an all-Polish "League for the Struggle Against Racism" that included such notables as Wladyslaw Bartoszewski and the noted Catholic author Jerzy Andrzejewski, began to address these issues in publications and in the broader public discourse (Borwicz 1947; Bartoszewski 1989, 243-254). The organization and its members were committed to examining the legacy of anti-Semitism in Poland, and the violent anti-Jewish agitation in the first months after the war made their efforts all the more timely.

It is particularly tragic that anti-Semitism would be so pervasive and violent in the very country that had suffered the most at the hands of the Nazi regime. Of the few Jews remaining in Poland or having returned to Poland after the war,[3] a sizable percentage attempted to reorganize themselves as a legitimate national minority with religious, educational and cultural institutions. In fact, many of these Jews, believing that they would be secure as long as a socialist or communist government was in control, were quite optimistic about the future (Dobroszycki 1973, 65; Borwicz 1986, 190; Institute of Jewish Affairs 1968, 6). Conditions in Poland, however, were not as friendly as they had perhaps anticipated, as a wave of anti-Jewish attacks swept across the country between 1945 and 1947. In 1945 alone 355 Jews were killed. Pogroms took place in Rzeszow and Crakow in the summer of 1945, and in the July 1946 Kielce pogrom 41 Jews were killed and 59 were wounded (Borwicz 1986, 193; Shneiderman 1947). By the end of 1947 nearly 1,500 Jews had died as the result of violent attacks (Dobroszycki 1973, 66-67). Not surprisingly, many of the surviving Jews chose to emigrate to western Europe, the United States, or to Palestine.

Part, but only part of the explanation for this vicious anti-Semitism in post-war, post-Holocaust Poland lies in a history of anti-Semitism in Polish culture and society that reached its apex in the years just prior to the war. In the words of one contemporary commentator, the national tradition of anti-Semitism "continues in Poland as a residual attitude, as a habit, and as a reflex" (*Zycie Warszawy* 1945, 15 April). In addition, the prevailing stereotype of the "*Zydokomuna,*" or Jewish-inspired communism, fueled anti-Semitism and violence against Jews. In Poland, as in many other European countries, much of the population associated the communist movement with Jewish conspiracy. Consequently, Jews in early postwar Poland were frequently identified with the unpopular Soviet-installed provisional government and especially the security forces (Checinski 1982, 7-18; Borwicz 1986, 192-193; Kersten 1991, 218-220; Adelson 1993, 405; Borodziej 1993, 76-77; Ossowski 1946). For Poles to immediately link a helpless Jew to the communist takeover in Poland was, of course, preposterous, but in the minds of many this view could be supported by easily available evidence, namely, that a disproportionately large percentage of the new governmental elite in Warsaw was of Jewish origin, as were many prewar Polish communists and socialists (Institute of Jewish Affairs 1968, 6; Checinski 1982, 8-10; Kersten 1991, 219-220; Szczypiorski 1982, 75).[4]

There were, however, more immediate and material causes for renewed discrimination and attacks against the Jews. According to several scholars, the appropriation and reclamation of former Jewish property was central to the problem (Deutscher 1946; Borwicz 1986, 191-193). Immediately after the war thousands of Jews were returning to their homes from refuge in the Soviet Union or from the camps. Much of their property, many of their homes, and even their synagogues had been appropriated by Poles who had assumed that they would never return. In his journalistic memoir, S.L. Shneiderman rather melodramatically describes the dilemma faced when Jews began to return from the camps and abroad:

> They were now returning to look for what was left of their homes or their relatives. But when a Polish peddler hands a Jew a loaf of bread or a bowl of soup, he wonders whence this Jew has come. He was persuaded that he would never again see a Jew. Many of these street peddlers have furnished their homes with the belongings of murdered Jews; some are living in Jewish apartments; others have inherited the workshops of Jewish tailors or shoemakers. Looking at the returning Jews, they wonder whether among their number there is not some relative of the Jews whose goods they had appropriated. In the smaller towns, where the inhabitants do not feel the hand of authority as directly as do those who live in the capital, such newly returned Jews have often been murdered (Shneiderman 1947, 24).

The existence and persistence of Polish anti-Semitism after the war was also rooted in a factor unique to the Polish situation: unlike in other countries under German rule where anti-Semitism was identified with fascist quisling governments, anti-Semitism in Poland was not wholly discredited by the experience of the occupation. As Alexander Smolar has perceptively noted: "Only in Poland was antisemitism compatible with patriotism [...]. Precisely because Polish antisemitism was not tainted by any trace of collaboration with the Germans, it could prosper – not only in the street, but also in the underground press, in political parties, and in the armed forces" (Smolar 1987, 41).

Despite the frightful character of relations between Jews and Poles in the first years after the liberation, the relative lack of censorship and government control in this period actually offered an opportunity for honest examination of the recent past and the meaning of the occupation. The advent of Polish Stalinism, however, put an end to this, and in subsequent years any discussion of Jewish-Polish relations was silenced even as anti-Semitism was consciously deployed by the Polish state for political purposes. This was apparent in Party rivalries during the so-called "Polish October" of 1956, and was especially evident in the context of the "anti-Zionist" campaign in the wake of the 1967 Six-Day War.

For years there had existed within the Party a so-called "Partisan" faction composed predominantly of former resistance fighters and veterans who, as they saw it, had established the foundation for the communist assumption of power in postwar Poland, only to lose their influence to a Moscow-trained elite. These nationally-minded, yet devoted communists had also been frustrated by the post-October reforms, such as Party leader Wladyslaw Gomulka's more liberal and tolerant stance towards critics of the regime. At the head of the "Partisan" group, which by the 1960s included many new and younger functionaries, stood General Mieczyslaw Moczar, Minister of the Interior, head of the Union of Fighters for Freedom and Democracy or ZBoWiD (a nationwide organization of veterans and former prisoners of the Nazi regime), and Gomulka's main rival for power within the Party apparatus.

Gomulka's policy towards Jews in the Party was aimed at their gradual dispersal from the echelons of power, either through attrition or an occasional demotion, but not through large-scale purges. A "Jewish question" therefore existed within the Party and state apparatus, but was not used as a political weapon. It was Moczar who transformed it into an instrument of power, and the Six Day War in June 1967 provided him and his faction with the perfect occasion to step up anti-Jewish measures, draw Gomulka into the fray, and destabilize the Party's upper cadres.

As Israeli troops defeated Nasser's Egypt, an ally of the Soviet Union, Poland quickly fell in line with its mentor in condemning "Zionism," and this new anti-Israel stance gave Gomulka cause to step up measures against Jews within the Party in the name of "anti-Zionism," "anti-imperialism," and the fight against "cosmopolitans." Polish citizens of Jewish descent were now associated not only with the so-called *Zydokomuna*, but more specifically with Stalinism. Jews were not true Poles, were cosmopolitans without a fatherland, and were, because of their Zionist and imperialist leanings, supposedly undermining the fabric of Polish socialism and the Polish nation. The defamation, discrimination, and purging reached their peak in March of 1968 when anti-government protests, led mostly by students and initiated in response to censorship and lack of democracy in public life, swept across the country. Seeking to identify the protesters, that is, dissent in general, with an unreliable Jewish element, the purges extended to nearly all areas of public life: the Party, bureaucracy, economic infrastructure, education, and the arts. Gomulka and Moczar were, however, using the anti-Jewish measures at cross purposes: Gomulka hoped to use the anti-Semitic frenzy as a form of "negative integration," thereby solidifying the regime and status quo in the country, while Moczar intended to destabilize Gomulka's hold on power and then fill the vacuum (Hirszowicz 1986, 202). The result was international condemnation from outside the Soviet block and, by the time the hysteria ended in late 1968, the exclusion of some 9,000 "Zionist traitors" from the ranks of the Party and the emigration of 20,000 Polish Jews. A prewar Jewish community of three million had numbered in 1967 only 30,000, and after the witch-hunts of the late 1960s, only some 10,000 remained (Hoensch 1993, 79). A nationalist movement in Polish communist politics that Jan Jozef Lipski has characterized as "xenophobia enmeshed with idiocy" (Lipski 1990, 56), the "anti-Zionist" campaign marked another low point in relations between Poles and Jews – not only Jews within Poland's borders, but abroad as well.

The campaign is also illustrative of the state's efforts to instrumentalize the past for the accumulation of political currency in the present, for it attempted to revise scholarship and public opinion on the issue of relative Jewish and Polish suffering during the Second World War and worked to distort the legacy of wartime Polish-Jewish relations. Publications emerged that speciously chronicled and celebrated selfless acts of Polish heroism on behalf of Jews during the occupation, and in the late summer of 1967 a number of articles appeared attacking the most recent (1966) edition of the *Wielka Encyklopedia Powszechna* (Great Universal Encyclopedia – a respected Polish reference work) for supposed inaccuracies regarding human losses suffered in Poland during the war. According to one journalist condemning the publication, the *Encyklopedia* entry on "Hitlerite Concentration Camps" had drastically understated Poland's non-Jewish losses by stating that "in the extermination camps approximately 5.7 million died (ca. 99 percent Jews, ca. 1 percent Gypsies and others)" ("Obozy Koncentracyjne Hitlerowski" 1966, 87-89). This "manipulation" of historical facts, the author implied, was the inspiration of imperialist West German and American anti-Polish propaganda bent on minimizing Polish losses during the war and defaming Poland's good name (Kulicz 1967).[5] This was followed by a press campaign in the Party organ *Trybuna Ludu* – a campaign that was little else than a clumsy effort to unmask the purported distorting claims of "Zionist" propaganda that 5.6 of 5.7 million killed in the extermination camps were Jews, as well as claims that the Poles are an organically anti-Semitic people who collaborated in their extermination (Pilichowski 1968, 23 May). A second article also advocated further investigation of the destructive activities of Jewish "administrative" prisoners in the camps, the role of the Jewish Councils in the ghettos, the activities of Jewish police in the extermination process, and Jewish collaboration with the Gestapo. Many of those "Zionists" and "nationalists" who collaborated, the author claimed, were now to be found in Western countries and Israel (Pilichowski 1968, 25 May).[6]

Marginalization of the Shoah had been an enduring characteristic of the postwar Polish memory of the occupation, and Poles had never been encouraged, whether in school curricula or at sites of wartime commemoration, to focus on Jews as a specific and the most numerous category of victim. Even if the conclusions intended to be drawn from publications such as these were not a major revision of the official historical record, they did represent a renegotiating of Polish considerations of the Shoah. At the very least, the reader was encouraged to regard statistics (and even *Polish* statistics such as those provided in the 1966 edition of the *Encyclopedia*) on Jewish wartime deaths with suspicion or, preferably, to dismiss them outright as "Zionist" fabrications. Moreover, it was implied that the behavior of Jews under the occupation and in the camps was not patriotic and self-sacrificing like that of Poles, but unpatriotic, self-serving, and ultimately treasonous[7] – in other words, like the treasonous behavior of the "Zionists" and "imperialists" currently working to undermine the reputation and integrity of the Polish nation and state.

The era of the "anti-Zionist" campaign provides a further example of how the history of the occupation, Polish-Jewish relations in wartime, and the history of, in this case, Auschwitz was distorted and deployed for political purposes. In April of that year an exhibition entitled "Martyrology and Struggle of the Jews" was opened at the State Museum at Auschwitz, the first large exhibition of its kind at the memorial site since its dedication in 1947. Most observers and analysts have assumed that this exhibit was opened prior to 1968 and closed as a result of the anti-Jewish campaign (Irwin-Zarecka 1989, 153-154; Young 1993, 130). In fact, the opposite is true. It was opened at the height of the campaign, in April 1968, in an effort to recoup for Poland some of its lost international credibility. In light of the purges, anti-Semitic rhetoric, and international protests leveled against the campaign, the Warsaw regime could exploit the new exhibition (and hence the memory of Auschwitz Jews) in the hope of redeeming its sullied reputation abroad. The exhibit was not intended as a memorial to Jewish suffering and death at the camp or in Europe as a whole. Nor was it meant to offer a rigorous historical presentation of the Shoah. Instead, simply put, the exhibit in Block 27 was intended as a testimony to the shared suffering of Poles and Jews and, more importantly, as a document of Polish aid to Jews during the occupation. It was to be an antidote (Iwaszko 1994; Szczypiorski 1999), but as an attempt to restore Poland's international credibility it was clumsy in its execution and tragically transparent in its hypocrisy.

This exhibition and the themes conveyed in it were also significant because they illustrated some of the salient trends in communist historiography at the time: anti-Semitism was a fascist tool that had been nearly eradicated under the watchful eye and increasingly classless society of communist Poland; during the occupation, both Poles and Jews shared a common fate; Polish and Jewish suffering was equal, or at the very least, Poles were next in line for extermination; Nazi occupation policy towards the Poles was brutal, but despite the risks involved, many Poles assisted Jews in acts of solidarity, altruism, and bravery. This is not to suggest that every Pole subscribed to these interpretations of the recent past, or that every historian of the occupation was instrumental in propogating them. What these distortions of the historical record do suggest is the crippling absence of open and fruitful debate over these issues.

In fact, it took nearly forty years for an honest and open conversation over issues of Polish-Jewish relations to emerge in the Polish People's Republic, and there are several reasons why this occurred in the 1980s. First, the independent trade union movement "Solidarity" encouraged not only the revival of traditional Polish nationalism and the Polish insurrectionary spirit. It also called for greater cultural openness, thereby encouraging a more thorough and honest historical self-examination. There were, to be sure, anti-Jewish elements in the Solidarity movement, but its condemnation of the regime's anti-Semitism in 1968, as well as the limited freedoms won from the state, allowed for the emergence of a fruitful, if painful, reassessment of relations between Poles and Jews during and since the war. It is, then, no accident that so many of the participants in the debates over Jewish-Polish relations in the 1980s and 1990s were intimately connected with Solidarity.

A second factor spurring a new assessment of the occupation and Polish-Jewish relations was the airing of Claude Lanzmann's film *Shoah*. Condemned by both the official press and many Polish critics abroad as tendentiously anti-Polish in its characterization of Poles as indifferent and ignorant "bystanders" to the Holocaust, the film nonetheless caused Poles to reassess their assumptions about the nature and character of Nazi occupation policy. One might be angered by the boorishness, ignorance, prejudice, or apparent indifference of the Polish peasants and villagers appearing in Lanzmann's interviews, but one is also aware of a certain incapacity on the part of those bystanders to comprehend, come to terms with, or even discuss the murder of Jews in their midst. Were their responses to the camera somehow indicative of their own ambivalence, horror, indifference, or fear as these events were transpiring? Lanzmann's agenda may be clear, but his film does leave room for interpretation.

Third, the Carmelite Convent controversy of the late 1980s brought not only the Auschwitz memorial site, but also the meaning and legacy of the war years in Poland into the international public eye. In 1984, the Carmelite order established a small convent in an abandoned building bordering the *Stammlager*, or base camp of the Auschwitz complex. This move was met with vocal protest on the part of Jews in Europe, Israel, and the United States, resulting in what one analyst has referred to as a "turf war" over "sacred space" (Modras 1991, 54). The controversy was acrimonious and proceeded at times more on the level of emotional accusation than reasoned debate. Jewish groups and publicists saw in the establishment of the convent yet another example of Polish anti-Semitism, and charged Poles with "polonizing" the site of Nazi Germany's largest extermination center. Polish defenders of the convent pointed out that it was located adjacent to the Auschwitz base camp, not Birkenau, which was the site of nearly a million Jewish deaths. Moreover, some Poles, including the Roman Catholic primate Jozef Glemp, regarded the Jewish protests as meddling in Poland's internal affairs. "Jews," the Cardinal stated, should not speak to Poles "from a position of a nation above all others," but should put an end to the anti-Polish campaign in the media, "which are," the Cardinal claimed, "in many countries, at [the Jews'] disposal." Several weeks later, the Israeli Prime Minister Yitzhak Shamir maintained that the Cardinal's remarks mirrored an organic Polish anti-Semitism that the Poles "suck . . . with their mother's milk" (cited from Rittner and Roth 1991, 24, 224). Thus, what had begun as a controversy over the appropriate use of memorial space at Auschwitz had become a revisitation of stereotypes.

Exchanges such as these were certainly unseemly, but the convent controversy did bring some broader questions into the public discourse, both in Poland and abroad. Why is the symbolic value of Auschwitz, as both terminus and as memorial site, so different for Poles and Jews? What aspects of the history of Auschwitz, or more broadly, what aspects of the history of the occupation have led to such divergent Polish and Jewish memories? What did the controversy suggest about the current state of Polish-Jewish relations? Must Auschwitz, this powerful symbol of the occupation and suffering, function only as a source of strife, or is it possible that it can serve as a locus for dialogue and understanding?

These questions were subsequently addressed in the context of a debate sparked in 1987 by the publication of an article entitled "The Poor Poles Look at the Ghetto" in the oppositional weekly *Tygodnik Powszechny*. Its author, the literary critic Jan Blonski, argued that to the extent that Poles have attempted to confront or discuss the Nazi destruction of Jews, their responses have generally been limited to apologetics and attempts to justify Polish behavior during the Holocaust. Poles, he claimed, were fearful of being accused of participating in the crimes or having regarded it with indifference. The way out of this fear, and the way to avoid reflex defensive reactions was, according to Blonski, for Poles to "stop haggling, trying to defend and justify ourselves. We must stop arguing about the things that were beyond our power to do, during the occupation and beforehand. Nor must we place blame on political, social and economic conditions. We must say first of all – Yes, we are guilty" (Blonski 1990, 44). Blonski did not claim that the Poles were guilty of any direct involvement in the genocide of the Jews (making, of course, the obvious exception for blackmailers and informants). Rather, the Poles were guilty of inadequate resistance against the persecution of Jews. "[I]f only," Blonski wrote, "we had behaved more humanely in the past, had been wiser, more generous, then genocide would perhaps have been 'less imaginable', would probably have been considerably more difficult to carry out, and almost certainly would have met with much greater resistance than it did. To put it differently, it would not have met with the indifference and moral turpitude of the society in whose full view it took place" (Blonski 1990, 46).

The article prompted passionate responses in the Polish press (Turowicz 1988), and the debates that ensued were even the subject of academic conferences in Poland and abroad. One powerful response expressing the sentiments of many Poles was that of the Solidarity activist Wladyslaw Sila-Nowicki, who enumerated several of the common defenses against accusations of Polish complicity or indifference: Poland had traditionally been a haven for Jews; before 1939, Jews dominated certain professions and disproportionately controlled wealth, yet at the same time retained their separateness and alien character; no European nation did more to help the Jews than Poland, and it was in Poland that the risks associated with assistance to Jews were the greatest; it was not only Jews who were killed under the occupation, but Poles as well; there were no quislings in Poland and no collaborative government, but there was a massive underground resistance that sentenced to death those who betrayed Jews to the Nazis. Sila-Nowicki's defense concluded with the following: "I am proud of my nation's stance in every respect during the period of occupation and in this include the attitude towards the tragedy of the Jewish nation. Obviously, the attitudes towards the Jews during that period do not give us a particular reason to be proud, but neither are they any grounds for shame, and even less for ignominy. Simply, we would have done relatively little more than we actually did" (Sila-Nowicki 1990, 62).

Responses such as these were not unusual, nor were the attitudes expressed therein particularly new. But the controversy in the late 1980s over relations between Jews and Poles during the occupation marked a turning point. For the first time in forty years, scholars and publicists, both in Poland and abroad, were participating in a relatively open (and certainly contentious) re-evaluation of history. Like the West German historians' debate of the same decade, the debate in the aftermath of Blonski's article was an effort to come to terms with or even "master" the past. This is probably where the similarities between the two controversies end, but the fact remains that both marked the beginning of a painful, and at times cathartic process that continues to the present day, albeit in different forms.

The fall of communism in 1989 has offered even greater openness to intellectual and cultural debate in Poland, bringing with it new opportunities to reassess the issue of Jewish-Polish relations. An open society, however, also presents new challenges. Most Poles are eager to build a society free of xenophobia, racism, and anti-Semitism, yet in post-communist political culture we have seen the growing tendency to draw distinctions between the "national" and the "foreign," between the "true Pole" and the "other" (Blatman 1997, 27-30). The notion of the *Zydokomuna* is certainly not as strong as it was in the interwar or early postwar years, but it has not disappeared. In Poland, as elsewhere, conspiracy theories die hard.

There also exists in contemporary Poland a tendency to condemn the former communist regime to the point of uncritically and ahistorically rendering it analogous to the Nazi regime during the occupation. Moreover, we have witnessed a growing tendency to dismiss postwar Polish anti-Semitism and its ugliest manifestations, such as the Kielce pogrom or the discrimination and purges of 1968, as responses to or manifestations of Soviet manipulation, while ignoring the fact that a certain level of animosity towards Jews among segments of the Polish population was necessary for the anti-Semitic excesses of 1945-1947 and the "anti-Zionist" state policy less than twenty years later. To generalize or stereotype the Poles or contemporary Polish national character on the basis of these excesses is unfair. They are cruel evidence of a pervasive anti-Semitism among Poles. They are not necessarily evidence of an organic and broadly-based anti-Semitism among Poles, and they are not concrete evidence of broad Polish complicity in or indifference to the extermination of Jews.

Debates will certainly continue – debates over the reality of the German occupation and its meaning, debates over the relative level of Jewish and Polish suffering, debates over the extent of Polish indifference, complicity, or instigation of crimes against Jews, and even debates over the meaning and use of symbols of the occupation. The emerging controversy over Jan T. Gross' account of the massacre of Jews at Jedwabne (Gross, 2000a), recent strife over the presence of crosses at Auschwitz, or criticism of so-called "Schindler tourism" in Cracow's former Jewish quarter are only a few examples of this. These debates and the introspective processes associated with them are painful, yet as Antony Polonsky has argued, all parties should strive to advance beyond the standard and reflex condemnations of Polish behavior during the Holocaust or justifications for it (Polonsky 1997). It is reassuring that as bitter or unseemly as some of the conflicts over Jewish-Polish relations have been, they have nonetheless brought us closer to the historical truth. They also place a new and welcome burden on the purveyors of public and academic history. Tour guides at Majdanek are now much more explicit about the numbers of and reasons for Jewish deaths in that camp complex. Many Poles may vehemently disagree with Jewish objections to the presence of a cross at an execution site at the Auschwitz base camp, but it is safe to say that most Poles now understand the reasons for those objections. The relative wartime suffering of Poles, Jews, and other victim groups is now less frequently discussed in terms of a fruitless and insulting zero-sum game according to which an acknowledgment of one group's suffering at the hands of the Nazis is regarded as detracting from the extent of another's.

To conclude on such a hopeful note is perhaps unjustifiably optimistic, for the issue of Polish-Jewish relations remains bitter and burdened. Indeed, the appearance of Jan Gross' aforementioned work has unleashed in Poland what is probably the most significant historical controversy since the fall of communism. Gross' account of the murder of 1,600 Jews by their Polish neighbors in July 1941, apparently without the participation of the Germans, is a horrific story unto itself. But the sensation that it has created is also characteristic, for it is yet another illustration of the broader and seemingly inexorable burdens of the Polish-Jewish relationship. The truth about Jedwabne was evident in the archives and memories of the townspeople, and postwar court proceedings were undertaken against a number of the perpetrators, yet the massacre was, for decades, officially commemorated as simply another instance of Nazi brutality against Poland's Jews. The monument at the site had simply stated: "A site of torment of the Jewish population – the Hitlerite Gestapo and Gendarmerie burned 1600 people alive, 10 July 1941" (Gross, 2000a, 120). This commemorative text, and the official amnesia at its source, are further evidence of the efforts of the Polish communist state to repress the truth about Polish complicity in the persecution and murder of Jews; they testify to the crippling effects of communist historiosophy. The inscription points, however, to a larger, decades-old problem in the Polish collective memory. In the words of the essayist and Warsaw Jewish leader Stanislaw Krajewski, the truth about Jedwabne was simply "not part of Polish historical consciousness" (Krajewski 2001). Not limited to the nationalist fringes of Polish politics, the historical consciousness to which the author refers remains rife with dated notions of traditional Polish tolerance of minorities, national messianism, and the innocent suffering of, to employ the trope of 19th-century romanticism, the "Christ among nations."

The story of the Jedwabne massacre and the controversy that the publication of Gross' book has awakened marks yet another turning point in the public discourse and historiography of Polish-Jewish relations, for at issue here is not the relative suffering of the two victim groups, or the indifference of Poles to the destruction in their midst, or even Polish complicity in the crimes of the Shoah. At issue is the active and enthusiastic participation of Polish villagers in the murder of their Jewish neighbors. Subsequent research will undoubtedly put Gross' broader generalizations and conclusions under scrutiny, but the foundation of Poland's postwar commemorative cult of righteous suffering has been severely weakened. If, as Gross claims, the story of Jedwabne marks a "new opening" in Polish historiography, and if this is, in fact, a moment when the historiographical "sedatives" (Gross, 2000a, 100) of the past fifty years can finally be put aside, then it will become ever clearer that the experience of the occupation only partially confirmed the collective perception of a nation suffering and resisting, in the words of the underground's motto, "for your freedom and ours."

The foregoing analysis has been descriptive rather than prescriptive, but in conclusion, it is not inappropriate to express a certain hope. In light of emerging research and a growing public discourse on the reality of the occupation, Poles will be forced to undertake a broader and more precise reading of their past. Jews, both in Poland and beyond, will also have to confront a history of the occupation that is perhaps no less brutal, but certainly more complex and nuanced with respect to relations between the two victim groups. A memory simplified or distorted, as useful or therapeutic as it may be, does not light the path to historical redemption. As Primo Levi has reminded us: "It is naive, absurd, and historically false to believe that an infernal system such as National Socialism sanctifies its victims" (Levi 1988, 40). For Levi, struggling in his final work to come to terms with the "gray zone" of moral culpability, there was little sense in attaching any sort of redemptive value to the victimization of Poles, Jews, or any other group suffering under the Nazis. The burdens of Polish-Jewish relations, and the pain and prejudice that are their legacy, suggest that sanctification of the victims is undertaken at great risk, for it inevitably leads to their instrumentalization, whether for the perpetuation of a condemnatory myth of inveterate Polish anti-Semitism, or a salvific myth of Polish national virtue.

Notes

[1]The essay is based in part on a lecture given in June 2000 for the Center for Holocaust Studies at the University of Vermont.

[2]I rely here on Smolar's characterizations of "historic discontinuity" and "historic continuity," but unlike Smolar, have refrained from labeling these interpretations "Polish" and "Jewish," respectively. See Smolar, 34-35.

[3]The *New York Times*, in an article of 22 February 1946, set the Jewish population at war's end at approximately 50,000. The historian Krystyna Kersten estimates that there were, in July 1946, approximately 245,000 Jews in Poland, mostly in the so-called "recovered territories" of western Poland that had been put under Polish administration by the terms of the Potsdam Conference (see Kersten 1991, 215 and Adelson 1993, 387). While estimates of Holocaust survivors, the number of Jews residing in Poland, or the number of Jewish immigrants to Poland after the liberation vary greatly, the point is that these figures represent only a small fraction of the prewar population of more than three million.

[4]While acknowledging the prevailing public perception of the *Zydokomuna* in early postwar Poland, Jan Gross has recently made a strong case against the traditional claims that Jews welcomed the Soviet occupation of eastern Poland in 1939, that Jewish survivors in Poland enthusiastically and disproportionalely supported the goals of the Soviet-inspired regime in the early postwar years (see Gross, 2000b, 92-105).

[5]See also Wilczur 1967; *Zycie Literackie* 1967. For a thorough account of the distortion of Jewish and non-Jewish losses in the press and in government propaganda efforts see Lendvai 1971, 188.

[6]Arguments similar to those of Pilichowski are also to be found in Walichnowski, 1968.

[7]This theme was echoed a month later for publication abroad in the foreign-language editions of *Polska*. See Piorkowski 1968.

Literature Cited

Adelson, Jozef. 1993. W Polsce zwanej ludowa. In *Najnowsze dzieje Zydow w Polsce*, ed. Jerzy Tomaszewski, pp. 387-477. Warszawa: Wydawnictwo Naukowe WDN.

Bartoszewski, Wladyslaw. 1989. The Founding of the All-Polish Anti-Racist League in 1946. *Polin* 4:243-254.

Blatman, Daniel. 1997. Polish Antisemitism and 'Judeo-Communism': Historiography and Memory. *East European Jewish Affairs* 27, no. 1:23-43.

Blonski, Jan. 1990. The Poor Poles Look at the Ghetto. In *'My Brother's Keeper?': Recent Polish Debates on the Holocaust*, ed. Antony Polonsky, pp. 34-52. London: Routledge.

Blonski, Jan. 1996. Polish Catholics and Catholic Poles: The Gospel, National Interest, Civic Solidarity, and the Destruction of the Warsaw Ghetto. *Yad Vashem Studies* 25:181-196.

Borodziej, Wlodzimierz. 1993. Polen und Juden im 20. Jahrhundert: Zum Fortleben von Stereotypen nach dem Holocaust. In *Polen nach dem Kommunismus*, ed. Erwin Oberländer, pp. 71-79. Stuttgart: Fritz Steiner Verlag.

Borwicz, Michal, ed. 1947. *Organizowanie Wscieklosci*. Warszawa: Wydawnictwo Ogolnopolskiej Ligi do Walki z Rasizmem.

Borwicz, Michal. 1986. Polish-Jewish Relations, 1944-1947. In *The Jews in Poland*, ed. Chimen Abramsky, Maciej Jachimczyk and Antony Polonsky, pp. 190-198. Oxford: Basil Blackwell.

Browning, Christopher. 1992. *Ordinary Men: Reserve Police Battalion 101 and the Final Solution in Poland*. New York: Harper Collins.

Checinski, Michael. 1982. *Poland: Communism – Nationalism – Anti-Semitism*. New York: Karz-Kohl.

Deutscher, Isaac. 1946. Remnants of a Race. *The Economist* (London) 150, no. 5342 (12 January):15-16.

Dobroszycki, Lucjan. 1973. Restoring Jewish Life in Post-War Poland. *Soviet Jewish Affairs* 3, no. 2:58-72.

Fein, Helen. 1984. *Accounting for Genocide: National Responses and Jewish Victimization During the Holocaust*. Chicago: University of Chicago Press.

Gross, Jan T. 1998. *Upiorna dekada: Trzy eseje o stereotypach na temat Zydow, Polakow, Niemcow i komunistow 1939-1948*. Krakow: Universitas.

Gross, Jan T. 2000a. *Sasiedzi: Historia zaglady zydowskiego miasteczka*. Sejny: Pogranicze.

Gross, Jan T. 2000b. A 'Tangled Web: Confronting Stereotypes Concerning Relations between Poles, Germans, Jews and Communists. In *The Politics of Retribution in Europe*, ed. Istvan Deak, Jan T. Gross, and Tony Judt, 74-129. Princeton, New Jersey: Princeton University Press.

Gutman, Yisrael and Shmuel Krakowski. 1986. *Unequal Victims: Poles and Jews during World War II*. New York: Holocaust Library.

Hilberg, Raul. 1992. *Perpetrators, Victims, Bystanders: The Jewish Catastrophe 1933-1945*. New York: Harper Collins.

Hirszowicz, Lukasz. 1986. The Jewish Issue in Post-War Communist Politics. In *The Jews in Poland*, ed. Chimen Abramsky, Maciej Jachimczyk and Antony Polonsky, pp. 199-208. Oxford: Basil Blackwell.

Hoensch, Jörg. 1993. Gegen 'Revisionismus' und 'Zionismus': Gomulka, die 'Partisanen" und die Intellecktuellen, 1964-1968. In *Zwischen Tauwetter und neuem Frost. Ostmitteleuropa 1956-1970*, ed. Hans Lemberg, pp. 79-92. Marburg: Herder.

Institute of Jewish Affairs. 1968. *The Anti-Jewish Campaign in Present-Day Poland*. London: Institute of Jewish Affairs.

Irwin-Zarecka, Iwona. 1989. *Neutralizing Memory: The Jew in Contemporary Poland*. New Brunswick: Transaction Publishers.

Iwaszko, Emeryka. 1994. Interview by author. 17 November.

Kersten, Krystyna. 1991. *The Establishment of Communist Rule in Poland, 1943-1948.* Berkeley, California: University of California Press.

Krajewski, Stanislaw. 2001. Teszuwa. *Wiez* 44, no. 2 (February).

Krakowski, Shmuel. 1988. Relations Between Jews and Poles during the Holocaust – New and Old Approaches in Polish Historiography. *Yad Vashem Studies* 19:317-340.

Kulicz, Krzysztof. 1967. Falsz w encyklopedii. *Stolica*, 13 August 1967.

Lendvai, Paul. 1971. *Antisemitism Without Jews.* New York: Doubleday.

Levi, Primo. 1988. *The Drowned and the Saved.* New York: Simon and Schuster.

Lipski, Jan Jozef. 1990. Two Fatherlands, Two Patriotisms. In *Between East and West: Writings from Kultura*, ed. Robert Kostrzewa, pp. 52-71. New York: Hill and Wang.

Modras, Ronald. 1991. Jews and Poles: Remembering at a Cemetery. In *Memory Offended: the Auschwitz Convent Controversy.* ed. Carol Rittner and John K. Roth, pp. 53-61. New York: Praeger.

Obozy Koncentracyjne Hitlerowskie. 1966. In *Wielka Encyklopedia Powszechna* 8:87-89. Warszawa: Panstwowe Wydawnictwo Naukowe.

Ossowski, Stanislaw. 1946. Na tle wydarzen Kieleckich. *Kuznica* 38(56).

Pilichowski, Czeslaw. 1968. Straty i lokalizacja. *Trybuna Ludu*, 23 May.

Pilichowski, Czeslaw. 1968. Pomoc i wspolnictwo. *Trybuna Ludu*, 25 May.

Piorkowski, Jerzy. 1968. Aus dem Notizbuch des Redakteurs. *Polen* 6, no. 166 (June):2.

Polonsky, Antony. 1997. Beyond Condemnation, Apologetics and Apologies: On the Complexity of Polish Behavior Toward the Jews During the Second World War. *The Fate of the European Jews, 1939-1945: Continuity or Contingency?* Studies in Contemporary Jewry, ed. Jonathan Frankel, 13:190-224.

Rittner, Carol and John K. Roth, ed. 1991. *Memory Offended: the Auschwitz Convent Controversy.* New York: Praeger.

Shneiderman, S. L. 1947. *Between Fear and Hope.* New York: Arco.

Sila-Nowicki, Wladyslaw. 1990. A Reply to Jan Blonski. In *'My Brother's Keeper?': Recent Polish Debates on the Holocaust*, ed. Antony Polonsky, pp. 59-68. London: Routledge.

Smolar, Alexander. 1987. Jews as a Polish Problem. *Daedelus* 116, no. 2 (spring 1987): 31-73.

Symonowicz, Antoni. 1960. Nazi Campaign against Polish Culture. In *1939-1945 War Losses in Poland*, ed. Roman Nurowski, pp. 73-105. Poznan: Zachodnia Agencja Prasowa.

Szczypiorski, Andrzej. 1982. *The Polish Ordeal: The View from Within.* London: Croom Helm.

Szczypiorski, Andzrej. 1999. Letter to author, 29 December.

Turowicz, Jerzy. 1988. Polish Reasons and Jewish Reasons. *Yad Vashem Studies* 19:379-388.

Walichnowski, Tadeusz. 1968. Die Rolle der zionistischen Bewegung in der antikommunistischen Kampagne und der Rehabilitation der Bundesrepublik. *Polen* 6, no. 166 (June):17-22, 39-44.

Wilczur, Jacek. 1967. Prawda obowiazek koniecznosc. *Za Wolnosc i Lud*, 1-15 September.

Young, James E. 1993. *The Texture of Memory: Holocaust Memorials and Meaning.* New Haven, Connecticut: Yale University Press.

Zycie Literackie. 1967. 6 August.

Zycie Warszawy. 1945. 8 April.

Zycie Warszawy. 1945. 15 August.

Aspects of the Transition Between the Living Memory and the History of the Holocaust

Carroll McC. Lewin

Our postmodern condition, with its attendant criticisms of rationalist and empiricist theories, attests to a seeming inescapability of cognitive and moral ambiguity and lack of consoling and redemptive metanarratives. At the same time, our more than half-century confrontation with the Holocaust cries out for an authoritative version of the events and a narrative wholeness and coherency which rejects the traducing of the terrors of history. Irony is situated in these waning years of the living memory of the Nazi genocide, a critical phase in the transposition of memory into history. The acute and palpable tension at this juncture between memory and history marks the competition between a desire for grand narrative and the evident propogation of variant versions of momentous events. Hegemonic struggles emerge in the discourse of memory even as the historian strives to make a promise to the dead to tell the truth about the past (Wyschograd 1998, xi). Present-day memory-work, the reconstruction of the past, helps shape the future antithesis between memory and history. What is required is a self-consciousness about this process as it now takes place, along with a commitment to analyse carefully the contemporary quest for meaning. Not to fulfill this obligation will impact future representation and remembrance. That is, unintended distortions could emerge to imprint indelibly, future recognition of the significance and meaning of the Holocaust. While the interpretation of the past serves the present, we cannot allow any one particular interpretation "to be made sacred and be transformed into a pious image" (Todorov 1996, x). This is because memory is not neutral and can serve a number of agendas and symbolic discourses, just as grand narrative can be appropriat-

ed and contested as strategies for separate political, cultural, and other interests. Increasingly, however, the contradiction may become not so much
between memory and history, but between memory and the metaphors that
now are replacing the events of which they are a reminder. While it may be
very human to reduce catastrophe to symbols, and to exhibit a sort of moral
laziness in "a growing lapse of memory disguised as devotion" (Finkelkraut
1998, 59), it is our obligation to engage in acute awareness about such tendencies and understand their implications for the future. Otherwise, we risk
passing on simplistic and mythic renditions of a major node in western historical consciousness.

A major requirement is to document carefully the present cultivation of
collective memory, that is, the determination of how the past will provide
the narrative content of what is to be shared in memory (Osiel 1997, 18).
This requires fighting against collective memory's tendency to essentialize
what had been the actual experience of the Holocaust which, as we have
learned from the survivors, was marked by fragmentation, discontinuity,
ambiguity, and ambivalence. While the cultivation of collective memory
attempts to assign common meaning to disparate individual memories, we
need to pass onto future generations that there is something else at stake here
– a self-consciousness about a still shifting dialogue between the past and the
present. Because communal debate continues to be heated, we, the occu-
pants of the transitional phase between memory and history, must make
apparent the significance of this phase in the waning years of the living
memory of the Nazi genocide. This includes recognizing the irony of the
hunger for redemptive wholeness in the face of alternative and competing
narratives, and passing on this recognition to subsequent generations as they
participate in their own memory-work. Our recognition that history is politically situated and that "history must be written from the standpoint of the
present so that one can see where a past event is leading" (Wyschograd 1998,
24), should be a legacy to the future. While there are no "national schools of
thought" in Holocaust scholarship (Jäckel 1998, 23), we should depict the
cultivation of collective memory as it is politically situated. Otherwise, relativization and falsification can slip through and seep into historical consciousness. We must neither over privilege the notion that there is no one
privileged discourse, nor abandon the ethical task of truth telling. In other
words, like Saul Friedländer, we should resist closure and totalization without succumbing to the perils of relativization posed by postmodernism
(Friedländer 1992). Because memory-work always bears on the present and
the future, we cannot oversimplify the issue of the binary opposition
between memory and history. Our present function is not only to adjudicate

truth claims, but to transmit critically tested memory as best we can (LaCapra 1998, 20).

To counter essentializing and totalizing tendencies is to document important communal differences, Jewish and non-Jewish, in present-day memory-work and cultivation of collective memory. A comparison between Germany and France highlights such differences as these communities work through their separate agendas, addressing them through different narrative strategies and discursive practices. With the end of the Cold War, all European countries are reevaluating their roles in World War II. Separate collective memories are now situated in a wider context of the so-called "New Europe," with an accompanying demise of ethnic nationalism questioned, nonetheless, by a resurgence of such nationalism, most notably in the former Yugoslavia. The dialogue between past and present continues to shift. To explore both particularities and commonalities in collective memory is to recognize the need to document these closing years of the living memory of the Holocaust in order to inform future processes of representation and remembrance. We need to pass on an understanding of present dialogic shiftings.

If collective memory consists of stories about momentous events in the history of a group from which common lessons are to be drawn (Osiel 1997, 19), the evolution of dialogue in Germany about the Holocaust forcefully demonstrates the vicissitudes of remembering. Significant generational splits and the reunification of the two Germanys are two major sources of dialogic shifting in coping with what Charles Maier terms "the unmasterable past" in German national identity (Maier 1988). Foci for debate have included, among others: (1) sites of memory and their possible commemorative purpose; (2) the role of the *Wehrmacht*, industrial corporations, and other institutions in the Nazi era; (3) the German historiographical perspective in the interpretation of Nazism, and (4) conflict between East and West German viewpoints on the historical context of Nazism. Public discourse on these topics has had an intense inter-generational component centering on coming-to-terms with the past in ways that can include or exclude the possibility of collective guilt and its expiation. An example of ambiguity and conflict in public discourse was the debate generated by the promulgation of a new immigration law, passed in May 1999, requiring a psychological shift from a volkish view of nationality to a more republican view of citizenship. This recent debate is significant because it addresses both the present reality of Germany as a multicultural society and highlights the issue of national identity which always has suffused German discourse about the Holocaust.

Reunification and the infusion of Jews from Russia, along with legislation promoting a transition from a "land of the German people" to a "land of immigration," has complicated Jewish identity in Germany and the role of the Jewish community in German coming-to-terms with the Nazi genocide. Ambivalence marks both Jewish identity and the Jewish-German dialogue: Germans may need the Jews in order to atone for the Holocaust, but Jews may be reluctant to play such a therapeutic role (Mittleman 1999, 314). The question is how long Jews will continue to remain a factor in the symbolic economy of German culture (Mittleman 1999, 318). At the same time, the construction of ethnic identity within the Jewish community is marked by some ambivalence and contradiction, producing what has been termed a "negative symbiosis" between Jews and Germans (Rapaport 1997, 145). The linked phenomena of reemergent Jewish culture and philo-semitism have come to affect both the symbiosis and the role of Jews in present-day Germany. Sander Gilman, among others, argues strongly that younger Jews in Germany are articulating a new Jewish cultural identity (Gilman 1996; Gilman and Remmler 1994). Others stress the continuing ambiguity of Jewish status in Germany and maintain that any vital or substantial Jewish social life is "a highly illusory phenomenon" with an almost exclusively non-Jewish German audience (Stern 1997, 229). Philo-semitism is a complex aspect of the Jewish-German dialogue, harking back to a long debate (notably between George Mosse and Gershom Shollem) as to whether there ever was such a thing as a German-Jewish dialogue and true cultural symbiosis. Tellingly, some Jews in Germany regard present philo-semitism as a modified form of anti-semitism (Rapaport 1997, 177).

Discourse on the Holocaust also has been marked in the commemorative sphere, notably in debates over the Holocaust Memorial in Berlin. Intertwined with issues of national identity in the context of the architectural rendering of the new capitol, these debates are of a series in which public memory catalyzes the larger issue of collective memory. Indeed, Holocaust memorial-work in Germany always has constituted "a tortured, self-reflective, even paralyzing preoccupation" (Young 1993, 20). Torn between forgetting and remembering, Germans of different generations continue to exhibit ambiguity and conflict in their discourse on the Holocaust. Concern about "public, consciously elaborated interpretive frameworks" addresses the possible alternatives of the persistence or the extinction of public memory (Herf 1997, 10; Fox 1999). It may be that for non-Jewish Germans the memory of the Holocaust is "not so much suppressed as negatively freighted," with feelings of shame and guilt transformed into defense mechanisms rather than reflection (Benz 1994, 104). While the political culture of the Federal Republic may be rooted in wishes for closure and redemption, younger (and future) generations require "new forms of discussion, confrontation, and understanding" (Benz 1994, 104). This is particularly so given the legacy of separate pre-unification discourses about the Holocaust. While East Germany repressed and "explained" the Holocaust in anti-fascist, Marxist terms, West Germany had been obliged at the outset to remember the Holocaust as the price for post-war entry as a democracy in the western European alliance. As current German history is dominated by the West German discursive agenda, serving, in part, to reinforce the idea of German identity, debate about Holocaust commemoration continues. The irony of the legacy of two German discourses is that the reemergence of Jewish cultural life in Germany is dominated by (East) Berlin young intellectuals in search of a previously submerged Jewish identity (Stern 1997, 228). Meanwhile, it is unresolved whether German public memory serves the purpose of public self-analysis and mourning, or acts to absolve feelings of guilt and shame (Domansky 1992, 82).

In an essay first published in 1959, Theodor Adorno questions the meaning of German "coming-to-terms with the past," concluding that the phrase does not imply "a serious working through of the past, the breaking of its spell through an act of clear consciousness," but, rather, a "wishing to turn the page and, if possible, wiping it from memory" (Adorno 1986, 115). Adorno also questioned whether German attempts at public enlightenment and exploration of the past might not bring about the opposite of what is intended, and actually awaken resistance to such an insistence on the past (Adorno 1986, 126). More recently, Charles Maier, in his consideration of the seminal 1980's *Historikerstreit*, or "historians' conflict," questions the unreflective belief that "identity is reducible to history" and that knowledge of identity can be captured only by the historian (Maier 1988, 149). Because the issues raised by the historians' debate and the need to come-to-terms with the past have transpired in an easily discernible generational context, it is clear that future generations in Germany will devise their own forms of confrontation and understanding. It is important that they be informed of what has been taking place during the present era of the living memory of the Holocaust. In the absence, nay the impossibility, at this time of a full resolution of the working-through of the vicissitudes of memory in Germany, to focus on the present irresolution is an appropriate task at this juncture.

That memory-work (reconstruction of the past) helps shape the future can be seen in the ways in which the Holocaust impinges on the social and political agendas of nation-states as they attempt to (re)write history to fit a national self-image. Thus, British resistance to a national memorial of the Holocaust suggests conflict with the mythological narrative of Britain "standing alone" during the War (Kushner 1998, 226). Thus, Israeli dialogues on the Holocaust have played sometimes contradictory roles in the self-conscious determination of the right to statehood (Segev 1993). Like Germany, France has had to confront its past, although, of course, under different circumstances and in keeping with different social and political agendas. Germany had no choice as to whether or when to confront its past, while France's confrontation evolved more slowly and has been more "voluntary." More to the point, while revisionism and negationism about the Holocaust always has been federally disallowed in German public fora, France has been a major seat of revisionist "scholarship" (Finkelkraut 1992). Moreover, issues of Jewish identity differ between the building up from a small remnant the Jewish community in Germany and the expansion of a much larger Jewish community in France. Lastly, memory-politics, public memory, and collective memory function differently in France and in Germany.

While there may be a map of the uses and abuses of the concept of collective memory (Gedi and Elam 1996), it is not inappropriate to point out that the concept is rooted in French scholarship. It is Pierre Nora's notion of "the dialectic of remembering and forgetting" (Nora 1989, 8), that informs the politics of memory and expectation in France both during and after the War (Cowans 1998). Visions of both the past and the future have suffused the complex political situations of both eras, culminating in a long postwar confrontation with the Vichy episode. As difficult as this confrontation has been, complicated by postwar French politics, it may be that the "reluctance" of the French to engage in historical examination of Vichy is now a thing of the past (Marrus 1995), or not (Wood 1999). Whatever, just as the Eichmann trial played an important role in the incorporation of the Holocaust in the construction of Israeli identity, the Barbie, Touvier, and Papon trials in France provided compelling social dramas allowing for self-examination and a hoped-for possibility of reconciliation. In part due to the trials, consensus has been reached both that Vichy bears a heavy responsibility for the deportation of Jews in 1942, but that 76 percent of the Jews of France survived, due to either the "passive benevolence" or the "benevolent indifference" of the French (Zuccotti 1998, 504). While the trials might not have served as vehicles of historical explanation, they demonstrated a distinct hierarchy of memories about Vichy, about the Resistance, and about the fate of the Jews in France.

Even if collective memory is but a metaphor, a new name for "myth" identified with "collective" or "social" stereotypes (Gedi and Elam 1996, 47), much has been done to pierce the evolution of the separate Vichy, Communist, and Gaullist legends which have dominated postwar political and cultural discourses (Paxton 1972; Rousso 1991). Here are found exemplary indications of the power of the multiplicity of competing narratives and ideologies. Just as the evolution of German coming-to-terms with the past has a generational component, so too have generational differences informed the evolution of myths and countermyths about Vichy and about the Resistance. In both countries, the so-called "generation of 1968" played a key role in the demand for a reevaluation of wartime activities. What is depicted with considerable empirical evidence by Henry Rousso is the diversity of collective memories that constitutes "the Vichy syndrome" with all its "disparities, tensions, and contradictions" between different ways of structuring memory (Rousso 1991, 302). As in Germany, debate within the realm of collective memory has had a good deal to do with issues of national identity, situating that identity within a wider, European context, and, simultaeously, dealing with the contemporary reality of a multicultural society.

Parallel to the politics of memory and expectation in "the Vichy syndrome," French Jews have subscribed to myths built up out of negotiation with the French historical past that helped shape their own responses to the Holocaust (Cohen 1998). While differences between native French Jews and East European immigrants belie a monolithic response, the fact of both collaboration and resistance by leaders of the Jewish community in Vichy and in occupied France forms the historical backdrop for subsequent attempts to forge Jewish identity (Cohen 1987). Intergenerational issues also abound in ethnic strategies in "the narrowness of the space available for ethnic expression in France" (Boyarin 1991, 154). The problem for the younger generations has been that of living as Jews tied to a secular Republican Frenchness inculcated by the French school system. Several sources of identity have been promulgated in the context of building Jewish identity consistent with commitment to France. In the 1980's, a "memory strategy" developed in which the Holocaust became a center of Jewish debate involving a symbolic transformation of sacralization. Encouraged by secular Jews intent on forcing a recognition of the specificity of Auschwitz, including its ritual commemoration, sacralization, in which the memory of a martyrdom is apprehended as a form of transcendence, paradoxically became a basis for new, secular, Jewish identity (Trigano 1977, 313). A second ethnic strategy involves immersion in *Yiddishkeit*, a nostalgic retreat to an imagined Eastern European world which had been abandoned by the parental generation (Boyarin 1991, 166). However, Alain Finkelkraut, a prominent French Jewish intellectual, regrets that such nostalgia runs the risk of regression, providing a "repetitive, pretentious and vain proclomation of our alterity" (Finkelkraut 1990, 178). Clearly, his concern stems from the conflict between Jewish identity and French citizenship. A third, neo-Judaic, strategy involves the Sephardic community and embraces ultra-orthodox observance, more or less ignoring the Holocaust and sealing off the community from "modern" Europe (Trigano 1977, 315). Lastly, prominent intellectuals, like Finkelkraut, have turned to historians and philosophers of Lithuanian origin (notably Emmanuel Levinas) and serve as mediators between those of East European background, their children, and the general French population and intellectual circles (Friedlander 1990).

This all too brief excursion into recent sources of French Jewish identity, not even elaborating on the important role of Zionism (Wolf 1999), suggests that is makes no sense to essentialize a collective Jewish community in France, nor, for that matter, anywhere else. Just as Jews in France did not have a common response to the Holocaust as it was happening (Cohen 1998), so neither do contemporary sources of ethnic identity express a monolithic response to the Holocaust. In various forms, however, the memory of the events has played a central role in how the past will be shared in memory in the future. That the discourse has been shifting is the processual moment worthy of attention, the same holding true for the evolutionary process characterizing the deconstruction of the myths and countermyths in "the Vichy syndrome."

Shifting dialogues about the Holocaust are not solely internal to the nation-states within which they take place. Outside pressures can force a reexamination and questioning of mythic structures erected in the postwar era. Two prominent examples are Austria, where the Kurt Waldhein affair pricked the apologetic myth of "annexation", and, more recently, Switzerland, where the banking industry has been forced to expose secretive, and allegedly politically neutral, practices. External pressure and attendant publicity in both cases forced a confrontation with deep-seated mythic structures. Germany, of course, has had, and continues to have, the foremost pressure exerted from the outside to confront the past in a context of moral and monetary reparation. That there is an evolutionary quality to this pressure is demonstrated in the complex and often ambivalent relationship between Germany and the American Jewish community. American Jewish organizations, in all their variety, have attempted with varying degrees of success to exert influence on American foreign policy toward Germany (Shafir 1999). A prominent occurrence was the Bitburg incident in 1985 which came to take on enormous symbolic significance for both Germans and Americans. The impossibility of either remembering or forgetting saturated the ceremonial "reconciliation" at Bitburg which, fueled by controversy and publicity, ended up perpetuating ambivalence and ambiguity for all concerned

(Hartman 1986). For those with living memory of the Holocaust, the time clearly was inappropriate for the sort of absolution at least suggested at Bitburg. The remnant of those with living memory have no way of knowing if, or how, reconciliation could be negotiated in the future. Saddled with their own agendas, future generations will need to understand that there could not have been authentic closure during this still transitional period.

Jews of the future should not receive a view of their predecessors which suggests an essentialist or reified Jewish community in the second half of the twentieth century. While it may be that the Holocaust has enforced a common narrative making all twentieth-century Jews characters in a shared and inescapable metanarrative, it also may be that Jewish history is contestable and that Jewish narratives are written and rewritten according to what each generation finds salient (Krausz 1993, 272). While the role of memory in Jewish history always has been preeminent, we cannot predict with certainty how the Holocaust will be incorporated in future collective memory, nor how it will play a role in future Jewish identity. It remains to be seen, for example, whether or not traditional textual responses to catastrophic events can remain preeminent in the face of increasing secularism and the loss of the East European Jewish cultural strand (Roskies 1984). It also remains to be seen whether this loss can be countered by the present nostalgia in some quarters for a now imagined East European world. Whether genuine or spurious, nostalgia can be very powerful in shaping the idea of memory and perpetuating a sense of community. That there is now a wide spectrum of opinion as to whether or not the Holocaust, accompanied or not by cultural nostalgia, should constitute the dominant trope in Jewish collective memory and narrative, suggests that essentialist views of Jewish community are both empirically unfounded and inappropriate. There can be no one priveleged discourse at this time to transmit to future generations for purposes of constructing their own collected or collective memories.

There is another piece to the lack of monolithic communal response which helps to explain the continuing debate over representation and the feeding of memory. Future German collected or collective memory about the Holocaust partly will be shaped by the future memory constructed by the Jews, both internal and external to Germany. Dialogue will continue, and it should prove to be multifaceted, but there is no certainty at this juncture about its exact foci and nuances. Germany's confrontation with the past will certainly involve internal communal dialogues, but it also will reflect responses to the German Jewish community (whatever shape it takes in the future), as well as awareness of other diaspora communities, and of Israel. Just as the separate generations in the present era of still living memory have their own agendas, so too will the generations to come. Any possible closure and possible modes of the implementation of closure will be up to them to formulate.

Because cultural and historical distinctions between Jewish communities cannot be effaced, despite the Holocaust suggesting a powerful tool for the homogenization of cultural identity, a proliferation of Holocaust discourses exists, suggested in the cases of Germany and France. In France, the fracturing of meaning in Holocaust discourse stems in part from the tension between the universal and the particular significance of the Holocaust (Wood 1999). Just as French Jews have had to reconcile their status as Jews and supporters of Israel with their French citizenship, so too German Jews have had to grapple with the German and the Jewish content of their identity in the context of the continuing debate over German-Jewish symbiosis. Whether contemporary Jewish culture in Germany represents a sort of "renaissance" or, rather, a piece of German public imagination expressed in philo-semitism, remains to be seen. While thematic and narrative possibilities are now several in France and in Germany, after the passing of the generations with living memory of the Holocaust, the shape of Jewish culture will be determined by the evolution of separate and different circumstances.

Whether or not the Holocaust will remain as a master trope in Western European Jewish identity, and, more pointedly, whether or not a viable Jewish community can be sustained in Western Europe, are somewhat open questions. One pessimistic view holds that demographic decline and increasing assimilation may lead to the disappearance of the community within just several generations. That is, in an increasingly multicultural and pluralist Europe (evidenced in Germany and France), the lack of necessity to efface "Jewishness" paradoxically could have a disintegrative effect, leading to the "disappearance" of the European diaspora as a population group, as a cultural entity, and as a significant force in European society and in the Jewish world (Wasserstein 1996, 289). One suspects, however, that this chain of events would need to be accompanied by the demise of the "Jewish question" as a serious theme in (non-Jewish) European public discourse. If, in the future, the Jewish community in Europe is so fragmented as to question its cultural and demographic viability, what will happen to the memory of the Holocaust? Substantive predictions are inappropriate, but it may be that the universalistic, rather than the particularistic, "message" of the Holocaust would come to hold sway, with the Nazi genocide increasingly lumped in with other (and future) genocides. On the other hand, a more amorphous ethnic identity might come to commemorate the uniqueness of the Holocaust, much in the same way that Irishness is conveyed by commemoration of the potato famine which led to the Irish diaspora. If all that would be left were a disembodied memory of catastrophe, a "pseudoreligion of victim-hood" could arise in which public acknowledgment of the Holocaust would function as a primary signifier of ethnic identity in the face of a dearth of alternative sources of communal identity in an increasingly secular and internationalist world (Buruma 1999, 289). If this scenario were to transpire, we still need to transmit to future generations that a multiplicity of dialogues and agendas have characterized the present transition during the waning years of a living memory of the Holocaust and that redemptive closure has not characterized this transition.

Representations of the Holocaust, cultural texts in various forms, in late twentieth and early twenty-first-century development of consciousness, will have considerable impact on future Jewish and non-Jewish configurations of collective memory. The metaphors surrounding the Holocaust presently available must be examined in the light of contemporary agendas and cultural circumstances. Communal solidarity is not to be presumed, despite the fact that various media with their self-conscious commemorative purposes may give the impression of communal solidarity. While public fora of collective memory, notably memorials and museums, very consciously elaborate interpretive frameworks, they do so in the context of concerns and agendas predominant at at the time of their conception. There is no assurance that their symbolic messages will speak meaningfully to future audiences who will have their own concerns and agendas. In other words, present-day commemorative devices are compromised in their ability to provide measures of stability and closure (Brower 1999). The effacement of ambiguity and ambivalence through public commemoration is illusory, representing an attempt to work through trauma and discord at the time of the conception of commemoration.

The process of creating fixed interpretations of the past through commemorative devices and accompanying debates over the translation of traumatic memory into postmemory are evident in both France and Germany. The history of commemoration at Drancy, at the Velodrome d'Hiver, and other sites of memory significant to the deportation of Jews from France, suggests how programmatic memorialization has the tendency to bury historical understanding under layers of "national myth and idealization" (Wiedmer 1999, 36). Indeed, much of the history of Holocaust commemoration in France has had to do with the evolution of an "official" coming-to-terms with Vichy and with French anti-semitism. The creation of static representations at memorial sites has a linked tendency to ignore the multiplicity of memories in the face of a continuing demise of living memory. This is perhaps unavoidable given that collective memory, "it would seem, begins where the individual memories of a group cease, along with its members, to exist" (Wiedmer 1999, 57). A different set of distinctive visions emerges in representation and commemoration in Germany with its own public memories and memory politics. The chronicle of the long debate over the Jewish Museum in Berlin encapsulates not only memory politics, but the attendant issues of Jewish identity and cultural symbiosis in today's Germany. "Was the Museum to be Jewish or German?" became a key focus of debate. The architectural task became one of dealing with the conundrum of representing the excision of Jewish life in a building that "had as its mandate the demonstration of the allegedly inextricable enmeshment of the Jewish and German cultures" (Wiedmer 1999, 128). For this reason there appears to be some ambivalence within the Jewish community in Berlin about the Museum, with many wanting a "positive" message, rather than a depiction of "voids," to emanate from the structure. Fearful of backlash and anti-semitism, members of the Jewish community may be like other Berliners in their desire for architecture "to fill voids instead of making them" (Kramer 1999, 64). Critics focus on the idea that Berlin appears as a city that "still seems more comfortable with the idea of monuments to dead Jews [...] than with the tragic complexities of its own interrupted and ongoing Jewish story" (Kramer 1999, 64). The tortuous competitions for the design of a National Memorial to the Murdered Jews of Europe attest to other complexities and competing dialogues. Was the Memorial to commemorate only Jewish victims of the Nazi genocide? Was the Memorial to mourn the loss of a civilization for the sake of the murdered Jews, or for the sake of the Germans, "who had to contend with a fragmented, 'impoverished' postwar culture?" (Wiedmer 1999, 140). Unsurprisingly in the context of issues surrounding German reunification, issues of national identity loomed large in the convoluted controversy over the Memorial, with different expectations, along with different tensions between experience and history, on the part of Jews and Germans of both East and West German background.

The process of debate and controversy over memorialization in both France and Germany is as significant and telling as the final, complete memorials themselves. The process has taken place in the context of the passing of living memory, while future observers of memorials and participants in commemoration will have their own sets of representational requirements and agendas for memory work. Two things need to be kept in mind: that a memorial site is only one of many Holocaust narratives in today's (and tomorrow's) media-saturated world, and that there is a theoretical bind in commemoration between too little representation leading to limited memory and too much interpretation leading to the distortion and fragmentation of memory (Wiedmer 1999, 166). Any balance here may be difficult to achieve, but in any case, future generations will respond to sites of memory in ways we are in no way able to predict with assurance.

While France and Germany have unique relationships with their own sites of memory and commemorative devices which are informed by separate political and cultural requirements and agendas, they also must contend with elements of culture, popular and otherwise, stemming from an increasing, so-called "Americanization of the Holocaust." The politics of memory and representation have become more complex as American mass media have penetrated European historical consciousness, bringing along American sensibilities in which "it gets harder and harder to render the Holocaust without incorporating American themes of multiculturalism, ethnicity, and cultural identity" (Flanzbaum 1999, 13). Holocaust memory gradually has been integrated into American civic culture (epitomized in the Memorial Museum in Washington D.C.), just as Holocaust memory has become central to American Jewish identity (Young 1999, 80-81; Novick 1999). As France and Germany cope with their own increasing multicultural realities, what are the implications of the pervasive influence of American mass media and styles of representation on the future of Holocaust memory and representation in Europe? Just as the "heritage of the Holocaust" has come to provide a way for secular Israelis to express a connection to their Jewish heritage (Segev 1993, 516), increasing assimilation in Europe and America has led to the Holocaust becoming a tag of communal identity in a search for cultural authenticity in an increasingly homogenized, global culture. Herein lies the possibility of a "pseudoreligion of victimhood," with all its emphasis on kitsch and death, eroding the remnants of the "kitchen comforts of ethnicity" in Europe (Buruma 1999, 6). As much as it might be resisted in some quarters in Europe, the Americanization of the Holocaust, with all its influence in mass media and cultural globalization, may spur on the use of the Holocaust in Europe as a means of cultural identity in the face of secularism, assimilation, and demographic decline in the Jewish community. This is why it is crucial to document the dialogic shiftings and narrative strategies which have taken place over the last half-century. If an ever increasing homogenization of Holocaust memory is going to occur, it should be understood that it was preceded by an evolution of separate hegemonic struggles over the cultivation of collective memory, both Jewish and non-Jewish. While future generations will have imagined, rather than real, relationships with the events of the Holocaust, what we have been experiencing are the waning years of a proliferation of discourses on the part of those still imbued with the living memory of catastrophic events for all participants. To ignore these processual moments in the cultivation of collective memory is to ignore that "memory cannot be divorced from actions taken on its own behalf, and that memory without consequences may even contain the seeds of its own destruction" (Young 1999, 82). For these and other reasons, it is not only premature, but unwarranted, to suggest in any manner that a redemptive, narrative wholeness and coherency, a closure of memory, is a legacy to future representation and remembrance of the Holocaust.

Literature Cited

Adorno, Theodor W. 1986. What Does Coming to Terms with the Past Mean? [1959], In *Bitburg in Moral and Political Perspective*, ed. Geoffrey H. Hartman, pp. 114-129. Bloomington Indiana: Indiana University Press.

Benz, Wolfgang. 1994. Auschwitz and the Germans: the Remembrance of the Genocide. *Holocaust and Genocide Studies* 8: 94-106.

Boyarin, Jonathan. 1987. *Polish Jews in Paris*. Bloomington Indiana: Indiana University Press.

Brower, Benjamin. 1999. The Preserving Machine. *History and Memory* 11: 77-103.

Buruma, Ian. 1999. The Joys and Perils of Victimhood. *The New York Review of Books* XLVI: 4-9.

Cohen, Richard I. 1987. *The Burden of Conscience*. Bloomington Indiana: Indiana University Press.

Cohen, Richard I. 1998. Remembering and Invoking 1789 During the Holocaust: the Trials and Tribulations of French Jews. In *The Holocaust and History*, eds. Michael Berenbaum and Abraham J. Peck, pp. 601-615. Bloomington Indiana: Indiana University Press.

Cowans, Jon. 1998. Visions of the Postwar. *History and Memory* 10: 68-101.

Domansky, Elisabeth. 1992. Kristallnacht, the Holocaust and German Unity: the Meaning of November 9 as an Anniversary in Germany. *History and Memory* 4: 60-94.

Finkelkraut, Alain. 1990. *The Imaginary Jew*. Lincoln Nebraska: University of Nebraska Press.

Finkelkraut, Alain. 1998. *The Future of a Negation*. Lincoln Nebraska: University of Nebraska Press.

Flanzbaum, Hilene. 1999. Introduction, In *The Americanization of the Holocaust*, ed. Hilene Flanzbaum, pp. 1-17. Baltimore Maryland: Johns Hopkins University Press.

Fox, Thomas C. 1999. *Stated Memory: East Germany and the Holocaust*. Rochester New York: Camden House.

Friedlander, Judith. 1990. *Vilna on the Seine*. New Haven Connecticut: Yale University Press.

Friedländer, Saul. 1992. Introduction. In *Probing the Limits of Representation*, ed. Saul Friedländer, pp. 1-21. Cambridge Massachusetts: Harvard University Press.

Gedi, Noa, and Yigal Elam. 1996. Collective Memory – What Is It?, *History and Memory* 8: 30-49.

Gilman, Sander L. 1996. Negative Symbiosis: the Reemergence of Jewish Culture in Germany. In *The German-Jewish Dialogue Reconsidered*, ed. Klaus L. Berghahn, pp. 207-232. New York: Peter Lang.

Gilman, Sander L., and Karen Remmler, eds. 1994. *Reemerging Jewish Culture in Germany*. New York: New York University Press.

Hartman, Geoffrey H., ed. 1986. *Bitburg in Moral Perspective*. Bloomington Indiana: Indiana University Press.

Herf, Jeffery. 1997. *Divided Memory: the Nazi Past in the Two Germanys*. Cambridge Massachusetts: Harvard University Press.

Jäckel, Eberhard. 1998. The Holocaust: Where We Are, Where We Need to Go, In *The Holocaust and History*, eds.Michael Berenbaum and Abraham J. Peck, pp. 23-29. Bloomington Indiana: Indiana University Press.

Kramer, Jane. 1999. Letter From Europe: Living With Berlin. *The New Yorker*, July 5, 1999: 50-63.

Krausz, Michael. 1993. On Being Jewish, In *Jewish Identity*, ed. David Theo Goldberg, Philadelphia Pennsylvania: Temple University Press.

Kushner, Tony. 1998. Remembering to Forget: Racism and Anti-Racism in Postwar Britain, In *Modernity, Culture and "the Jew,"* eds. Bryan Cheyette and Laura Marcus, pp. 226-241. Stanford California: Stanford University Press.

LaCapra, Dominick. 1998. *History and Memory after Auschwitz*. Ithaca New York: Cornell University Press.

Maier, Charles S. 1998. *The Unmasterable Past*. Cambridge Massachusetts: Harvard University Press.

Marrus, Michael R. 1995. Coming to Terms With Vichy. *Holocaust and Genocide Studies* 9: 23-41.

Mittleman, Alan. 1999. The German Jewish Community Between Adjustment and Ambivalence. In *Jewish Centers and Peripheries*, ed. S. Ilan Troen, pp. 303-322. London: Transaction Publishers.

Nora, Pierre. 1989. Between Memory and History: Les Lieux de Memoire. *Representations* 26: 1-25.

Novick, Peter. 1999. *The Holocaust in American Life*. New York: Houghton Mifflen.

Osiel, Mark. 1997. *Mass Atrocity, Collective Memory and the Law*. New Brunswick New Jersey: Transaction Publishers.

Paxton, Robert O. 1972. *Vichy France: Old Guard and the New Order, 1940-1944*. New York: Knopf.

Rapaport, Lynn. 1997. *Jews in Germany after the Holocaust*. Cambridge: Cambridge University Press.

Roskies, David G. 1984. *Against the Apocalypse*. Cambridge Massachusetts: Harvard University Press.

Rousso, Henry. 1991. *The Vichy Syndrome*. Cambridge Massachusetts: Harvard University Press.

Segev, Tom. 1993. *The Seventh Million: the Israelis and the Holocaust*. New York: Hill and Wang.

Shafir, Shlomo. 1999. *Ambiguous Relations: the American Jewish Community and Germany since 1945*. Detroit Michigan: Wayne State University Press.

Stern, Frank. 1997. Breaking the 'Cordon Sanitaire' of Memory. In *Thinking about the Holocaust*, ed. Alvin H. Rosenfeld, pp. 213-232. Bloomington Indiana: Indiana University Press.

Todorov, Tzvetan. 1996. *A French Tragedy*. Hanover New Hampshire: University Press of New England.

Trigano, Shmuel. 1997. The Jews and the Spirit of Europe, In *Thinking About the Holocaust*, ed. Alvin H. Rosenfeld, pp. 300-318. Bloomington Indiana: Indiana University Press.

Vidal-Naquet, Pierre. 1992. *Assassins of Memory*. New York: Columbia University Press.

Wasserstein, Bernard. 1996. *Vanishing Diaspora: the Jews in Europe since 1945*. Cambridge Massachusetts: Harvard University Press.

Wiedmer, Caroline. 1999. *The Claims of Memory*. Ithaca New York: Cornell University Press.

Wolf, Joan B. 1999. Anne Frank is Dead, Long Live Anne Frank. *History and Memory* 11: 104-140.

Wood, Nancy. 1999. Memory on Trial in Contemporary France. *History and Memory* 11: 41-76.

Wyschograd, Edith. 1998. *An Ethics of Remembering*. Chicago Illinois: University of Chicago Press.

Young, James E. 1993. *The Texture of Memory*. New Haven Connecticut: Yale University Press.

Young, James E. 1999. America's Holocaust: Memory and the Politics of Identity, In *The Americanization of the Holocaust*, ed. Hilene Flanzbaum. Baltimore Maryland: The Johns Hopkins University Press.

Zuccotti, Susan S. 1998. Surviving the Holocaust: the Situation in France, In *The Holocaust and History*, eds. Micael Berenbaum and Abraham J. Peck, pp. 492-509. Bloomington Indiana: Indiana University Press.

Abandonment, Adjustment, and Memory

Reflections on J. Presser, Elie Cohen and Gerhard Durlacher

Yehudi Lindeman

In some recent literature, the survivors of the Holocaust, and especially the child survivors and hidden children who began to emerge from silence and powerlessness during the 1990s, are profiled as a "group of irritating people" for remembering and reminding the world of the outrage committed against them (Krell 1999, 95). Elie Wiesel, addressing a conference of hidden children, calls them people whose stories are reluctantly tolerated and who force their memory "on the memory of the world" (Wiesel 1999, 45). But what is at the root of this memory that survivors force upon the world? It is in part a personal need to unburden the mind and release accumulated pain after decades of silence. But it is also a long suppressed indictment of the world's silence in the face of Jewish suffering and need, a silence of indifference and complicity that has been amply documented over the past twenty years. One might call it the shame that one feels for the world. The presence of shame helps explain the decades of reluctance to listen to survivors, on the part of otherwise well meaning people. Yet isn't the shame traceable as well to people's appalling lack of understanding? Arguably, one of the first items needed to confront the unimaginable events that make up the Holocaust is a historical imagination. Maybe that is a tall order, but for the stories and the voices of victims and survivors to be heard, the listeners' imagination needs to be freed. That way the world can begin to share their memories, hear the long since silenced voices of those no longer able to speak, and repair the imaginary relations with the victims.

As a child survivor of the Shoah, I spent most of my adult life "underground," unable to face the events that broke up my childhood and haunted me for the rest of my life. The process of opening up and "coming out" could not have been navigated without the help of those pioneers whose own journey became a kind of path for me to study and confront. J. Presser, Elie Cohen, and Gerhard Durlacher were among the first to help stir up my own historical imagination which had at one point turned rock-solid in the face of a past I could not endure. Fellow child survivors from around the world gave me the support and warmth to complete this journey to the past, allowing me to thaw out and dissolve much of the accumulated pain of loss and humiliation in the process. But a question occurs to me: If I as a survivor was unable to confront my past for the longest time, how can I possibly expect others, born later and outside of the European center of Nazi persecution and destruction, to contemplate these events? How can one expect them to gain or regain access to a historical imagination regarding these matters? The following observations about abandonment and adjustment are prompted by the insights of writers whose struggle with the memory of unimaginable events helped rekindle my own memory. I trust that they may be of assistance to others, in turn.

In the fall of 1986, only months after seeing Claude Lanzmann's *Shoah* which had left me moved, but confused, two events brought about a change in my life. The first was meeting the Dutch physician, writer, and Auschwitz survivor Dr. Elie Cohen, in Jerusalem. Then on my way back to Canada, a Dutch friend or relative gave me a copy of Gerhard Durlacher's newly published volume of stories *Stripes in the Sky*. It would be several more years before I started reading Durlacher's book, but the opening passage haunted me from the outset. It evokes the sensation of complete abandonment experienced by a sixteen-year old boy standing at an endless roll call at Auschwitz-Birkenau, in August 1944, as the Hungarian convoys keep coming in. This sensation remained burned into my memory, much as I tried to shake it off.

The meeting with Dr. Cohen which I have described elsewhere, shook me up, and caused radical changes in my life (Lindeman 2001, 208-209). Elie Cohen, an acknowledged authority on the Holocaust, had written openly about being a camp physician at Westerbork and Auschwitz. At a more personal level, he had been the general physician of my aunt, herself a survivor of Auschwitz. After hearing me speak at a Jerusalem conference, the elderly Dr. Cohen went out of his way to remind me that as a child survivor of the Holocaust, I had a special responsibility. He claimed I had been a witness to events that needed to be talked and written about, and I owed it to the world, and to myself, to do something with that knowledge and experience. This came as a shock: frankly, I had not been aware that my personal history singled me out for any particular actions or responsibilities. Now Dr. Cohen made it seem as if I had been running away from myself for all these years.

If viewing *Shoah* earlier that year had shaken me up, the encounter with Dr. Cohen and reading that one fragment from Durlacher's title story "Stripes in the Sky" were the factors that pushed me over the top, and into the kind of free fall from which I had always steered away. Suddenly I was confronted with memories that had been quarantined for over four decades. Maybe it was the airtight way in which they had been compartmentalized that made them so vivid and real. Memories started to pour out of me, especially late at night. At other times, I woke up in a sweat from oppressive dreams full of cramped places. I was six years old again, and lying in bed, struck down by some nasty child's disease that caused me to be yellow all over. I wanted to get up, but felt paralyzed and helpless. For days I lay sick and brooding in my attic room under the slanted roof of a small house, in the eastern part of the Netherlands. My protectors who ran a lovely flower shop on the bottom floor, but could not keep me, because they were afraid. I remember feeling stuck and at their mercy, with nowhere to go and the Germans hot on my trail. Moreover this was at least the fourth or fifth hiding place in so many months. Worst of all, I realized that I could no longer rely on these people who were kind enough, but whose overheard conversations (I was an expert at eavesdropping by now) indicated that I would not be able to stay much longer.

I relived being in a small group home, with at least seven other children, and two non-Jewish women in charge. The area was tranquil, but there was always the threat of being discovered. Sometimes we had to leave the house to go to a hiding place in the woods. I re-experienced our nature walks, which I adored. But under the threat of imminent arrest, the same walks became nightmarish. I see us going through those woods again, a procession of anxious children singing a song about the arrival of spring in an effort to appear nonchalant and cheerful. I recall a cold evening, and the feeling of abandonment as we buried each other under tree branches which we covered with armfuls of dead leaves. And I remember hearing sounds from the small German prison camp nearby, and catching glimpses of German soldiers on patrol in the forest, as they marched along the narrow path in their black uniforms and tall shining boots, singing a German military song that I still know today: "Erika," marching in step to the beat. Suddenly that relived memory, untouched for all those years, surged over me with such clarity that for a few moments I heard those words and experienced the swing of those boots again, "E-ri-ka, zwei drei vier [...]."

How to find words for what happened to me as a result of these and other remembered experiences that I had buried for so a long? The immediate effect was to render me more open to the experiences of others. One account that had always eluded me was the narrow escape from being gassed on the part of my aunt, my mother's older sister. I couldn't make sense of it, though my aunt had told the story often enough, how within weeks after arrival in Auschwitz she had stood in line in front of the gas chamber. I had always reacted to it with a mixture of awe and disbelief. But I could not visualize it: it remained an abstract account. Now the details fell into place: it hurt a lot, but suddenly I was able to see her standing there, lined up alongside hundreds of other women selected to die, waiting for her turn, possibly hearing the shouts and sobs of those who were being gassed before her. For the first time I had an inkling of what she had gone through. And that included the sudden announcement, whispered through the lines, that the Germans had run out of gas. After waiting for what seemed like hours in the cold September night, in the certain knowledge that this would be the end, the women received a command to return to their barracks.

In short, I had become a listener. I started to admit to myself my personal connection to the victims and the survivors, and to share, however faintly and vicariously, something of their agony and fear. This new ability to listen also helped redefine my relationship to those who were murdered, including the almost one and a half million Jewish children and the dozens of gassed cousins and second cousins in my own family, most of whom had no one to speak for them; and to those who were saved after surviving in camps, ghettos, and various hiding places all over Europe; and finally to the children of persecuted minorities and warring factions everywhere in the world. It also brought back unexpectedly vivid memories of the first person to evoke some of these sentiments in me, however indirectly and subversively, namely the eminent Dutch historian Professor Jacob Presser.

II

"The Humanities don't humanize." With these frank but cryptic words Professor J. Presser of the University of Amsterdam summed up his thoughts at a point where his argument about an aspect of modern European history had reached a particularly knotty stage (see van der Zee, 106). I can't recall what country we were discussing, but I can still see him standing there, hands folded in front of his body, the shoulders sloping a bit, or in the even more characteristic position of having the arms folded across his chest, both proud of his insight and provocative, at once seducer and challenger, his eyes scanning the rows of students for a reaction. At such a moment he was above all eager to put up for close examination his own statement, to gauge it for whatever amount of validity or insight it might contain.

These were the early sixties when I more or less faithfully attended, first as an undergraduate and then as a graduate student, the Wednesday afternoon lectures of Professor Jacob Presser in Modern European History. I believe there were many dozens of others who did the same. Though we were neither majoring in History, nor students of Political Science (Professor Presser's chair was in the Faculty of Political and Social Sciences), for many of us those two hours of weekly lectures we audited became part of our curriculum. For me this unusual state of affairs continued for three years while Presser covered French, German, and British Modern History (I can't remember in what order) in front of an audience that was steadily increasing in size.

Whatever the focus of any given lecture, it was never about the Holocaust. The term did not exist, and neither did the subject. The Second World War was about certain treaties, invasions, and battles, while the persecution of the European Jews was relegated to an area quite separate from the main war narrative, if it was mentioned at all. Only in Dutch literature, especially in poetry, considerable attention was paid in high schools to what was called the literature of resistance. But WW II was not part of the curriculum of Modern European History, either in high schools or in the University. As in other countries, it would take time, and the contributions of scholars like Raul Hilberg and Presser to change that.

What most people did not know was that Professor Presser had long been engaged in research on the history of the Holocaust. His much acclaimed *Ondergang*, a two volume study of the persecution and destruction of the Dutch Jews, was published in 1965, to great academic and popular acclaim: it sold 140,000 copies within the first eight months. An abbreviated version was published in the U.S. in 1969, as *The Destruction of the Dutch Jews*. During a visit to my native country I picked up a copy, but I rarely opened it. Over one hundred members of my immediate family had passed through camp Westerbork on their way East, and to read about the details of their deportation was more than I could handle. But some of the things I remember from the lectures can be found there. These included Presser's struggle with the participation in criminal behavior on the part of German people of the highest intellectual caliber (hence his formulation that "the humanities don't humanize"), his need to give a voice to the victims, i.e., those no longer able to speak for themselves, and his early insistence on studying what he called "ego documents," i.e., letters, memoirs, and other personal sources as part of historical documentation.

To Jacob Presser (known as J. Presser by the Dutch public, and as Jacques by his friends), the Second World War was of course a terrible thing, and not only for personal reasons. He had lost his wife to whom he had been extremely devoted, and all of his immediate relatives. At a personal level he never got over that. But collectively and culturally, he could not absorb what had happened. That this had occurred, that this had been possible in the twentieth century! And that from the side of the much admired Germans! For it is important to understand what Germany and Germans stood for, for Presser and his generation. It is quite hard to evoke that in plain words today. In practically every field, in music, architecture, the arts, science, medicine, the Germans were plainly the most advanced and admired people of all. That is how it was perceived. When Presser and his wife played piano pieces for four hands by Mozart or Brahms, they were worshipping at the altar of German culture.

I remember how during one of those legendary Wednesday afternoon lectures, Professor Presser once took us on an imaginary tour of the River Rhine, and all those magical places and towns, and how he went on and on about the art, the museums, the buildings, the music, the people. And then he suddenly stopped, and you could hear the proverbial pin drop. That was before the big overhaul of the Universities in the later sixties. He had this habit of moving around the lecture hall, probably as a result of teaching high school for many years. So he stood very stiff and still, and none of the 300 or so students fidgeted or even coughed. It seemed as if he had caught himself in the middle of some very private thought. In retrospect, I suspect that he had been talking about places he had visited and admired together with his first wife. Then he opened his arms as if he were dropping something, or in some kind of apologetic gesture. And then he said something like, "Yes, all of that is of course permanently gone." And then again that silence, as if we were at some solemn commemorative ceremony. And then he continued his lecture at the point where he had broken off, and as if nothing had happened.

Presser could not get over the fact that the Germans, of all the people in the world, had been willing and able to do those terrible things. It was there as an ongoing context for our study of Modern European History, so to speak. I myself experienced it as an indictment of the society in which I was growing up, which had failed its Jewish citizens badly in the years of their abandonment, a sentiment not widely shared in the early sixties. The fact that all those thousands of well educated Germans, the physicians, lawyers, judges, University lecturers, the cultural elite of the German nation, that so many of those high minded people had been willing and able to descend to those levels. He could never get over that. About Eichmann and others like him, Presser, in a published interview, is dismissive, calling them the proto-types of the low-life criminal, people of the very lowest level mentally and culturally. "But that so many people of the highest caliber, winners of Nobel Prizes from the 'country of poets and philosophers' turned out to be capable of participating in the extermination of six million people, [...] that was of course a terrible, terrible blow" (Bregstein 1981, 23).

As I said before, Presser needed to speak on behalf of those who perished. Hence his decision, from the outset of writing *Destruction*, to speak on behalf of those who had been killed: "I had to be a spokesman for those people, [...] it became an obsession for me" (van der Zee 1988, 237; see Bregstein 1972, 119 and 125). In one extreme instance, Presser allows the vic-tims to address the two leaders of the Amsterdam Jewish Council, the busi-nessman A. Asscher and Professor David Cohen. He has a lot of sympathy for their position, and understood and respected their basic integrity and good will (Bregstein 1981, 36). But at one crucial point he changes sides. Speaking on behalf of the poor and abandoned Jews, he indicts their leaders because they allowed the deportation of those who had no one to protect them, while the leaders themselves and their associates were able to keep themselves from being deported (Presser 1969, 269-270; see Bregstein 1981, 55-56).

Some have considered this accusation a flaw in Presser's book. It certain-ly became an issue. Elie Cohen was among those who attacked him because Presser, through his position as a teacher at the Jewish High School, had himself enjoyed the Jewish Council's protection. There is logic to this posi-tion, but it is also beside the point. Presser wanted to present the viewpoint of the masses who were deported, but who had nobody to speak on their behalf. His decision to give a voice to the victims fitted in with the impor-tance he attached to personal accounts, a position he had first outlined years earlier (see Bregstein 1981, 57). There and elsewhere he formulates the notion of the "historical ego document," and its important relation to ordi-nary historical documentation. To him the historical ego document is part of a genre that encompasses, among other things, letters, diaries, and mem-oirs. According to this view, history can be truly registered only through the personal, subjective experience of individuals. As we will see, this theoretical view is put to work and tested in Elie Cohen's *The Abyss* which Cohen calls an "ego document" (Cohen 1973, 9).

III

Elie Aaron Cohen was born in 1909 in the town of Groningen, in the north of the Netherlands. He grew up in a lower middle class Jewish milieu.

His father was a waiter in an upscale restaurant, which served as a gathering place for some of the town's most respected citizens. His humble social origins were a cause of frustration and shame to him. During his years of medical study the ambitious Cohen was embarrassed about being a scholarship student, and envious of those who joined one of the fashionable student fraternities. It is interesting to notice that Presser, who had been a scholarship student as well, never fretted about his childhood poverty, for he was already a militant socialist, and firmly rooted in the very special, largely socialist Jewish district of Amsterdam in which he grew up. Since both Presser and Cohen have been spokesmen for the destroyed Jewish communities from which they hailed in an attempt to give a voice to those who died, it is worth mentioning these differences in background. Presser who was certainly no less ambitious than Cohen, can be seen as a representative of the city's socialism that became the secular focus for at least half of Amsterdam's more than one hundred thousand Jews. Cohen, a Jew from the provinces, with his middle class orientation, represents what is known in Dutch-Yiddish jargon as the "mediene." One clue to Cohen's character, and to the nature of *The Abyss: A Confession* (its full title), is the account of how he avoided meeting his father (embarrassingly dressed in his waiter's suit), by quickly crossing to the other side of the square, along with a fellow student. From the outset the brutally frank Cohen aims to show how he had always been motivated by a desire to advance himself (Cohen 1973, 21). Cohen views himself as someone who squarely helped himself. This becomes evident once he has been arrested, which is the beginning of his Darwinian struggle to survive. His "confesssion" is also a study of identity change and depersonalization, as a result of his adjustment to a system designed to (intentionally, according to Cohen) destabilize and fragment the normal personality.

Dr. Cohen had his own medical practice which he was forced to give up in May 1941, as a result of the German occupier's anti-Jewish measures. The deportations began in the summer of 1942. In a bungled attempt to flee abroad, he and his wife were betrayed and arrested. Too trusting and naive for their own good, they walked right into a trap. Dr. Cohen was then sent to the notorious police transit camp Amersfoort, while his wife ended up in Westerbork, where he would join her, in December 1942. Though marked for immediate deportation to the East, as was standard procedure for those who were *Straf* (punishment) cases in Westerbork (their dossiers were marked by an "S"), Dr. Cohen managed to get a reprieve for himself and his wife. From there on he quickly rose in the camp's social hierarchy to become a transport doctor who could get persons off the transport to Auschwitz even hours prior to their departure. He fully used this position to help his relatives and friends stay off the dreaded transport trains. He had so much confidence in his own staying power that he persuaded his own sister to come to Westerbork, though she had been perfectly safe in Amsterdam, where she lived under a false identity. As one of the camp's "prominent persons," he thoroughly enjoyed his role and his status, as he unabashedly admits.

But in September 1943 his luck turned. An insignificant incident was all it took to cancel his vaunted "protection." Together with his wife and young son (who had joined them, in spite of the pleas of the hiding family), he was sent to Auschwitz on personal instructions from the camp commander, Obersturmführer Gemmeker. If Cohen survived, it was because of his frequent good luck and, as he never tires of pointing out, his medical training. In his own words, his privileged status as a physician was the "red thread you can trace through all my war years" (Cohen 1973, 74). After the war, Cohen set up as a general practitioner once again, and remarried. He completed his Ph.D. degree in 1952. His dissertation, published in Dutch and several other languages, was published in English as *Human Behavior in the Concentration Camp: A Medical and Psychological Study*. In 1968, he introduced the Netherlands to the so-called "post-concentration camp syndrome." Dr. Cohen attended the Eichmann trial in Jerusalem, and was a regular publicist for a variety of newspapers about subjects related to the Holocaust. After suffering a heart attack in 1966, he gave up his general practitioner's practice in order to dedicate the remainder of his public life to researching and publishing about the Holocaust. He wrote about the return of the survivors from the liberated camps to Holland, and about the fate of the more than 2500 Jews of the once flourishing Jewish community of his native Groningen (Cohen 1968; 1975), and he published three books, *The Abyss* (Cohen 1973), *The Nineteen Trains to Sobibor* (Cohen 1979), and *Night Images* (1992). Elie Cohen died in 1993.

My discussion will concentrate on *The Abyss*. Unfortunately, the other major work, *The Nineteen Trains to Sobibor*, is unavailable in English. Based on years of research, it contains a careful analysis of among other things the 1970 trial of camp commander Franz Stangl, and the extensive (second) 1973 trial of the notorious guard Hubert Gomerski, as well personal interviews with fifteen of the thirty known survivors of the Sobibor extermination camp in which over thirty-four thousand Dutch Jews were killed. In both works the aim is to evoke the conditions that reigned in the camps, to fathom the mentality of the perpetrators, and to describe and analyze the attitudes of those who survived. By always referring back to his own personal experiences and attitudes, Cohen succeeds in keeping the focus on what happens to human beings in the extreme conditions of the camp, and what identity changes result from the need to adjust to a world where there was no room for empathy or pity. Having any feelings when someone was killed in front of you, or selected for the gas, would only destabilize and weaken you, and "you wanted to stay alive, you had to adjust," and above all, you had to get used to it:

> You had to learn to watch horrifying events with "empty" eyes, you could not afford to feel pity, you had to get calluses on your soul, in brief, you had to pass through a *process of customization*. (Cohen 1979, 175; Cohen's italics)

In the end the most terrible things are reduced to everyday events, resulting in a process of hardening and an absence of any emotional reaction. Cohen considers this third, deadening stage as the ultimate phase in the process of adjustment (Cohen 1979, 175-176).

Cohen deals in an open and direct manner with what it took to survive, once the first shock of being in captivity has been registered and absorbed. The sense of complete abandonment is recorded through a naive persona who is rather surprised that life goes quietly on for everybody else, but that nobody volunteers to be of help. Even before the forcible shut-down of his practice in May 1941, the Dutch Medical Association had done nothing for him and his Jewish colleagues. Now, with plenty of physicians ready to pounce on his practice, but none willing to pay, the professional organization looked passively on. This discouraging state of affairs prompts Cohen to use the first of several animal images in the book: "They swooped on my practice like vultures on carrion. The Aryans. They all wanted to take it over" (Cohen 1973, 29), before concluding that "the Medical Association completely let me down" (30).

Real abandonment does not come until after his arrest. The truth of his situation begins to sink in when he is being taken from the Amersfoort police station to the camp of that name. Walking through the town under a police escort, he still indulges in self-pity as he notices "mothers sitting round the table with their children," and couples "drinking tea" (Cohen 1973, 45). But he is hardly inside the dreaded camp before he sees labor gangs coming back from work looking "practically like corpses" (45), and an SS man who knocks down a man and kicks him until he stops moving and is "probably dead." This quickly prompts him to start looking out for himself:

> It was then that I began to look to my own protection. I called that 'depersonalization.' You looked on, as though through a peephole, taking no part in things yourself. You watched. It didn't concern you. (46)

At this point the feeling of abandonment (which is centrifugal and disorienting) has made place for a keen detachment from others, Cohen's self-described "depersonalization," and a more focused sense of self-protection and self-possession. To protect himself he is unhooking himself from traditional feelings of empathy. The first phase of adjustment has just begun.

It is easy to listen to Cohen's voice as we witness him climbing the social ladder, first in Amersfoort, and ever more successfully in camp Westerbork. There his star rises as he becomes a "prominent" person (62), even reaching the distinguished position of "transport doctor," one who is able to decide who should be free from deportation. Cohen admits that in retrospect he was fooled by the Germans whose "system" had subverted them all, and made them act in a despicable manner, in their quest for personal survival:

> I saw that man is an egoist. Someone who thinks only of his own safety. The Germans had a cunning system, and the more I have read about it, the clearer it has become to me that it was a system. [...] They would say to a few people, 'No, you don't have to go on transport, you'll get a suspension [a *Sperr* was their word for it] but, of course, the others do have to go on transport, and you'll have to help with that.' So that's what I did. [...] I myself collaborated. I was obedient and did the job I had to do, [...] it wasn't decent, and it wasn't courageous. It is a fact, one of the facts, of which I am ashamed. [...] I'm tarred. (61)

Full of self-recrimination as these sentiments may be, they are also free from any moral judgment or condemnation. Every one of his actions is guided by one inner logic, that of survival. The only time Cohen feels guilty is when he can no longer protect his own sister and family, whom he had persuaded to come to Westerbork from relative safety, in the first place. For the rest he is shown as a contented man who has become a master in the art of impersonal detachment and adjustment.

Of course there is always the threat of the next transport train, with its weekly (and during the Sobibor period, bi-weekly) scenes of human cargo being shipped to the East. Dr. Cohen is always there, for every transport that leaves requires his professional presence. We only have to recall some of the images of human disarray in Etty Hillesum's most famous letter from Westerbork, of 24 August 1943, to realize the extent of the pain and suffering during those transport nights. But apparently Cohen's process of adjustment has advanced just far enough to make him immune to human misery. What he calls the "curse" that is the next transport evokes for him mostly images of overcrowding, influence peddling, and last minute deals, as "the closer that Tuesday came, the more things began to buzz like a beehive, an ant heap" (73). By using these terrifying, but emotionally detached insect images to reflect human confusion and despair, Cohen reflects his position of safety and detachment. It does not make for a pretty picture, but it is (I believe) part of his honest attempt at showing the world how devilishly clever the German system was, how relatively well things were going for himself, and how far his own rapid adjustment had already succeeded in changing and subverting him.

Once that Tuesday train had left, a sigh of relief went through the entire camp, as people relaxed and started looking for some form of amusement, strange and even surreal as that may seem. And if you were one of the prominent, you enjoyed yourself in style:

> Westerbork. Life there was agreeable. When the transport had left, on Tuesday morning, I went to the bathhouse (I was privileged), took a shower, went to my small room, and slept for an hour. And in the evening we went out. Then Willy Rosen would perform. [...] There was a good orchestra. [...] In short, we were out for the evening. (73)

And again:

> You were cheerful. You enjoyed yourself. And after that you did your work [...] in a white jacket, of course: there always had to be status. (70)

There is something akin to nostalgia here, as if Westerbork were some tranquil and almost pleasant interlude. And who would say that it wasn't, compared to the next stage of the journey?

With Cohen's arrival in Auschwitz, the descent into the "abyss" is almost complete. Again, his adjustment is immediate. By at once stepping forward when he hears a call for physicians, he is able to escape selection. When an inmate who is a former friend of his tells him his family (including his wife and son) has already been gassed, he believes it right away. As a physician, he gets a job as a nurse, which "signified an enormous protection since the other men had to go off to labor squads where the conditions were frightful" (84). Though still in a state of shock, he holds on to the knowledge, acquired in camp Amersfoort, that his only chance for survival is through his profession, and he is eager to live: "The maddest thing of all is that you go on fighting. You go on fighting" (84). Soon he seizes the opportunity to become a "room doctor" in a lunatic ward filled mostly with non-Jewish Poles, the first phase of enjoying some real "protection:"

> As room doctor, you immediately had a better time of it. You got the good food, and your portions were never the smallest. [...] There were no medicines. If the lunatics became too troublesome, you shoved them into a strait jacket. (87)

But when a lunatic escapes from the ward and walks into the main camp at night, he is made responsible for ensuring it won't happen again. If it does, six hundred people will go to the gas, doctors and orderlies included. By giving an overdose of insulin to the potential troublemaker, he ensures that "from then on it was quiet on our block." Though Cohen struggles with this decision for ethical reasons, he has less trouble when the same situation occurs again, a few weeks later. The second man also dies as a result of his injection, "but by that time I had far fewer scruples" (88).

His job also involved writing progress reports about the Jewish inmates on the ward to the notorious Dr. Klein. Klein would be condemned at the Bergen Belsen trial, and hanged. After glancing at the chart handed to him by Dr. Cohen, Dr. Klein would pass it on to an SS man standing at his side. All of this was done with a great show of politeness. Then the men whose charts had been collected, were picked up by an army truck that took them to the gas. The first time it happened, Cohen was devastated and broke down in sobs, but he soon adjusted: "Oh, I was beside myself the first time. But well, you get over it" (90-91). His promotion from the rank of "room doctor" to that of "case reporting doctor," gave him enough of an "important, prominent position" (106) to ensure him of protection and good food, and shield him from having to stand at roll call. Thus he can exclaim: "We got good food, of course. I say 'of course,' but it was a fact. You looked after yourself" (97). And again, "Our life was a good one ('good' between inverted commas) in that place Auschwitz" (98).

As I said before, Cohen is careful not to condemn those who collaborated with the German imposed system to save their own lives. That applies both to his assessment of himself, in Auschwitz I, and of those who survived against even greater odds, and in more extreme situations: the *Arbeitsjuden* of Sobibor I and II, who "lived to work, who worked to live" (Cohen 1979, 176). Impressed with the degree to which most inmates and especially the women helped each other, he quotes with approval one woman survivor who reports that you "got used to it, it was terrible, but the unimaginable became habit, it just became so natural, it was your work." And again, in a moving passage that leaves the survivors much ethical space, the inmates, robotlike, did their work as best they could, since it was "the only passport for the small Realm of Life which was situated inside the Realm of Death. The fear of Camp III was their constant companion" (Cohen 1979, 176). But although he doesn't judge or condemn, he does not excuse his own actions either, and acknowledges that he is at times haunted by the sense of not having "lived very nicely" (Cohen 1973, 98). And he freely admits that he never refused to work on behalf of the system; worse, that he never considered refusing, but always did the job he was asked to do: "Although as a physician I knew that the selections performed by the camp doctor that took place in the clinic amounted to death sentences, I kept on cooperating" (Cohen 1979, 162).

I believe that Cohen's report on borderline human situations which straddle the boundaries between what can and cannot be done (a line that he
strongly believes should not be crossed) leaves more room for changes and
adjustments in human identity than is normally granted in the literature on
these matters. His lack of moral condemnation is striking when compared to
Primo Levi's rather moralizing comments on himself and other prisoners in
Auschwitz. Levi's guilt and shame for not sharing the precious water from
the two-inch pipe with the young Daniele is represented as a "costly" moral
failure (Levi 1989, 80-81). By Cohen's standards he is being unfairly and
unnecessarily hard on himself. Set beside his own milder assessment, Levi's
view of human nature seems cramped and defined by unalterable notions
about dignity and ethical taboos. When members of the *Sonderkommando*
play soccer against the men of the SS, they are perceived as having been successfully "corrupted," and "dragged [...] to the bottom" along with the SS
themselves (Levi 1989, 55). Interestingly, the account of the soccer game is
itself based on a report by a Hungarian camp physician who rose to the rank
of "chief physician" in Auschwitz-Birkenau. Cohen, no doubt as a direct
result of serving as a camp doctor in Westerbork and Auschwitz, views
human identity as looser, more changeable, and less ruled by ethical imperatives. An equally open and unconfined version of human behavior permeates the accounts of persecution and imprisonment by Gerhard Durlacher,
but with a difference: Durlacher never enjoyed the status of a "prominent"
person, and toiled at the very bottom of the camp system.

IV

"Eli, Eli, lama sabachthani." (My God, my God, why hast thou forsaken
me!) With this epigraph from the Gospel of St. Matthew, Gerhard Durlacher
opens his first book *Stripes in the Sky* (Durlacher 1985; 1991). The four stories of this slim volume are based on memories of war experiences and are
narrated with a quiet and precise intensity. In the first story the sixteen-year
old boy is seen standing at an interminable roll call, while allied planes fly
overhead and the crematoria are burning without a pause. In the second
story he relives the early years of the war, from the German invasion
and occupation of May 1940 till his arrest and arrival in transit camp
Westerbork, in the fall of 1942. Of the family and friends who arrived there,
he will be the only survivor. "The Illusionists," a tale of Jewish make belief
and German deceit, recounts the May 1944 journey from Theresienstadt to
the ill-fated Family Camp of Auschwitz-Birkenau. In the moving fourth
story, the boy relives his liberation by the Soviet troops, and his repatriation
to the Netherlands. The words "Eli, Eli, Lama sabachthani" form a suitable

subtext, because central to the situations in all these stories are questions about the almost total abandonment of the Jewish victims during World War II, questions that have haunted the narrator for decades. In an attempt to answer these questions, the narrator has to tell and retell what has happened, and to probe his memory for events many of which are "etched" on his retina like "underexposed images" or "overexposed scenes" in order to absorb and understand them (Durlacher 1991, 9). He goes to archives and libraries to conduct research, and talks with fellow survivors. That way he hopes better to absorb and understand what happened, and be able to place his own personal history within the context of "history."

Gerhard Durlacher was born in 1928, in the German town of Baden-Baden. In *Drowning: Growing Up in the Third Reich*, published in Dutch in 1987, and in English in 1993 (Durlacher 1993), Durlacher describes his childhood and youth in Germany, and evokes through specific scenes the manner in which his early years are slowly undermined and poisoned by the rise of the Nazis, the spread of anti-Semitism and the taunts of the uniformed boys of the Hitler Jugend. After moving from Baden-Baden to Rotterdam, in the mid-1930s, the family lived in relative peace and prosperity. This was shattered by the invasion of Holland and the bombardment of Rotterdam which made their house uninhabitable, and turned them into refugees once again. Resettled in the town of Apeldoorn, the Durlachers were arrested in October 1942, and taken to Westerbork. Though long protected by fellow-Germans who held key positions in Westerbork, they were sent to Theresienstadt in January 1944. In May 1944 they arrived in Auschwitz as part of the "Family Camp." After liberation, Gerhard returned to Apeldoorn as the only surviving member of his family and tried to put his life together again. Until his early retirement in 1983, he was a respected senior lecturer of Sociology at the University of Amsterdam. *Stripes in the Sky*, his first book, was published in Dutch in 1985, and in English in 1991. After *Drowning* he wrote three more books, including *De Zoektocht* (1991) and *Quarantaine* (*Quarantine*, 1993), neither of which are available in English at this time. Gerhard Durlacher died in 1996, at the age of sixty-seven.

Durlacher's literary style is supple and direct and uses images from nature, especially animal imagery. A few of the earlier stories contain references to books and historical documents, in an effort to connect personal narrative with the larger historical perspective. The setting of the story that opens *Stripes in the Sky* is Auschwitz-Birkenau in the late summer of 1944. While the prisoners are lined up in rows of five at roll call, and are counted again and again during a long and sadistic ritual that lasts all day, they view, caps in hand, the trails of smoke, "white strands of sheep's wool" (the title's stripes in the sky). As they see the allied planes whose bombing targets are the nearby I.G. Farben factory and the oil refineries of Blechhammer, and maybe their crematoria and rail road lines, the inmates' sense of expectation and abandonment is described in moving detail.

The roar of the allied planes gives the exhausted men the strength to stand up, and brings an "imperceptible grin" to their faces (Durlacher 1991, 10). But their contentment doesn't last long. For apart from a few stray bombs that accidentally fell from the sunny sky, nothing further happened. "Had they forgotten us?" they ask in tired resignation. The answer is left hanging in the summer air, as they realize that the allied planes have no mandate to attack the crematoria after all. Then the *Rollwagenkommando* with its overburdened carts, "with us as sled dogs" pulling the heavy load, resumes its exhausting grind (12). It is August 1944. After laboring to capacity for three months, the ovens are now burning the last remaining convoys of Hungarian Jews. In the second part of the story, the narrator draws on publications by Walter Laqueur, Martin Gilbert, and David Wyman to detail the Allied Forces' policy of systematic abandonment of the Jews, at the diplomatic and military level. The author comments dryly: "No wonder we felt abandoned" (14).

In the third story, "The Illusionists," we witness the journey, in May 1944, from Theresienstadt to the Family Camp of Auschwitz-Birkenau. There the inmates live in fearful expectation. What will happen to them next? They are overworked and occasionally beaten, but still united with their families, dressed in civilian clothes, and reasonably well fed. But when the narrator asks himself what is happening in the rest of the camp, terror and disbelief compete for his attention, as "night and day my senses record what's happening on the other side of the barbed wire" (Durlacher 1991, 51). Neither his fifteen months in Westerbork, nor his four months in Theresienstadt have prepared him for watching scenes not even dreamed of in Dante's *Inferno*:

> There's no language in hell to describe what I see, hear, smell or taste. Terror and dread have cordoned off my emotions. [...] I see and hear trains, the stumbling masses of people en route to the flames, the dull blows, the naked and shorn women, [...] but I don't understand. (51)

Who are these people, the narrator asks, and how is their fate related to ours? Animal imagery abounds. The inmates are a "herd" of animals chased along registration tables. Kapos dressed in stripes behave like animal trainers, and beat them on their heads and backs with their heavy walking sticks. In another image, Block B II B, the Family Camp is compared to an animal "reserve" where no systematic hunt is allowed to take place, but where "game may be thinned out and shot" (52).

The illusion that they may perhaps be saved from what happens on the other side of the barbed wire lasts until July 1944, when the dreaded selections put an end to everybody's illusions. His father's number is called which means that he will live, at least for now. But the narrator, along with all other men under sixteen and over forty-five years of age, is assigned to the flames. They are considered unfit for productive work. He manages to say good-bye to his mother who has also survived the selection. For a moment their eyes meet, but then everybody scatters in panic as they are chased by guards with clubs, and must run away "like wounded animals in a forest fire" (54). He is now resigned to dying. But some of the boys want to live, and won' t give up. In a sudden reversal, about a hundred boys are allowed to present themselves before the Block leader. Then Mengele arrives on a bicycle, to size them up, "like a farmer inspecting his livestock" (56). He passes the selection. Considered fit to live, he is assigned to the Männerlager (Men's Camp) B II D:

> We're counted again as we go through the gate. The walking stick goes up and down with every fifth row. And then we march toward the sun, which sharply outlines the silhouette of the crematoria against the pale blue sky. (57)

They shower and change into their gray-blue striped uniforms and caps. Their initiation ritual over, they enter the Männerlager. From here on the emphasis is no longer on abandonment, but on adjustment and survival.

Animal images are used once again, but this time they do not to indicate panic or flight, but adjustment to a new, more savage state, as a prerequisite for survival on the part of the defenceless young man. An inkling of understanding comes to the not-yet-sixteen-year-old narrator when he scans the faces of the older prisoners, some of them outfitted with leather boots, or dressed a cut above the norm: to survive in this place, he realizes, you have to be "as a wolf among wolves" (58). This insight is further reinforced when he looks at the Russian prisoners, with their muscular, tanned torsos that are "tattooed all over with tanks, artillery [...] and birds," who stare at them without any sign of interest and behave like "old monkeys in a monkey colony" (59). In the morning, there is the ritual of counting, and the same happens the next day. By then, all that remains of the other seven thousand inmates of the Family camp is ashes and smoke.

Except for the fourth and final story ("After 1945") which picks up where the final story "Liberations" from *Stripes in the Sky* leaves off, the stories in *Quarantaine* (1993) are all about scenes of impending arrest and detention. There are the usual animal images ("Our herd is driven into the corral," 21; the locomotive, already under steam, waits "like an impatient horse," 35), and there are other images from nature. Above all, there are many images of

hands, among them those of the lawyer Heinz Gabel, the German refugee
from the St.-Louis who used to be so proud of his clean hands and finger-
nails. In Westerbork, it is only Heinz Gabel's no-longer clean hands which
are able to shield them from deportation by sifting through the card cata-
logue and removing, at great personal risk, their name cards, prior to each
Tuesday night's deportation train.

At this point, the young protagonist's own hands are useless. Though he
tries hard to learn how to stand up for himself during boxing lessons from
the great Bennie Bril in Westerbork (in "Forbidden Lessons," Durlacher
1993, 59), his gloved hands won't do the necessary work. Later in Theresienstadt, surrounded by aggressive adult men, the fifteen year old is completely vulnerable, and finds no protection, not even from his own father.
The only real comfort during this bleak period comes from the lessons of Dr.
Belinfante who speaks to him about "free will and determinism" and teaches him algebra inside a barracks (Durlacher 1993, 65-66). These gestures by
Bennie Bril and Dr. Belinfante give him some of the necessary warmth and
protection, and lift his spirits, even if they can't protect him from the ever
present threat of further deportation. Another such small, but significant
gesture can be found in the hands of Dr. Logeman, the high school principal, who was allowed to hand him a mathematics book through the bars of
the detention cell in the police station in Apeldoorn, after his arrest
(Durlacher 1993, 67; see also Durlacher 1991, 41).

After surviving Auschwitz, and coming back to Holland as the only surviving member of his family, the protagonist finds safety, but no lack of
humiliation. In an episode from "After 1945" the narrator rings the doorbell
of the house where the family had lived until their arrest. The woman who
opens the door is less than friendly when he explains who he is and why he
is there, and closes the door abruptly. On his visit to the couple next door,
the husband walks in dressed in his father's stylish pin-striped suit, to their
mutual embarrassment. So much for his homecoming! Most of his efforts at
adjustment fail as an atmosphere of corruption seems to have seeped into
almost every layer of Dutch post-war society.

There are also some heart-warming episodes which slowly begin to melt
the "river of ice" that had been carrying him along (Durlacher 1993, 87).
The money left by his parents with the family notary is just enough to get
him started in high school. Music is a revitalizing force in his life, together
with his discovery of books. His fellow students increasingly accept him as
one of theirs, but when one of them innocently inquires about the number
on his arm, he clams up and withdraws behind a "wall of glass" (99). Slowly,
he begins to realize that he will be able to cope in the post-war world, but

the emblematic fate of the wife of the Biblical Lot sends a powerful signal, warning him of the dangers involved in glancing back too soon at the realm of the dead.

Finally, there is the problem of silence and communication. Gerhard Durlacher was conscious, right from the moment of his return, that words could not capture the reality of what he had lived, and that there was nobody interested in listening to him anyway. But ever so slowly, and also "thanks to understanding therapists," the structure he had erected between himself and the past started to come apart. The turning point came in 1983 when he retired from the University in order to write. The resulting five books were all composed during the final decade (1985-1995) of his relatively brief life. They are short books that ask irritating questions, including how it is possible that the world "discreetly turns the other way or watches unmoved" while hundreds of thousands are being killed (Durlacher 1991, 24). Like the book handed to him in prison by the school principal, every one of Durlacher's books is a small gesture which has the power to reach those susceptible to the less than comfortable questions they pose.

Literature Cited

Bregstein, Philo. 1972. *Gesprekken met Jacques Presser*. Amsterdam: Athenaeum-Polak & Van Gennep.

Bregstein, Philo. 1981. *Dingen die niet voorbijgaan*. Amsterdam: Meulenhoff.

Cohen, Elie A. 1973. *The Abyss: A Confession*. New York: W.W. Norton.

Cohen, Elie A. 1979. *De negentien treinen naar Sobibor*. Amsterdam: Sijthoff.

Durlacher, Gerhard L. 1991. *De zoektocht*. Amsterdam: Meulenhoff.

Durlacher, Gerhard L. 1991. *Stripes in the Sky: A Wartime Memoir*. London: Serpent's Tail.

Durlacher, Gerhard L. 1993. *Drowning: Growing up in the Third Reich*. London: Serpent's Tail.

Durlacher, Gerhard L. 1993. *Quarantaine: Verhalen*. Amsterdam: Meulenhoff.

Krell, Robert 1999. The Psychologic Challenges Facing Child Survivors. In *Messages and Memories: Reflections on Child Survivors of the Holocaust*, ed. Robert Krell, pp. 87-96. Vancouver: Memory Press.

Levi, Primo. 1989. *The Drowned and the Saved*. New York: Random House Vintage International.

Lindeman, Yehudi. 2001. In Hiding in Holland. In *The Holocaust: Personal Accounts*, eds. David Scrase and Wolfgang Mieder, pp. 193-209. Burlington, Vermont: The Center for Holocaust Studies at the University of Vermont.

Presser, J. 1969. *The Destruction of the Dutch Jews*. New York: E.P. Dutton and Company.

Van der Zee, Nanda. 1988. *Jacques Presser.* Amsterdam: Balans.

Wiesel, Elie. 1999. Hidden Memories. In *Messages and Memories: Reflections on Child Survivors of the Holocaust,* ed. Robert Krell, pp. 41-48. Vancouver: Memory Press.

"Vox Populi – Voces Populi"

Proverbial Revelations in Victor Klemperer's *Diaries of the Nazi Years (1933-1945)*

Wolfgang Mieder

Scholars of language and culture who study the use and misuse of the German language during the twelve years of the Nazi reign have regarded the philologist and literary scholar Victor Klemperer as a key figure for decades. After all, as early as 1947, Klemperer was the first to publish his now famous book *L[ingua] T[ertii] I[mperii]: Notizbuch eines Philologen*, which started the still ongoing debate about the role of the German language during the Third Reich (see Bauer 1988; Berning 1964; Bork 1970; Maas 1984; Mieder 1996; Seidel and Seidel-Slotty 1961). While this book, based on diary entries, is still read with scholarly interest and deep compassion for the Jewish author who escaped the horrors of the Nazi era, a two-volume edition of Klemperer's diaries has been published in 1995 under the title *Ich will Zeugnis ablegen bis zum letzten. Tagebücher 1933-1945*. In much greater detail, these volumes present disturbing images of the Second World War and the Holocaust from a victim's perspective. To a large extent, this is done through linguistic observation and analysis. The philologist Klemperer turns his own contemporary history into a "source of linguistic history" and "this philological interpretation is needed to understand contemporary history as cultural history" (Kämper 1996, 328-329). However, those who interpret "linguistic history as cultural history and cultural history as linguistic history" (Schober 1988, 188) in Klemperer's sense will not only study individual elements of Nazi vocabulary, but will include the problematic phraseology of that time into their analysis as well. Naturally, proverbs and proverbial expressions are an important partial aspect of such an analysis, particularly since pre-set linguistic formulas played such an important role in Nazi propaganda from war mongering to the persecution of the Jews (see Mieder 1983 and 1993).[1]

Victor Klemperer, born on 5 October 1881, in Landsberg as the son of a rabbi, began to write a diary when he was sixteen. Even if he did not make daily entries, he continued writing a regular diary until his death on 11 February 1960 in Dresden. He began to compile the most important aspects of his life and time by assembling a *Vita* out of dozens of diary notebooks. The first part of this *Vita* was published posthumously in 1989 in two volumes under the title *Curriculum vitae. Erinnerungen 1881-1918*. In his introduction, Klemperer muses about his manic obsession with writing a diary in typical openness:

> Those who write a *Vita* [...] are concerned about permanency, and want to stay here longer [...]. The wish to stay here means: The wish to play a role [...]; I studied and have achieved a professorship, a rather modest one at that. That is quite an average achievement, and if I were to use it as a claim for an autobiography, it would be bound to be ignored. [...]. Yet, I have often argued that the average has a special right to receive attention, since it is the fate of the majority to be average. (Klemperer 1989, 1,7-8)

Of course, Victor Klemperer was far more than an average person. This is evident from four more volumes of diaries now available in print, *Leben sammeln, nicht fragen wozu und warum. Tagebücher 1918-1932* and *So sitze ich denn zwischen allen Stühlen. Tagebücher 1945-1959* (see Klemperer 1995b, 1996, and 1999), which on several thousand pages present almost 70 years of history experienced and interpreted by Victor Klemperer. It is therefore hardly surprising that the journalist Volker Ullrich entitled his review of the diaries describing life in East Germany with the well-deserved headline "The Chronicler of the Century" (Ulrich 1999, 19-20).

In 1935, Klemperer had lost the professorship bestowed upon him in 1920 at the Technical University of Dresden and then had to spend torturous years of absolute isolation and daily fear for his life in Nazi Germany, courageously assisted by his non-Jewish wife Eva (née Schlemmer) who stood by him as an "Aryan" even after the couple was expelled from their residence in Dölzschen (near Dresden) and forced to live in various "Jew's houses" after 1940. Apart from the forced labor he had to perform in factories, Klemperer had little else to do but manically to give expression to his fate as a former German citizen (see Elon 1996). As the editor of the diaries Walter Nowojski has noted, the core of the diaries in the period from 1933 to 1945 is a "chronicle of the isolation, incapacitation, harassment, and finally, the systematic annihilation of the Dresden Jews" (II,866).[2] Only the catastrophic air attack on Dresden of 13 February 1945, saved Victor Klemperer from deportation with the last resident Jews and from sure death in a concentration camp. By the death of his companion and fellow sufferer Eva on 8 July 1951, Klemperer had regained a much deserved professorship at Berlin after teaching at Greifswald and Halle universities. In 1952, Klemperer married Hadwig Kirchner (collaborator in the large project of editing the diaries). In 1953, he became a member of the German Academy of Sciences in Berlin. Until his death, he was held in high esteem in East Germany as a victim of National Socialism and as an established scholar.[3]

"I will bear witness, precise witness!" (II,99)

The interpreters of Klemperer's diaries from the Nazi years have repeatedly quoted the following characteristic entry of 27 May 1942, which has also found its way into the title of the two volumes of the book *I Will Bear Witness*: "But I continue to write. That is *my* heroism. I will bear witness, precise witness!" (II,99) (see Kämper 1996, 329; Reiss 1998, 84; Würzner 1997, 173). Nevertheless, it has not been noted that this expression is of course alluding to the proverbial Eighth Commandment: "Thou shalt not bear false witness against your neighbor" (2. Moses 20,16). Klemperer is able to add bitter irony to the Biblical expression "to bear false witness." While the ruling Nazis repeatedly bear false witness against him and all his fellow Jews, he intends to "become the cultural historiographer of the current disaster. To observe until the last, take notes without asking whether the notes will be used" (II,12) (see Fries 1996, 5) by bearing truthful and precise witness. It comes as no surprise that his books *Language of the Third Reich* and *Curriculum vitae* have been praised as "exemplary excerpts of everyday communication in the Third Reich" (Lang 1986, 72) as well as for their "openness, honesty, and bluntness" (Christmann 1993, 19). With regard to the *Diaries of the Nazi Years (1933-1945)*, critics have spoken of "semantic exposure strategies" (Kämper 1996, 340) and "kaleidoscopic stock taking" (Przyrembel 1998, 314).

Throughout the diaries, "bearing witness" becomes a psycholinguistic *leitmotif*, as is evident from two more references:

> *11 June 1942:* I will continue to dare writing the diary. I want to bear witness to the last. (II,124)

> *8 April 1944:* Conversation with Stühler senior: "I want to bear witness." – "What you are writing is all well known, and you don't know about the big events, Kiev, Minsk etc." – "The big events don't matter. It is the everyday life of tyranny that is forgotten. A thousand mosquito bites are worse than a hit to the head. I observe, I note the mosquito bites [...]." (II,503)

Quite obviously, in the latter instance, Klemperer not only uses the "witness" expression, but also adds the proverb "A thousand mosquito bites are worse than a hit to the head," which in the *Deutsches Sprichwörter-Lexikon* (1867-1880) by Karl Friedrich Wilhelm Wander can only be found as "A thousand can do more than one" (Wander 1867-1880, 4,1051; see Dirschauer 1998, 71; Turner 1999, 386). Klemperer's proverb variant has significantly more metaphorical power and expresses vividly what his main concern for bearing witness is: to register the normal events of the "everyday life of tyranny." As early as 10 December 1940, Klemperer had come to the same conclusion: "But the changing details of everyday life are precisely what is most important" (I, 565; I,364).

Repeatedly he characterized his work as a tool to fight his fear of death and as a psychological escape mechanism. Thus, he writes on 29 November 1942: "Work, to get intoxicated with work!" (II,285), and on 15 March 1943: "It is difficult to continue working as if I had enough time to complete anything. But working is the best way to forget" (II,344). In a certain way, the absurd Nazi slogan found on several concentration camp gates, "Work makes free" (see Brückner 1998; Doerr 2000), has been positively true in the case of Victor Klemperer, whose unrelenting will to work and to bear witness about the crimes of the Nazi period fueled his will to survive and gave him the strength to offer valuable services for humanity in spite of the inhuman treatment he received. Martin Walser, in his informative *Laudatio for Victor Klemperer* (1996), correctly speaks of the "professional courage" (Walser 1996a, 53 and 1996b, 58) Klemperer displayed as a scholar and diary writer for twelve years in the face of constant deadly danger. As an outsider and outcast he only had his pen to bear precise witness about human and inhuman behavior during the Nazi period.

"I keep coming back to it: in lingua veritas" (II,75)

On 25 April 1937, Klemperer wrote to his brother-in-law Martin Süßmann in regards to his National Socialist language study "that its motto would be: *In lingua veritas*" (I, 345; I,216), which precisely defines the base of his socio-psychological language analysis by using a so-called anti-proverb. There are many humorous parodies and innovative alterations of the classical proverb "In vino veritas," but no other instance exists of the very logical phrase "In lingua veritas" (see Mieder 1998, 311-318). Five years later, on 28 April 1942, Klemperer returned to this phrase which completely explains his philological point of view: "But will not my history of language just be a 'disguised' cultural (intellectual) history? No, I have to maintain this: *in lingua veritas. Veritas* belongs to cultural history; and *lingua* offers a general confirmation of the facts under discussion" (II,75).

Of particular interest in this context is Klemperer's variation of the proverb "The sun will bring it to light" in the *LTI*-book: "Language will bring it to light [i.e., bring out the truth]":

> Whatever someone is trying to hide, be it from others, or from himself, or be it carried around unconsciously: language will bring it to light. That must be the meaning of the phrase: *Le style c'est l'homme*; what a person says may be a lie – but the language style reveals character without fail. (Klemperer 1987 [1947], 16; see Maas 1984, 216; Reiss 1998, 75)[4]

Klemperer first uses this fitting expression on 31 March 1942, in his diary, and he may have remembered it when he was preparing the *LTI* manuscript, but he did not take over this exact quote:

> *LTI.* Language brings it to light. Sometimes, people will try to hide the truth by speaking. But language does not lie. Sometimes, people will try to give expression to the truth. But language will prove truer than they. There is no remedy against the truth of language. (II,58)

As a language critic and "judge," Klemperer takes it upon himself to write a "sociolinguistic analysis" (Schober 1988, 190) of the Nazi era and "interprets it primarily in a psychological way (language as the mirror of the damnable actions of human beings; language in the service of irrationality)" (Techtmeier 1987, 321).

"The shameless shortleggedness of their lies" (II,580)

It should not be overlooked that, in spite of his own intellectual scholarship, Victor Klemperer repeatedly resorted to proverbs and proverbial expressions to get his frustration metaphorically speaking "off his chest." This is particularly evident in his descriptions of the political situation, where he loves to "play" with proverbs by rephrasing them to characterize the fascist mind set. The following two references illustrate the way Klemperer sometimes accumulates proverbial expressions in his political musings to "vent his anger" about the steadily deteriorating situation. In this context it is interesting to see that in the first example, he already recognizes the collective guilt of the German people:

> *2 October 1938:* I have an expression in my ear that we have kept hearing for years now: "We don't know what games they are playing." Politics, more than ever, has become a secret game of a few who make decisions affecting millions and claim to represent the people. Grammatical despair, subconscious despair. But I quote from Bernadin de Saint-Pierre: "If the government is

corrupt, then the corrupted people are to blame." (I,427; text omitted in English version)

14 March 1939: But now that according to today's evening paper the fixed game appears to have been so very swiftly and smoothly and completely won by Germany, while England and France take it all lying down, I feel as sick as a dog again. (I,465; I, 296)

Those are thoughts about world politics in vernacular language we might not necessarily expect from an intellectual. And yet, expressions such as "to be a fixed game," "to take it lying down," or "to feel as sick as a dog" are very well suited to give expression to the whole dilemma. Klemperer's own emotional state lets him resort to proverbial expressions in contrast to his usual abstract style. This phenomenon was also apparent in the case of the eloquent Winston Churchill of whom we know that he used his persuasive and often proverbial linguistic power to fight Hitler's Germany in verbal and written form (see Mieder 1997a; Mieder and Bryan 1995).

The diaries' main task is to present information about the Nazi state. This is also true in the case of an apparently obvious statement such as the following, where the well-known proverb "Whoever whispers, lies" on a propaganda poster serves to characterize the way Nazi propaganda style is based on fear:

1 June 1943: Eva was telling me, that there is a poster all over town – two people whispering – with the caption: "Whoever whispers, lies." And now it occurs to me that they have been writing a long time, a very long time about whisper propaganda, and that *whisper propaganda* is a very characteristic word of LTI and that it must be used in the context of a bad conscience [...]. (II,386)

The mere mention of a proverb abused for the purposes of propaganda is enough to provide the philologist Klemperer with a new idea for his *LTI* research. All this is happening at a time when such actions became increasingly risky for Jews.

Particularly impressive is Klemperer's use of the proverb "Lies have short legs" of 10 September 1944, in order to point out the insincerity of the German regime and its impending downfall: "A special characteristic of the *LTI* is the shameless shortleggedness of their lies. They forever coolly deny any claims that were made the day before" (II,580). Apparently, Klemperer liked this re-phrasing of the old proverb, and in his *LTI*-book we read two years later: "What astonished me was the shameless shortleggedness of their lies, which became apparent in the numbers: The foundation of the Nazi doctrine includes the conviction that the masses are thoughtless and easy to stupefy" (Klemperer 1987 [1947], 230-231; see Jäger and Jäger 1999, 45).

However, what Klemperer writes down on 14 December 1944, as a proverb riddle involving the most popular German proverb "The morning hour has gold in its mouth" seems to prove that the masses couldn't be completely fooled after all: "A new joke-riddle is going around, Neumark's secretary, Mrs. Jährig, told us: What is that? It has silver in its hair, gold in its mouth, and lead in its limbs. Answer: The 'Volkssturm' [the forced drafting of all capable males in 1944 to protect Germany resulting in a so-called 'people's army']" (II,627). In this joke-riddle, the original proverb is combined with the popular expanded variant "Morning hour has gold in its mouth and lead in its legs (limbs, butt)" (see Mieder 1997b and 1998, 198-207).

Yet how revealing is Klemperer's statement of 1 May 1945, where the following scene in an inn a week before the end of the war already shows how the majority of Germans will deny that they share any guilt in the Nazi regime:

> The innkeeper was loquacious, he told us [...] that he had never been a member of the Party and how he had wrangled with the SA and claimed their respect. How far will the sails be trimmed to the wind, how far can one trust? Now, everyone has been an enemy of the Party. If only they had *always* been [...]. (II,761)

Of course, "the feeling of having been saved dominates" (II,761), but from the point of view of Klemperer and all other victims of Nazi terror, the old expression "to trim one's sails to the wind" is understood as a clear sign of consent, if not of active participation. Shortly before the end of the war, as can be expected, a lot of opportunists' sails are being trimmed to the wind, and excuses are available all too readily. On 5 May 1945, Klemperer notes with distress: "Everything now comes to light triumphantly that had been most fearfully hidden before 28 April [U.S. troops liberate the concentration camp at Dachau] [...]; no one wants to have been a Nazi among all those who doubtlessly played a part. – Where is the truth, how can it even be approximated?" (II,768). What came to the proverbial light of day were primarily brazen claims of innocence, and the search for the truth, despite the large scholarly body of literature written about the war and the Holocaust, is incomplete to this day. Klemperer's accusing question of 25 May 1945, remains valid today: "Which part of this not-knowing is the truth?" (II,797).

"An eye for an eye, and a tooth for a tooth" (II,470)

Of course, there is no question about the massive guilt of Adolf Hitler and Joseph Goebbels, and Klemperer denounces both men on many pages of his diary. Among other remarks, he gives evidence of their manipulative use of proverbs and proverbial expressions. With distress, Klemperer reacts on 31 March 1933, to the general boycott against shops in Jewish ownership proclaimed that day by the Nazi authorities:

> Ever more hopeless. The boycott begins tomorrow. Yellow placards, men on guard. Pressure to pay Christian employees two months salary, to dismiss Jewish ones. [...] – They murder coldly or "with delay." "Not a hair is harmed on someone's head" – they only let you starve to death. (I,16; I, 10, text partially omitted in the English version)

By putting the expression "not to harm a hair on someone's head" in quotation marks, Klemperer expresses a certain irony. He is quoting Adolf Hitler, whose "Boycott Call Against the Jews to all Party Organizations of the NSDAP" of 28 March 1933, was the first official step to exclude Jews from public life in Germany. Hitler seems to have been convinced that his proclamation was going to cause the Jewish population to leave Germany:

> The action committees are responsible for ensuring that this entire struggle [against the Jews] is carried out with utmost calm and discipline. Continue not to harm a single hair on a Jew's head! We will overcome this plague, simply by the drastic power of these measures. (Domarus 1962, 1,248 and 251)

Today we know how fast Hitler turned the expression "not to harm a hair on someone's head" into its opposite by ordering the physical torture, the murder, and finally the complete annihilation of all Jews. Hitler used the expression with devilish irony, as he knew in advance that he would go much further than merely harming the hair of the Jewish citizenry.

On 20 July 1933, Klemperer quotes another expression used by Hitler, which actually characterizes the latter as a paranoid psychopath who hates nothing more than to get laughed at and not to be taken seriously. Those who still laugh literally receive the threat that they will stop doing so sooner or later:

> A sound film recording of Hitler, a few sentences in front of a big meeting – clenched fist, twisted face, wild bawling – "on 30 January [1933; Hitler takes power] they were still laughing at me, they won't be laughing anymore [...]." It seems that perhaps for the moment he is all-powerful – but the voice and gestures expressed impotent rage. Doubts of his omnipotence? Does one talk incessantly about a thousand years and enemies destroyed, if one is certain of these thousand years and this annihilation? (I,42-43; I, 26) (see Klemperer 1987 [1947], 38)

This is evidence of Klemperer's ability as an insightful psycholinguist with profound understanding of Hitler's psyche. Later, in his *LTI*-book, Klemperer returns to this expression and shows how Hitler and his companions turned it from a metaphorical phrase into horrible action:

> One of the frequently repeated and paraphrased *Führer* phrases is the threat
> that the Jews would stop laughing, which later evolved into the also fre-
> quently repeated statement that they really had stopped laughing. That is
> true and is confirmed by the bitter Jewish joke that the Jews are the only
> group for whom Hitler really has kept his word. (Klemperer 1987 [1947],
> 190-191)[5]

Hitler was obsessed with his idea of "Jewish laughter," and kept returning to
his threat that those who failed to take him seriously would stop laughing
soon. In a speech of 8 November 1942, he claimed that "the National
Socialist prophesies are not just phrases," and repeated at the same time:

> If the Jews think they can bring about an international world war to annihi-
> late the European races, the result will not be the annihilation of the
> European races, but the annihilation of the Jews in Europe (see Hilberg 1961
> and 1992). They laughed at me as a prophet. Many of those who laughed
> back then are not laughing any more, and many of those who still do may
> soon stop as well. (Domarus 1962, 2,1937)

The only surprise left here is the word "may" inserted by Hitler, who knew
that his own unthinkable murder policy, which ended the lives of millions
of innocent people, was already consequently underway.

The otherwise eloquent Klemperer can only respond to Hitler's menda-
cious politics on 25 December 1941, with a half-quoted proverb: "Doesn't
he [Hitler] know the proverb: 'Those who lie once [...]'?" (I,700). Contrary
to the other half of the proverb, "[...] will not be believed again," millions of
Germans continued to believe in the lying demagogue for several more years!

As a last example for Hitler's crazed "populism" it should be mentioned
how he blasphemously abused the Biblical proverb "An eye for an eye, and a
tooth for a tooth." On 8 January 1944, Klemperer notes as part of his collection of references on the language of National Socialism:

> *LTI. [...] Hitler:* "Jewish world dictatorship" – "Annihilation of the Jews in
> Europe" – "with the healthy and fanatical hatred of a race fighting for sur-
> vival, which, at least in this case, professes to the old Biblical phrase: 'An eye
> for an eye, a tooth for a tooth'." (II,470)

Hitler had used this Biblical proverb before, in a speech held 30 January
1942. What had been a metaphorical proverb or drastic phrase had now
been turned into physical reality. The proverb "An eye for an eye, a tooth for
a tooth" (2. Moses 21,24; Matthew 5,38) had been perverted into a popular
justification for the actual annihilation of the European Jews:

> We are sure that the war can only end when either the Aryan people have
> been eliminated or when the Jews disappear from Europe. [...] the result of

this war will be the annihilation of the Jews. This time, for the first time, the authentic old Jewish law will be applied: "An eye for an eye, a tooth for a tooth!" (Domarus 1962, 2,1828-1829)

The Holocaust has shown that all of Klemperer's linguistic observations were only too true. This perversion of the ancient proverb of revenge eventually led to genocide, for which there is no proverbial lore.

"The Jewish Question is the A and O" (II,385)

The linguistic registry of antisemitism is at the core of the *Diaries 1933-1945* and the *LTI*-book. In this context, Klemperer mentions the many proverbial placards and headlines, and concludes his entry of 12 September 1937, with the telling statement: "And the people are so stupid that they believe everything" (I,378; I, 237). Obviously, Klemperer was aware that the National Socialist propaganda machine was subtle enough to base its hate slogans on well-known proverbial structures. This is particularly evident in such antisemitic proverb collections as Julius Schwab's *Rassenpflege im Sprichwort* [Racial Hygiene in the Proverb] (1937) and Ernst Hiemer's *Der Jude im Sprichwort der Völker* [The Jew in International Proverbs] (1942).

Such horrific collections were not known to Klemperer, but some of his diary notes give clear evidence of the proverbial antisemitism of his times:

> *25 April 1933:* Notice on the Student House (likewise at all the universities): "When the Jew writes in German, he lies," henceforth he is to be allowed to write only in Hebrew. Jewish books must be characterized as "translations." (I,24; I,15) (see Klemperer 1987 [1947], 35)

> *17 April 1935:* Der Stürmer is displayed at many street corners; there are special bulletin boards, and each one bears a slogan in large letters: "The Jews are our misfortune." Or: "Whoever knows the Jew, knows the devil." Etc. (I,192; I,118)

> *29 May 1943:* Stylistically, each sentence, each phrase of the speech [by Prof. Johann von Leer] is essential. The pretended objectivity, the obsession, the popular touch, the common denominator, the emphasis: *The Jewish Question is the A and O.* (II,385)

Repeatedly, Klemperer uses expressions which highlight the increasing antisemitism and the Jewish persecution emphasized by the propaganda:

> *27 February 1943:* Note on *LTI*: "Emigrated" for "has been emigrated." Harmless word for "rape," "send away," "send to death." We can be certain now that no Jews will return from Poland alive. They will be killed before the retreat. Besides, word has it that many of those evacuated never even reach Poland alive. It is said that they are gassed in cattle wagons on their way, and then, the wagons stop at a prepared mass grave. (II,335)

These examples make it amply clear that Klemperer in Dresden had full knowledge of the gassing in concentration camps. On 16 March 1942, we find the first mention of Auschwitz: "As the worst KZ I heard mention Auschwitz (or some such name) near Königshütte in Upper Silesia. Work in the mines. Death after a few days" (II,47). Then, on 14 January 1943: "The permanent awful fear of Auschwitz" (II,312). And finally, on 20 August 1944, Klemperer writes the following entry, even if he cannot comment with certainty on the rumor because of his isolation, as is indicated by the attached Italian proverb: "I heard: Some time ago, a great number of older Jews (three hundred? three thousand?) had been transported out of – Theresienstadt, and after that, the English broadcast had reported the gassing of the transport. True? *Forse che sí, forse che no*" (II,565) (see Klemperer 1962, 165).

Klemperer's diaries have justifiably been called "stenographs [shorthand notes] from Purgatory" (Reemtsma 1997, 170), and Klemperer himself has been referred to as a "seismograph of Jewish persecution" (Przyrembel 1998, 313). The contextualized examples show that proverbs and proverbial expressions served the cause of antisemitism only too well, which on the other hand is also a clear indication that these traditional phraseological units are much more than mere simplistic formulas.

"Vox populi breaks down into voces populi" (I,513; I, 329)

The classical proverb "Vox populi, vox dei" serves Klemperer as a logical *leitmotif* to characterize his philological observations of the Nazi language (see Boas 1969, 3-38; Militz 1998, 214-215). Throughout his notes, Klemperer wants to record the voice of the people to preserve impressions of the general atmosphere during the Third Reich. During this process, he sometimes doubts who and what represents the "German voice," and whether such a generally applicable voice even exists. All this, of course, leads to the larger question of the guilt and responsibility of the German population whose *Führer* Hitler understood himself as the "voice of God" for National Socialism. In a speech held 16 March 1936, Hitler already referred to this originally democratic proverb: "German people [...] I await your decision, and I know I will be proven right! I will accept your decision as the voice of the people, which is the voice of God" (Domarus 1962, 1,607). Of course, Hitler once again only understood this proverb literally, which is to say, "the voice of the people" for him only meant the National Socialist German segment of the population and all other dissenting voices were excluded. Klemperer, on the other hand, speaks in his *LTI*-book of the insolent lies that were spread by the Nazi leaders under the guise of the "people's voice" and notes: "However, there is no *vox populi*, only *voces populi*; and it only can be determined after the fact which of these different voices is the true one, that is to say, which of them determines the course of events." A dozen pages later follows this remark: "*Vox populi* – always the question of the observer which of the many voices will determine events!" (Klemperer 1987 [1947], 236 and 248). However, the voice prevalent at the time was only that of Hitler himself who claimed the right to be the "*Führer*-God" based on his arrogant interpretation of the entire proverb "Vox populi, vox dei."

Klemperer knows the power held by Hitler and his associates, and their manipulating and propagandistic language is of much concern to him. But the "voice of the people" is of equal interest to him, for "nothing brings us closer to the soul of the people than language" (Klemperer 1987 [1947], 168).[6] The following four textual examples may serve to show us how Klemperer wrestles with a correct view of the popular voice (see Jäger and Jäger 1999, 55; Kämper 1996, 339; Reiss 1998, 84):

> *29 September 1939*: Vogel, the grocer: "I don't believe it will last three years, the English will give in, or they will be destroyed. *Vox populi communis opinio*. It has proved in the right with the Russian alliance and the partition of Poland, it could prove in the right now too. There is absolute confidence and intoxication in victory everywhere here. There seems to be no war at all any more. (I,493; I, 314)

> *17 March 1940*: Rumors and mood change from day to day, from person to person. Whom do I see, to whom do I listen? Natscheff, Berger the grocer; the cigar dealer in Chemnitzer Straße, who is a freemason, the charwoman, whose forty-year old son is stationed in the West and who is on leave just now, the coal heavers. *Vox populi* breaks down into *voces populi*. (I,513; I, 329)

> *15 January 1944*: Always the same question: Which is the true *communis opinio*, which is the true *vox populi*, the true, determining voice affecting the people and the Army? Nobody knows. The decision comes from some impulse, some group, some prevalent mood; the decision comes from what can be called God, chance, fate, x, – not from consciously leading people. (II,473)

> *7 February 1944*: *Voces populi*: On the way to Katz, an older man in passing: "Judas!" In the hallway at the health insurance company. I am the only star bearer walking up and down in front of an occupied bench. I hear a worker say: "A [terminal] injection they should give them. Then, they'd be gone!" Does he mean me? The starred one? A few minutes later the man is called in.[...] I take his place. An older lady next to me, whispers: "That was mean! Maybe he'll have the same thing happen to him one day that he just wished for you. Who knows, the Lord will judge!" (II,483-484)

These ambivalent incidents of the popular voice may serve as evidence how Klemperer as a reporter not only varies the proverb "Vox populi, vox dei" as a *leitmotif,* but also how he describes the shifting opinions of the populace. This is enhanced by the many proverbs and expressions used by the individuals Klemperer quotes to document their language conventions. The formulas of popular language are used by antisemites and philosemites alike to react in a negative or positive manner to their fellow Jewish citizens. The ambivalent multi-functionality of proverbial language is particularly apparent here when it is employed to support opposing arguments.

Klemperer cannot get away from his principal question expressed as a proverb. As late as 15 February 1945, he speaks with understandable frustration about the "fickleness of the popular mood" (II,673), obviously a great problem for someone working as a philological eyewitness. M.H. Würzner has observed that "What Klemperer notes is 'oral history' in its truest sense. Historians tend to follow the larger outline of the politics of power, but are barely interested in the opinions circulating in everyday life" (Würzner 1997, 170 and 172). Terms such as "oral history" or "personal narrative" were unknown during Klemperer's time, but his own proverbial variation "Vox populi communis opinio" (I,493) comes very close to the results yielded by this type of social and folklore research, and his main interest is in this general opinion as the voice of the people. It is not at all easy to find a common denominator for this opinion, as was attempted, for example, by Daniel J. Goldhagen in his controversial book *Hitler's Willing Executioners. Ordinary Germans and the Holocaust* (1996) (see Heil and Erb 1998; Hilberg 1997; Schoeps 1996). Justifiably, Klemperer describes his research on the "mentality of a national community" (see Heer 1997) as "voces populi" or "the organ play of popular voices," since *one* true "vox populi" does not exist. On 22 January 1939, he notes in this regard: "No one, whether inside or outside, can fathom the true mood of the people – probably, no certainly there is no general true mood, but always only moods of certain groups" (I,459; I, 293). Here, among other things, lies the great value of the Klemperer diaries; they show us that there simply are no easy answers to the complex questions raised by the Nazi dictatorship and the Holocaust.

"*It can cost your head*" (II,633)

Of the many somatic expressions found in the *Diaries 1933-1945,* the group around the word "head" might well be analyzed in some detail. The use of proverbial expressions such as "to risk one's head" and "to cost one's head" in the diaries, even without context, point out that the National

Socialist state is a matter of life and death for the Jews. This also applies to Klemperer's non-Jewish wife Eva who engages herself for her husband and other Jewish friends:

> *1 July 1942*: Eva is increasingly occupied with errands. – For Frau Pick she literally risks her head, no, our heads. ("For your manuscripts, too," she counters my admonitions.) (II,150)

The word "literally" underscores the fact that the proverbial expression "to risk one's head" is not just a cliché. The actual danger for Eva to be intercepted on her errands with her husband's manuscripts was much too great.

Even more direct and drastic are two diary entries in which Klemperer uses the expression "to cost one's head" to characterize the difficult and dangerous situation through a very clear metaphor. In this context, the expression loses its metaphorical meaning and shows in the most obvious way the true danger those people lived in who were not welcome to the government for any reason:

> *12 April 1944*: [after a conversation with the optician Hahn]: I in the end: "But don't tell anyone, or else you don't need to bother making the glasses; it will cost me my head." (II,504)

> *22 April 1945*: And always: "But you know that our conversation will cost your head if [...]." (II,752)

Repeatedly, the deadly fear comes to the surface that both Klemperers suffered for years. When Klemperer in this context uses seemingly well-worn expressions, they never come across as clichés because of their frightening meaning.

At the end of this analysis of the somatic "head" expressions in the diaries, a few examples citing the positive and encouraging expression "to keep one's head [in English better: chin] up" must also be mentioned. These are all moments when German fellow citizens showed human compassion for the German Jew Klemperer. In spite of evil perpetrators and the many silent bystanders, there were also some decent people who had enough humanity and courage to help Jews such as Victor Klemperer or to at least give them a friendly word. The following diary entries seem to express a certain type of charity or, more abstract, an ideal of humanity in Lessing's sense (see Guthke 1999). Maybe such people remembered their old school reading of Lessing's *Nathan the Wise* and simply expressed their understanding of tolerance with the expression "to keep one's chin up." After reading these examples, it becomes apparent that the expression is not employed as a mere popular cliché. Rather, it is a popular way of expressing solidarity for one's Jewish fellow citizens which today moves us as evidence of human charity and sincerity, somewhat remindful of Goethe's request: "Noble be man, helpful, and good!" from his poem "The Divine [i.e., in humans]" (1783):

> *16 April 1943*: They [two helpful workers] were silent and left. Right after-wards, one of them stuck his head back through the half open door and said in a low voice: "Keep your chin up!" I looked at him with big eyes. Then he added: "Those damned pigs – what they are doing to people – in Poland – I am angry about that, too. Chin up, it will not be forever [...]. They cannot go through another winter in Russia – chin up, things will change [...]." (II,352)

> *24 August 1944*: Yesterday afternoon at the train crossing in front of our house, a wild looking worker came right up close to me and said loudly: "Keep your chin up! Those bastards will soon be done with!" – Stühler had a similar thing happen to him. But on the other hand, we have been seeing this type of event every few days for years, and we have also been experiencing the exact opposite every few days for the same number of years. Nothing can be concluded from that, and nothing from the war situation either, as desperate it may be in both East and West for Germany. (II,567) (see Klemperer 1987 [1947], 60)

Certainly, Klemperer is right in saying that not much can be concluded from all these positive and negative statements. They did take place, and if a work-man came back under threat of danger to encourage Dr. Klemperer in sim-ple folk language by using the proverbial expression "to keep one's chin up" three times, and if by doing so he managed to express a little bit of solidari-ty, we are most impressed with this sign of human decency. And even the scholar Klemperer resorts to the expression "to keep one's chin up" to con-tinue his own literary and language studies of the Third Reich with his head held high: "To study as if tomorrow were a sure thing! That is the only way to keep my chin up" (II,214).

"To escape with one's [naked] life" (II,235)

For twelve years, the life of Victor Klemperer oscillates between deep pes-simism and small hope, and the fear of a violent death accompanies his every step. On 14 January 1943, we read generally and proverbially: "I am sub-ject to the Gestapo, they are not good to eat cherries with [in English better: they are best not to tangle with]" (II,312), and this wisdom expressed with a certain amount of black humor is followed half a page later by the very realistic statement about the "permanent dreadful fear of Auschwitz" (II,312). The main focus of the *Diaries 1933-1945* is necessarily on life and survival, which of course is reflected in the proverbial expressions dealing with "life." The following chronologically arranged references contain the phrases "to pay with one's life," "to escape with one's [naked] life," "to be a

matter of life and death," and "to cost one's life," which, even without context, underscore the precarious situation of Victor and Eva Klemperer:

> *3 April 1933*: I have the impression of a swiftly approaching catastrophe. [...]
> There will be an explosion – but we may pay for it with our lives, we Jews.
> [...] I no longer believe in national psychologies. Everything I considered un-
> German, brutality, injustice, hypocrisy, mass hysteria to the point of intoxi-
> cation, all of it flourishes here.[7] (I,18; I, 11)
>
> *18 May 1942*: The general mood at Seliksohns was depressed. He keeps
> claiming that we will not escape with our [naked] lives. (II,87)
>
> *7 September 1942*: It is a matter of life and death, I wouldn't challenge these
> people [the Gestapo]. (II,235)
>
> *19 July 1943*: When I returned from the cemetery on Sunday afternoon,
> there was an older gentleman on the sidewalk at Lothringer Strasse – white
> goatee, around seventy, a retired higher official – who crossed over to meet
> me. He gave me his hand and said, with a certain formality: "I saw your star
> and I salute you; I do not approve of the ostracizing of your race, and many
> others agree with me." I: "Very kind – but you should not talk to me, it could
> cost my life and get you in prison." – Yes, but he had wanted and needed to
> say that to me. (II,406)

Thus, their life is always at the proverbial stake and it is astonishing how
Klemperer, with the help of his wife, can muster the ever so weak optimism
to somehow survive all his troubles. In this process, he seems to move from
one unlikely ray of hope to the next, and proverbs and proverbial expressions, in their popular simplicity, help him mentally to deal with his situation and to give him the courage to go on. An interesting example can be
found in the following diary entry of 24 November 1936:

> I now have the impression that war is unavoidable; every day brings it closer
> [...]. We have learned patience and were quite without hope and are still only
> halfway hopeful, but the pitcher has truly been going to the well for a very
> long time now, and every day with a greater (perhaps desperate?) foolhardi-
> ness. (I,322; I, 200)

Here, the medieval proverb "The pitcher goes to the well until it breaks"
serves to give metaphorical expression to the hope that the expected war will
also mean an end of Hitler's power and his policy of antisemitic persecution.
Such frail rays of hope quickly are followed by fatalistic thoughts, such as on
14 October 1940, where the expression "nobody gives a hoot" characterizes
the futility of his work:

> Day and night (literally) I am dogged by thoughts of death and futility [...].
> Only the end [of the war and Hitler] will show how I spent the last part of
> my life, whether I shall be considered irresponsibly indolent and unprinci-

pled or tenacious and self-assured or whether nobody will give a hoot, myself included. This last statement is 99 percent likely. (I,557; I, 359)

Besides its convincing honesty, this statement is of interest in the way Klemperer uses the word "literally" to indicate that there is nothing figurative about an expression such as "day and night," as the fear for his life is at every moment overwhelmingly real.

This honest observation of his own emotions and thoughts is also apparent in Klemperer's report about the week from 23 June to 1 July 1941, which he spent in "cell 89" in prison. Who would have thought that the intellectual Professor Victor Klemperer would have used three proverbs in that situation to do a self-critical appraisal of himself. He accuses himself primarily of having been driven by "hubris" (I,635; I, 411) and having brought danger not only upon himself but also his wife Eva. What follows are excerpts of his self-accusing thoughts written in prison expecting a certain death:

> But if one settles accounts with oneself, forgiveness is self-deception. Can the intention, to do better in the future, help me? First of all, it is very questionable whether I still have a future (at 60 and in the clutches of the 3. Reich), second doing better never wipes out what one has done badly before, and third, – I have always told myself that the opposite of every proverb is also true (the first step is always easiest, you can teach an old dog new tricks [...]), but one, about the road to hell being paved with good intentions is absolutely to the point. (I,635-636; I, 411)

Even though the term "anti-proverb" was unknown to Klemperer, he forms two such phrases in this short paragraph. Of even larger importance is of course the fact that Klemperer fully accepts the proverb "The road to hell is paved with good intentions" in regard to his own life. The proverbial lines actually represent an unexpected self-accusation in a very popular style. In addition, this triple proverbial statement shows how Klemperer reduced his entire fate and life to popular wisdom rather than attempting to convey abstract explanations and justifications.

Klemperer finally did "escape with his life." In the truest sense of the word, he was "granted" what he had wished on 9 October 1942: "Perhaps I will be able to survive and bear witness" (II,255). Like a Biblical prophet, Victor Klemperer proverbially "bore witness" in his *Diaries 1933-1945*, not a false, but an honest and exact witness to his life and survival during the Third Reich. Thus, his diaries represent the autobiography of one of the many Jewish victims, but they also are a document of their times of the highest value for linguistic and cultural history. Obviously, Klemperer intentionally used popular proverbs and proverbial expressions to add power to his observations and statements. The proverbial language he shows us is a two-edged sword, as it serves both perpetrators and victims of the Third Reich alike. In spite of that, or maybe because of that, the proverbial wealth of the *Diaries 1933-1945* is a sign of their linguistic and factual authenticity. As early as 15 February 1934, Victor Klemperer wrote with proverbial expressiveness "The truth speaks for itself" (I,87), and this is also expressed by the Biblical proverbial statement "I will bear witness to the last," written down by Klemperer on 11 June 1942, and ultimately chosen by the editors for the title of his *Diaries 1933-1945*. They are indeed particularly valuable documents of the proverbial *vox populi*, or better *voces populi*, of an infamous period in German history.

Notes

[1]This essay in the English language is based on my German book "*In lingua veritas*": *Sprichwörtliche Rhetorik in Victor Klemperers "Tagebüchern 1933-1945*" (Wien: Edition Praesens, 2000).

[2]All volume and page numbers refer to Victor Klemperer, *Ich will Zeugnis ablegen bis zum letzten. Tagebücher 1933-1945*, ed. Walter Nowojski, 2 vols. (Berlin: Aufbau-Verlag, 1995). Where the English translation was available in print, the second set of volume and page numbers refers to the corresponding English translation. The instances labeled with a Roman number III are cited from Victor Klemperer, *Und so ist alles schwankend. Tagebücher Juni bis Dezember 1945*, eds. Günter Jäckel and Hadwig Klemperer (Berlin: Aufbau Taschenbuch Verlag, 1995). At the time of writing this essay, only the first volume of the diaries was available in English translation by Martin Chalmers: *I Will Bear Witness: A Diary of the Nazi Years (1933-1941)* (New York: Random House, 1998).

[3]Of course, Klemperer continued his cultural linguistic research after the war. It was as early as 25 June 1945, two months after the end of the war that he entered the following remark in his diary: "It is about time I started paying attention to the language of the FOURTH REICH. It does not seem to differ much from that of the THIRD, as different as Saxonian spoken in Dresden and Leipzig" (III,31). Almost two months later, we find the term L[ingua] Q[uartii] I[mperii] on 16 August: "I don't see any difference between LTI and LQI" (III,94). And on 12 October: "Every day I observe the continuation of LTI in LQI" (III,157), and three days later proverbially: "LQI just takes over LTI, bones and all" (III,159), up to 26 October, where we find the equation "LTI=LQI" (III,168). See particularly Ehlich 1998, 287-289; Henke 1998, 17; Jäckel 1998, 55; and Watt 1998, 367-369.

[4]The German language edition of the book with many helpful English annotations should also be mentioned (see Watt 1997).

[5]On this joke on the expression "to keep one's word to someone" see also the bitter statement from 11 August 1935: "Pflugk told me: They say they haven't kept their word to anyone, except the Jews!" (I,213) (see Dundes and Hauschild 1983).

[6]In his pamphlet *Zur gegenwärtigen Sprachsituation in Deutschland*, Klemperer makes a similar statement: "In the language of a nation, its entire heritage is contained, it belongs to all as a common heritage and it informs all" (Klemperer 1953, 6).

[7]See also Klemperer's proverbial statement of 21 July 1935: "My principles about Germans and other nationalities have become as shaky as an old man's teeth" (I,211).

Literature Cited

Bauer, Gerhard. 1988. *Sprache und Sprachlosigkeit im "Dritten Reich"*. Köln: Bund-Verlag.

Berning, Cornelia. 1964. *Vom Abstammungsnachweis zum Zuchtwort: Vokabular des Nationalsozialismus*. Berlin: Walter de Gruyter.

Boas, G. 1969. *Vox Populi: Essays in the History of an Idea*. Baltimore, Maryland: Johns Hopkins University Press.

Bork, Siegfried. 1970. *Mißbrauch der Sprache: Tendenzen nationalsozialistischer Sprachregelung*. München: Francke.

Brückner, Wolfgang. 1998. *"Arbeit macht frei": Herkunft und Hintergrund der KZ-Devise*. Opladen: Leske & Budrich.

Christmann, Hans Helmut. 1993. Victor Klemperer und sein "Curriculum vitae." In *Literarhistorische Begegnungen. Festschrift Bernhard König*, eds. Andreas Kablitz and Ulrich Schulz-Buschhaus, pp. 17-28. Tübingen: Gunter Narr.

Dirschauer, Johannes. 1998. Zur Faszination Victor Klemperers. In *Leben in zwei Diktaturen: Victor Klemperers Leben in der NS-Zeit und in der DDR*, eds. Christoph Wielepp and Hans-Peter Lühr, pp. 70-76. Dresden: Friedrich-Ebert-Stiftung.

Doerr, Karin. 2000. "To Each His Own" (Jedem das Seine): The (Mis)Use of German Proverbs in Concentration Camps and Beyond. *Proverbium* 17:71-90.

Domarus, Max ed. 1962. *Hitler. Reden und Proklamationen 1932 bis 1945*. 2 vols. Neustadt a.d. Aisch: Schmidt.

Dundes, Alan, and Thomas Hauschild. 1983. Auschwitz Jokes. *Western Folklore* 42:249-260.

Ehlich, Konrad. 1998. ... "LTI, LQI" ... – Von der Unschuld der Sprache und der Schuld der Sprechenden. In *Das 20. Jahrhundert: Sprachgeschichte – Zeitgeschichte*, eds. Heidrun Kämper and Hartmut Schmidt, pp. 275-303. Berlin: Walter de Gruyter.

Elon, Amos. 1996. The Jew [Victor Klemperer] Who Fought to Stay German. *The New York Times Magazine* (March 24), 52-55.

Fries, Fritz Rudolf. 1996. *Lesarten zu Klemperer*. Berlin: Aufbau-Verlag.

Goldhagen, Daniel J. 1996. *Hitler's Willing Executioners: Ordinary Germans and the Holocaust*. New York: Alfred A. Knopf.

Guthke, Karl S. 1999. Lessing and the Jews. In *Shifting Paradigms in German-Jewish Relations (1750-2000). Harry H. Kahn Memorial Lectures (1995-1999)*, eds. Wolfgang Mieder and Hazel Kahn Keimowitz, pp. 35-58. Burlington, Vermont: Center for Holocaust Studies at the University of Vermont.

Heer, Hannes. 1997. *Vox populi*: Zur Mentalität der Volksgemeinschaft. In *Im Herzen der Finsternis: Victor Klemperer als Chronist der NS-Zeit*, ed. H. Heer, pp. 122-143. Berlin: Aufbau-Verlag.

Heil, Johannes, and Rainer Erb eds. 1998. *Geschichtswissenschaft und Öffentlichkeit: Der Streit um Daniel J. Goldhagen*. Frankfurt am Main: Fischer Taschenbuch Verlag.

Henke, Klaus Dietmar. 1998. Mutmaßungen über Victor Klemperers Leben in zwei deutschen Diktaturen. In *Leben in zwei Diktaturen: Victor Klemperers Leben in der NS-Zeit und in der DDR*, eds. Christoph Wielepp and Hans-Peter Lühr, pp. 15-19. Dresden: Friedrich-Ebert-Stiftung.

Hiemer, Ernst, 1942. *Der Jude im Sprichwort*. Nürnberg: Der Stürmer.

Hilberg, Raul. 1961. *The Destruction of the European Jews*. Chicago: Quadrangle Books.

Hilberg, Raul. 1992. *Perpetrators, Bystanders, Victims: The Jewish Catastrophe 1933-1945*. New York: HarperCollins.

Hilberg, Raul. 1997. The Goldhagen Phenomenon. *Critical Inquiry* 23:721-728.

Jäckel, Günter. 1998. "Zwiespältiger denn je": Dresden 1945 in Victor Klemperers Tagebuch. In *Leben in zwei Diktaturen: Victor Klemperers Leben in der NS-Zeit und in der DDR*, eds. Christoph Wielepp and Hans-Peter Lühr, pp. 52-60. Dresden: Friedrich-Ebert-Stiftung.

Jäger, Margret and Siegfried. 1999. Victor Klemperers Sprach- und Kulturkritik. In M. and S. Jäger, *Gefährliche Erbschaften: Die schleichende Restauration rechten Denkens*, pp. 13-62. Berlin: Aufbau Taschenbuch Verlag.

Kämper, Heidrun. 1996. Zeitgeschichte – Sprachgeschichte: Gedanken bei der Lektüre des Tagebuchs eines Philologen. Über die Ausgaben von Victor Klemperers Tagebuch 1933-1945. *Zeitschrift für Germanistische Linguistik* 24:328-341.

Klemperer, Victor. 1953. *Zur gegenwärtigen Sprachsituation in Deutschland*. Berlin: Aufbau-Verlag.

Klemperer, Victor. 1962. Einprägen! In *Victor Klemperer zum Gedenken von seinen Freunden und ihm selbst*, ed. F. Zschech, pp. 162-165. Rudolstadt: Greifenverlag.

Klemperer, Victor. 1987 [1947]. *LTI. Notizbuch eines Philologen*. Köln: Röderberg.

Klemperer, Victor. 1989. *Curriculum vitae. Erinnerungen 1881-1918*, ed. Walter Nowojski. 2 vols. Berlin: Rütten & Loening (paperback edition Berlin: Aufbau Taschenbuch Verlag, 1996).

Klemperer, Victor. 1995a. *Ich will Zeugnis ablegen bis zum letzten. Tagebücher 1933-1945*, ed. Walter Nowojski. 2 vols. Berlin: Aufbau-Verlag.

Klemperer, Victor. 1995b. *Und so ist alles schwankend. Tagebücher Juni bis Dezember 1945*, eds. Günter Jäckel and Hadwig Klemperer. Berlin: Aufbau Taschenbuch Verlag.

Klemperer, Victor. 1996. *Leben sammeln, nicht fragen wozu und warum. Tagebücher 1918-1932*, ed. Walter Nowojski. 2 vols. Berlin: Aufbau-Verlag.

Klemperer, Victor. 1998. *I Will Bear Witness: A Diary of the Nazi Years (1933-1945)*, trans. Martin Chalmers. 2 vols. New York: Random House.

Klemperer, Victor. 1999. *So sitze ich denn zwischen allen Stühlen. Tagebücher 1945-1959*, ed. Walter Nowojski. 2 vols. Berlin: Aufbau-Verlag.

Lang, Ewald. 1986. Victor Klemperers LTI. *Osnabrücker Beiträge zur Sprachtheorie* 33:69-79.

Maas, Utz. 1984. *Als der Geist der Gemeinschaft eine Sprache fand: Sprache im Nationalsozialismus. Versuch einer historischen Argumentationsanalyse.* Opladen: Westdeutscher Verlag.

Mieder, Wolfgang. 1983. Sprichwörter unterm Hakenkreuz. In W. Mieder, *Deutsche Sprichwörter in Literatur, Politik, Presse und Werbung*, pp. 181-210. Hamburg: Helmut Buske.

Mieder, Wolfgang. 1993. Proverbs in Nazi Germany: The Promulgation of Anti-Semitism and Stereotypes Through Folklore. In W. Mieder, *Proverbs Are Never Out of Season: Popular Wisdom in the Modern Age*, pp. 225-255. New York: Oxford University Press.

Mieder, Wolfgang. 1996. Language and Folklore of the Holocaust. In *The Holocaust: Introductory Essays*, eds. David Scrase and W. Mieder, pp. 93-106. Burlington, Vermont: The Center for Holocaust Studies at the University of Vermont.

Mieder, Wolfgang. 1997a. "Make Hell While the Sun Shines": Proverbial Rhetoric in Winston Churchill's *The Second World War*. In W. Mieder, *The Politics of Proverbs: From Traditional Wisdom to Proverbial Stereotypes*, pp. 39-66. Madison, Wisconsin: The University of Wisconsin Press.

Mieder, Wolfgang. 1997b. *"Morgenstunde hat Gold im Munde": Studien und Belege zum populärsten deutschsprachigen Sprichwort.* Wien: Edition Praesens.

Mieder, Wolfgang ed. 1998. *Verdrehte Weisheiten: Antisprichwörter aus Literatur und Medien.* Wiesbaden: Quelle & Meyer.

Mieder, Wolfgang. 2000. *"In lingua veritas": Sprichwörtliche Rhetorik in Victor Klemperers "Tagebüchern 1933-1945".* Wien: Edition Praesens.

Mieder, Wolfgang, and George B. Bryan eds. 1995. *The Proverbial Winston S. Churchill: An Index to Proverbs in the Works of Sir Winston Churchill.* Westport, Connecticut: Greenwood Press.

Militz, Hans-Manfred. 1998. "Wejen Ausdrücken": Redewendungen im *LTI* von Victor Klemperer. *Proverbium* 15:201-219.

Przyrembel, Alexandra. 1998. Die Tagebücher Victor Klemperers und ihre Wirkung in der deutschen Öffentlichkeit. In *Geschichtswissenschaft und Öffentlichkeit. Der Streit um Daniel J. Goldhagen*, eds. Johannes Heil and Rainer Erb, pp. 312-327. Frankfurt am Main: Fischer Taschenbuch Verlag.

Reemtsma, Jan Philipp. 1997. "Buchenwald wird von andern geschildert werden; ich will mich an meine Erlebnisse halten": Stenogramme aus der Vorhölle. In *Im Herzen der Finsternis: Victor Klemperer als Chronist der NS-Zeit*, ed. Hannes Heer, pp. 170-193. Berlin: Aufbau-Verlag.

Reiss, Hans. 1998. Victor Klemperer (1881-1960): Reflections on His "Third Reich" Diaries. *German Life and Letters* 51:65-92.

Schober, Rita. 1988. Sprache – Kultur – Humanismus: Victor Klemperer zum Gedenken. In R. Schober, *Vom Sinn und Unsinn der Literaturwissenschaft*, pp. 181-204. Halle: Mitteldeutscher Verlag.

Schoeps, Julius H. ed. 1996. *Ein Volk von Mördern? Die Dokumentation zur Goldhagen-Kontroverse um die Rolle der Deutschen im Holocaust*. Hamburg: Hoffmann und Campe.

Schwab, Julius. 1937. *Rassenpflege im Sprichwort. Eine volkstümliche Sammlung*. Leipzig: Alwin Fröhlich.

Seidel, Eugen, and Ingeborg Seidel-Slotty. 1961. *Sprachwandel im Dritten Reich*. Halle: Verlag Sprache und Literatur.

Techtmeier, Bärbel. 1987. Bedeutung zwischen Wort und Tat: Die Sprache des Faschismus im Spiegel von Victor Klemperers "LTI." In *Bedeutungen und Ideen in Sprachen und Texten*, eds. Werner Neumann and B. Techtmeier, pp. 315-324. Berlin: Akademie-Verlag.

Turner, Henry Ashby. 1999. Victor Klemperer's Holocaust. *German Studies Review* 22:385-395.

Ulrich, Volker. 1999. Der Chronist des Jahrhunderts. Mit Victor Klemperers Aufzeichnungen der Jahre 1945-1959 wird nun die Edition seiner Tagebücher abgeschlossen. *Die Zeit*, no. 13 (March 25), 19-20.

Walser, Martin. 1996a. *Das Prinzip Genauigkeit. Laudatio auf Victor Klemperer*. Frankfurt am Main: Suhrkamp.

Walser, Martin. 1996b. *Literatur als Weltverständnis. Drei Versuche*. Eggingen: Edition Isele.

Wander, Karl Friedrich Wilhelm Wander. 1867-1880. *Deutsches Sprichwörter-Lexikon*. 5 vols. Leipzig: F.A. Brockhaus.

Watt, Roderick H. ed. 1997. *An Annotated Edition of Victor Klemperer's "LTI": Notizbuch eines Philologen*. Lewiston, New York: Edwin Mellen Press.

Watt, Roderick H. 1998. Victor Klemperer's "Sprache des Vierten Reiches": LTI=LTQ? *German Life and Letters* 51:360-371.

Würzner, M.H. 1997. Das Tagebuch als "Oral History." *Amsterdamer Beiträge zur älteren Germanistik* 48:169-173.

Zionism, Antisemitism, and the Origins of the Final Solution

Francis R. Nicosia

The inspiration for this essay is rooted in recent debates over the nature of German Antisemitism and the ways in which it shaped attitudes of ordinary and not so ordinary Germans, and the policies of their government, during the Third Reich. Was there some special link between German Antisemitism and the decision of the Nazi state to exterminate the Jews of Europe? It also stems from the older debates between "intentionalists" and "functionalists," going back to the mid-1980s, over the origins of the decision by Hitler's regime to exterminate the Jews of Europe. Was the Final Solution part of a plan that pre-dated its actual implementation? The two questions are, of course, related. The nature of a pathological hatred aimed at a particular group must ultimately condition the manner in which that hatred becomes action or policy.

Over the years, historians and others have examined the manner in which Nazi perpetrators have translated Antisemitic ideology into a variety of policies during the Third Reich. These perpetrators ranged from Hitler to the bureaucrats in the Nazi party and state, from the professions to the leaders of business and industry, and finally to ordinary Germans. They have endeavored to understand from those actions who the perpetrators were and what motivated them. The relationship between concrete, identifiable practice, and the complex, contradictory, and often elusive ideology behind it, between the various anti-Jewish policies and actions of the Nazi state and the Antisemitism behind those policies, has been at the center of scholarly debate over the past two decades. To what extent were the perpetrators motivated by Antisemitic ideas or attitudes, or by other factors? And if they were motivated by a hatred of the Jews, what was the nature of that hatred? Was genocide its natural, logical, or, in the end, inevitable outcome?

The relationship between Antisemitism and Zionism in Germany, from the latter decades of the nineteenth century to the early years of the Second World War, is instructive in this regard. During that period of more than half a century, Zionism offered a useful and generally acceptable vehicle for German Antisemites to translate their antipathy toward the Jews, whatever its nature, into specific action or policies. Most of the important Antisemitic writers, political philosophers, and others came to view Zionism as an attractive and practical solution to the Jewish question because, unlike the dominant liberal-assimilationist Jewish community in Germany and in the west in general, Zionist ideology and the fledgling world Zionist movement essentially accepted some of the Antisemites' own basic assumptions. Zionists accepted the argument that the Jews were a distinct nation, and not merely a religious community. They agreed that the Jews were aliens, and concluded that the Jews should emigrate from Germany and from other countries in the Diaspora to their own state in Palestine. Therefore Theodor Herzl and other early Zionists believed that Zionism would neutralize a large part of their problem, namely Antisemitism, while many Antisemites came to the conclusion that Zionism might provide a useful mechanism for the elimination of their problem, namely the Jews. The question arises, therefore, whether the attitudes and policies of German Antisemites toward Zionism and the Zionist movement, from Bismarck's time through the Nazi period, tell us anything about the nature of German Antisemitism before 1945. More specifically, do the actual policies that the Nazi regime pursued toward Zionism and the Zionist movement in Germany between 1933 and 1940 tell us anything about the decision making process in Nazi Jewish policy that ultimately led to the Final Solution in 1941?

Support for Zionism in the non-Jewish world has been motivated through the years by a variety of factors. These have included the imperial interests of the Great Powers in the Middle East, a sense of idealism, justice, sympathy and guilt on the part of liberals, and, of course, Antisemitism. Often it has been a combination of these factors. During the First World War, British belief in a monolithic international Jewry, a common myth among gentiles throughout history, provided part of the rationale for using Zionism to promote Allied interests in the Middle East, central and Eastern Europe (Vital 1987, 286-293, 297-302). During the era of Jewish emancipation in Germany in the nineteenth century, even liberal gentiles often found Judaism and Jewish culture objectionable and degenerate. They were willing to grant their Jewish fellow-citizens civil equality only if the latter ceased to be Jews (Rose 1990). One important study of the origins of modern Antisemitism sees it not as a reaction to, but as a part of, the Enlightenment and French Revolution (Hertzberg 1990). For those who could not accept Jewish assimilation, however, Zionism also offered an attractive solution to the Jewish Question in Europe, by offering possibilities for Jewish redemption through emigration to Palestine, a return to agriculture and to the land (Doron 1983). In this regard, Zionists and even some Antisemites were inclined to regard Zionism as the path to Jewish redemption.

It appears that some Antisemitic thinkers of the nineteenth century wavered between notions of an inherent and unchanging inferiority and evil of all Jews, and the possibility of something positive, indeed redemptive, emerging in Jewish life as a result of emigration and settlement in Palestine. Most of them, however, the direct precursors of the Nazis at the turn of the century, usually rejected the possibility of Jewish redemption, and simply demanded the removal of the Jews from Germany as a practical matter. In any case, the Antisemitism of all of them was, to use more accurately Daniel Goldhagen's term, usually "eliminationist" in its multiple manifestations, in most places, and at most times. It was an ideology that demanded the elimination of Jewish life from German society. That demand took different forms, at different times, for different people. It could mean physically removing Jews through emigration, deportation, or mass murder, or by some other means, such as assimilation. "Eliminationist Antisemitism," therefore, was not necessarily synonymous with extermination, nor was it exclusively German or even National Socialist.

Important German philosophers, not always unfavorably disposed toward the Jews, saw merit in the idea of Jewish emigration from Germany to Palestine. Johann Gottfried Herder concluded that Jewish emigration to Palestine was an appropriate option (Rose 1990, 101-105). Friedrich Schiller, an advocate of equal rights for Jews in Germany, nevertheless advanced the idea of setting up a Jewish state in Palestine, while Immanuel Kant, arguing that Judaism was an immoral and obsolete religion, and that the Jews were an alien nation, might have looked favorably on the idea of Jewish emigration to Palestine or some other destination (Rose 1990, 102). The liberal Christian theologian, Heinrich Eberhard Paulus, concluded that the Jews were a distinct people and belonged in the land for which they longed, Palestine (Katz 1980, 156). In France, Utopian Socialists such as Charles Fourier and Pierre-Joseph Proudhon rejected the continued presence of the Jews in Europe, and favored either assimilation or a return to Palestine (Rubinstein and Roth 1987, 71).

Among Jew-haters in the nineteenth century, specific reference to Palestine as a destination to which Jews ought to emigrate or be expelled was usually a part of their prescription for solving the Jewish question. Johann

Gottlieb Fichte warned against the evils of Jewish emancipation, and suggested the return of the Jews to Palestine (Graetz III n.d., 535-536; Nicosia 1992, 121; Treitschke 1975, 104-107; Poliakov 1971, 363). Wilhelm Marr often used Palestine as a point of reference in his Antisemitic writings. In his most famous work, *Der Sieg des Judenthums über das Germanenthum*, published in 1879, Marr described the German *Reich* as the "New Palestine" and the new "Promised Land," an example of the "alien conquest and domination" of Germany by the Jews. He lamented the fact that the Jews did not possess a fatherland of their own and that Palestine had become more and more alien to them as memories of it faded over the centuries (Marr 1879, 5-14). But he warned that the idea of return to Palestine was really a cover for a continued Jewish presence and domination in Germany, that the Jews were incapable of building a model state there, and that this was in any case not their intention (Zimmermann 1986, 87-88). Thus, Marr saw nothing inherently good or positive in the Zionist idea, beyond its practical capacity for eliminating Jewish life in Germany, thereby reversing the Jewish "victory" that he described in his well-known book.

Eugen Dühring also asserted that the Jews were incapable of anything original or positive, that they were intent only on exploitation and world domination (Dühring 1892, 43-44, 57-58, 106-107; Adler 1960, 99; Mosse 1978, 164-166). He advocated the "herding" of the Jewish people together in some form of Jewish state outside of Europe, possibly Palestine. But he warned that Zionism was misleading and dangerous because the Jews neither could nor would build a viable state, even if they were all assembled in their own land. Alluding to the alleged Jewish conspiracy, he argued that the fulfillment of Zionist aspirations would only enhance Jewish power throughout the world. Thus, for Duhring too, Palestine might serve as a useful instrument for eliminating the Jews from Germany. But because Zionism was another manifestation of Jewish evil, he ultimately raised the possibility of eliminating the Jews by other means, namely extermination. The evolution of Marr's and Dühring's application of theory to practice, of eliminationist Jew-hatred to concrete policy, provides a precedent for National Socialism. While Zionism might be used to eliminate the Jews in Germany, it was neither a good in itself, nor was it likely to be the ultimate solution to the Jewish "problem."

In his *Das Gesetz des Nomadenthums und die heutige Judenherrschaft*, published in 1887, Adolf Wahrmund, the Viennese orientalist, attributed the *Fähigkeit zur Staatenbildung* (ability to build states) to the rooted, Aryan peasant nations such as the Germans, and denied it to the Jews whom he described as rootless, wandering, aliens (Wahrmund 1887, 3, 106). Wahrmund agreed with Dühring and others that the Jews were not only incapable of building their own state, but that any attempt to do so would only result in the creation of an independent power base for the international Jewish conspiracy. Nevertheless, he favored their deportation to Palestine where, in apparent contradiction to his theories about nomads, their inability to build viable states, and the Jewish conspiracy, he implied that their resettlement might end their spirit of Nomadism and generate a more "humane and idealistic Jewry". Paul de Lagarde, in *Juden und Indogermanen. Eine Studie nach dem Leben* (1887), subscribed to all of the myths about the Jews and considered Zionism a useful instrument to achieve the "elimination" of Jewish life in Germany (Lagarde 1887, 303, 349-350).

The anti-Prussian political theorist Constantin Franz was favorably disposed to Jewish emigration to Palestine if the Jews continued to reject Christianity and, in effect, did not cease to be Jews (Friedman 1977, 6). Heinrich Class, the leader of the Pan German League, recognized the Zionists as Jews who understood the natural laws that precluded Jewish assimilation; he favored sending them to Palestine (Frymann 1913, 78). Hermann Ahlwardt, politician and editor of the Berlin organ *Der Bundschuh*, demanded the prompt removal of the Jews and Jewish influence, and favored their return to Palestine (Niewyk 1990, 361-362). Heinrich Pudor saw Zionism as the only solution to the Jewish problem, notwithstanding Jewish inferiority and treachery (Nicosia 1992, 127-128). Hans Leuss, a Reichstag delegate and Antisemite, felt that a state of their own, perhaps in South Africa, might improve the Jews and eliminate undesirable Jewish qualities (Niewyk 1990, 365-366). Ludwig Woltmann's political anthropology rejected the view of some that the Jews might be eliminated through assimilation, condemned inter-marriage, and supported Zionism and Jewish emigration as the most practical way of eliminating Jewish life in Germany (Woltmann 1903, 288-89, 308-309).

Theodor Fritsch and Houston Stewart Chamberlain were probably the intellectual links between nineteenth century Antisemitic thought and the Nazis. They stressed that Zionism was not indicative of anything good in Jewish life. They warned that the Jews were incapable of building a state, and that Zionism was merely a cover for the establishment of a Jewish power base in Palestine to promote the world Jewish conspiracy. Nevertheless, both favored Jewish emigration to Palestine (Frey 1893, 6, 19-20, 22-24; Chamberlain 1938, 386-388).

The nineteenth century Antisemitic approach to Zionism became an important part of Nazi ideology and policy toward the Jews from the early years of the movement to the onset of the Final Solution in 1941. At a minimum, it was part of a larger effort to eliminate Jewish life in Germany through the reversal of Jewish emancipation and assimilation, and the promotion of Jewish emigration. Alfred Rosenberg was primarily responsible for incorporating this approach to Zionism into an emerging Nazi policy toward the Jews during the early years of the movement (Rosenberg 1922). He identified Zionism and Bolshevism as the twin agents of a Jewish world conspiracy. Arguing that the Zionists had neither the intention nor the capability to build a state, he concluded that they would make Palestine a power base, a "Jewish Vatican" or "Jewish Comintern," from which their conspiracy would be directed. Nevertheless, he did recognize the utility of encouraging Zionism in Germany as a means of neutralizing the assimilationist culture of German Jewry, and eliminating the Jews through emigration. This approach was not lost on Hitler during the early years of the movement. He too saw the Zionist enterprise in Palestine as part of the Jewish conspiracy and the Jews as incapable of building states, but concluded that Zionism might prove useful in removing Jews from Germany (Hitler 1941, 447-448; Phelps 1968, 400-420; Phelps 1963, 305).

From 1933 through the first year and a half of the Second World War, the Nazi state consistently promoted Jewish emigration from Germany as rapidly as possible, preferably to destinations outside of Europe. In particular, the regime encouraged the Zionist movement in Germany and its efforts to facilitate Jewish emigration from Germany to Palestine. This was done at the expense of the activities of the far larger liberal-assimilationist Jewish organizations that had always fought for Jewish rights and equality as German citizens. Although the regime vigorously opposed the creation of an independent Jewish state, the logical and ultimate outcome of Zionist efforts to promote mass Jewish emigration to Palestine from Germany and the rest of Europe, it sought to remove Jews from Greater Germany by way of an existing Zionist movement and organization in Palestine and around the world. It was a movement and organization fueled by an ideology that rejected Jewish life in the Diaspora, assimilation among the nations of Europe, and followed the imperative of emigration to Palestine. In other words, there existed a level of common interest between the German Zionist movement, the World Zionist movement, and Hitler's National Socialist state. Moreover, as a destination, Palestine was preferable to other European countries because of Hitler's ultimate plans for conquest in Europe. The Nazi approach to Zionism was not based on a positive view of Zionism, or of the Zionist movement, nor did it exempt the Zionists from the brutalities of Nazi persecution after 1933 (Nicosia 1991, 243-265). It did, however, reflect the manner in which German Antisemitism at that particular time endeavored to eliminate Jewish life in Germany through legislation and emigration.

The policy toward Zionism annunciated by Rosenberg and Hitler in the early 1920s was incorporated into the Jewish policy of the regime in 1933. Government ministries were primarily responsible for the formulation and execution of Nazi Jewish policy before the end of 1938. The Ministry of Economics, the *Reichsbank*, the Ministry of the Interior, and the Foreign Ministry all supported the Haavara agreement which was concluded between Hitler's government and the Zionist movement in August 1933. Haavara enabled the Nazi regime to promote Jewish emigration to Palestine. At the same time, it promoted German exports, and neutralized the anti-German economic boycott that developed in response to persecution of Jews in Germany during the 1930s (Feilchenfeld 1972, 15-85; PA: 28 August 1933). Jews willing to go to Palestine were allowed to salvage a small portion of their assets in the form of German exports to Palestine. These goods were sold on the Palestine market, and part of the income from these exports was given to immigrants upon their arrival in Palestine for the purpose of beginning a new life. For the Zionists, more than 50,000 German Jews, or almost 10% of the Jewish population in Germany at the time of Hitler's appointment as Chancellor, and more than RM100 million were moved to Palestine between November 1933 and December 1939, and thereby saved.

In the Fall of 1933, as if to reiterate the importance the German government attached to the Haavara agreement, *Referat-Deutschland*, the department responsible for Jewish affairs in the German Foreign Ministry, declared: "The most important destination for emigrants is and remains Palestine" (PA: September 1933). In February 1934, the German Foreign Office argued that the support of Zionism in Germany was justified because of its rejection of assimilation and its promotion of Jewish emigration, and that: "Zionism comes closest to meeting the practical goals of Germany's Jewish policy. The National Socialist government henceforth will promote as a matter of practice the emigration of German Jews" (PA: no date). The German Consul-General in Jerusalem, Walter Döhle, described the role of Zionism and Palestine in German policy in 1937 in the following way: "In all of our efforts, the idea of promoting Jewish emigration from Germany and settling these emigrating Jews in Palestine was primary" (PA: 22 March 1937). Until the summer of 1937, there existed a general consensus among government and party agencies responsible for Jewish policy that Zionism and Jewish emigration to Palestine was a key to achieving the goal of a Germany that was *judenrein*, a Germany "cleansed" of Jews.

Zionist and other Jewish organizations in Germany were regulated and controlled by the police apparatus, the Gestapo and, beginning in the middle of 1934, the *Sicherheitsdienst* (Security Service, or SD), in Himmler's SS. The role of the police in the formulation of Nazi Jewish policy until 1938 was essentially an advisory one to the Ministry of the Interior, which was the responsible authority for the police in Germany. Supervision of Jewish organizations, including the posting of observers at Jewish functions, events, etc., followed by detailed reports on the nature and course of those events to Gestapo headquarters, constituted one of the major responsibilities of local Gestapo officials and offices. Jewish organizations were also required to provide a constant stream of information, forms, etc. to the Gestapo reporting on every aspect or detail of their operations and activities. This information provided the basis for the kind of advice that Himmler, as chief of the Gestapo, would give to the Interior Minister on the handling of the Jewish question.

Both the Gestapo and the SD remained consistent throughout the 1930s in the view that Jewish emigration was the fundamental, primary goal of Nazi Jewish policy, and the only feasible solution to the Jewish question in Germany. They judged every initiative, report, policy, action, etc. in terms of whether or not it facilitated the removal of Jews from Germany. As such, this approach dovetailed perfectly with the policies described above of the government agencies such as the Interior and Economic ministries, the Reichsbank, the Foreign Office, etc., agencies that formulated a Jewish policy predicated first and foremost on the promotion of Jewish emigration. The SS and the Gestapo favored anti-Jewish legislation that reversed Jewish emancipation by depriving Jews of their civil rights, and promoted dissimilation by ending social and cultural contacts between Jewish and non-Jewish Germans as a means of increasing pressure on Jews to emigrate. The police apparatus deemed approaches to the Jewish question, such as the boycott of Jewish businesses of 1 April 1933 and sporadic boycotts on a local level that followed for the rest of the decade, as well as the on-going acts of violence against the Jews favored by some in the SA, the Hitler Youth, and the Propaganda Ministry, as counter-productive and detrimental to an orderly and efficient emigration process. In the SS newspaper *Das Schwarze Korps*, Reinhard Heydrich outlined the SS position on what the role of Zionism in the Jewish policy of Hitler's government should be. He commended the Zionists for adhering to what he considered a strict racial position, while the "assimilationist" groups were denying their own race. In an article in the September, 1935, issue he described the German government's approach to Zionism in the following manner: "The government finds itself in agreement with that great spiritual movement within Jewry, Zionism, which recognizes the unity of all Jews throughout the world, and which rejects all notions of assimilation" (*Das Schwarze Korps*: 14 May and 26 Sept. 1935). Indeed, the police authorities expressed their satisfaction on a number of occasions between 1934 and 1938 that Zionism had become the dominant political force within German Jewry.

As early as November 1933, the Gestapo in Berlin expressed its approval of the philosophy and the mission of the Zionist movement. In a 23 November memorandum to its office in Frankfurt/Oder, the Gestapo observed that from a political perspective there was nothing problematic about Zionism, pointing to the traditional Zionist rejection of Jewish assimilation in the states in which they lived, and the Zionist preference for a Jewish national life in Palestine (USHMM: 23 November 1933). The earliest indication of active SD attempts to influence the formulation and execution of Jewish policy was a 24 May 1934 memorandum from Department IV 2 of the SD to its director, Reinhard Heydrich. Entitled "On Dealing with the Jewish Question," the memorandum stipulated at the outset that: "The aim of Jewish policy must be the emigration of all Jews" (Wildt 1995, 66-69; Wildt 1998, 241-269). The memo outlined the potential obstacles to this policy, realities that would have to be dealt with as a systematic *Judenpolitik* was developed and implemented in the future. These included the problem of securing adequate destinations to which the flow of Jewish emigrants might be directed, as well as the danger that Jews and Germans alike would adapt themselves to the new circumstances in which "[...] emigration as a final aim would be forgotten by Jews and Germans alike or that it would disappear as an unrealizable, distant goal." To avoid this likelihood, the Jews would be disenfranchised in every way, ultimately in the economy as well, so that Germany would become a country "[...] without a future for the Jews, in which the older generation will die off in their remaining positions, but in which young Jews are able to live so that the attraction of emigration is constantly kept alive." With all of this in mind, the memorandum concluded that the Zionist movement, because it openly and consistently promoted the end of Jewish assimilation in Germany and worked tirelessly to promote Jewish emigration to Palestine, should receive preferential treatment by the authorities over the majority, "assimilationist" Jewish organizations.

One of the most formidable obstacles to Jewish emigration was the deeply rooted, assimilationist character of the Jewish community in Germany, a community that had been overwhelmingly non-Zionist or anti-Zionist during the era of Jewish emancipation in Germany before 1933. The

Gestapo and SD were obviously aware of this, and generally accorded the Zionists preferential treatment over the non-Zionist Jewish organizations throughout most of the 1930s in an effort to neutralize the natural tendency of German Jews to ride out the storm and to avoid emigration if possible. The police considered one of its primary duties during the 1930s to be the crushing of the will of most German Jews to hang on in the hope that the storm would pass, and that they might remain in Germany. This became standard police practice, as indicated in the 24 May 1934 memorandum:

> It is the aim of the State Police (*Staatspolizei*) to support Zionism and its emigration policy as fully as possible. The German assimilationists are being restricted in their activities as much as possible in order to force them into the Zionist camp. [...] Every authority concerned should, in particular, concentrate their efforts in recognizing the Zionist organizations and in supporting their training and emigration endeavors; at the same time the activities of German-Jewish groups should be restricted in order to force them to abandon the idea of remaining in Germany. (Wildt 1998, 246-247)

Beginning on 26 June 1934, the Gestapo required Jewish organizations to register all of their events, meetings, etc. with the police (*Anmeldepflicht*), and soon after decreed that propaganda that counseled Jews to ride out the storm and to remain in Germany was prohibited (USHMM: 25 June 1935). The Gestapo was very much in the business of observing the meetings and other official functions, events, etc. of Jewish organizations in Germany throughout the 1930s, and sought to prevent all activities that might encourage Jews, directly or indirectly, to remain in Germany, or in any way weaken the pressures on Jews to emigrate from Germany. Organizations like the *Centralverein deutscher Staatsbürger jüdischen Glaubens* (Central Association of German Citizens of the Jewish Faith) were specifically targeted and closely scrutinized for any indication that they might promote their traditional assimilationist or *deutschnationale* agendas, while the police reports on Zionist functions usually mentioned with satisfaction that assimilationist tendencies were not in evidence. In the spring of 1937, section II-112 of the SD reiterated more strongly earlier recommendations to apply maximum pressure on all Jewish leaders and organizations to "forcibly nourish a will to emigrate and to bury once and for all the idea of remaining in Germany," and suggested an active policy of playing off Zionists against assimilationists as a means of neutralizing assimilationist tendencies by dividing the Jewish community internally (USHMM: 4 April 1937; Safrian 1993, 27). The SD also pointed to the need to exert pressure on *Scheinzionisten*, or "apparent Zionists," those Zionists who worked in various capacities for the Zionist movement, but who did not themselves intend to emigrate. It demanded the unified focus of German Jews on emigration, the removal of "assimilationists" from the leadership of Jewish political organizations, the *Gemeinden*, cultural organizations, Jewish schools, and retraining centers, the prohibition of assimilationist-oriented elements from public speaking, and the promotion of emigration in Jewish newspapers.

On the local level, police authorities worked to encourage Zionist ideals and aims on non-Zionist Jewish organizations such as the *Centralverein*, and the *Reichsbund jüdischer Frontsoldaten* (Reich Association of Jewish War Veterans) (NstA: 4 September 1933; GLA: 15 September 1933). For instance, there are hundreds of police reports on meetings of Zionist and non-Zionist organizations in Leipzig between 1933 and 1938 at which Zionism and emigration were the required themes for discussion. In particular, the SS promoted occupational retraining camps and other reeducation centers established by the Zionist youth movement and other Zionist groups throughout Germany. These centers and programs were designed to train and otherwise prepare Jews willing to emigrate and to begin a new life in Palestine. The police further encouraged Jewish schools, sports clubs, cultural and other groups and activities that promoted a distinctly Jewish national identity, while at the same time seeking to eliminate any tendencies that might reinforce the German identity of German Jews. Moreover, police authorities and the Foreign Ministry permitted foreign Zionists and other personnel of the Jewish Agency for Palestine, including Hebrew teachers, agricultural specialists, and others who helped prepare young German Jews for settlement and life in Palestine, to enter Germany with relative ease for much of the 1930s.

The preferences given to the Zionists were, of course, superficial to say the least. Zionists, like all Jews in Nazi Germany during the 1930s, were disenfranchised, gradually impoverished, publicly vilified, and deprived of their civil and human rights. They too were subject to periodic bans on meetings and public speeches, and were as much the targets of intimidation, violence, and arrests as were non-Zionists. But in small ways meant to facilitate Zionist work in Germany and the process of Jewish emigration in general, the police made certain exceptions to the rules, exceptions that helped the Zionists without in any way relieving their plight as Jews. In April 1935, the police made an exception to the ban on the wearing of uniforms at meetings of Jewish organizations for the militant youth organization (*Nationale Jugend Herzlia*) of the Revisionist State Zionist Organization (*Staatszionistische Organisation*) (Mommsen 1962, 80-81). Contact between Jews and non-Jews, an almost pathological fear of the regime especially after 1935, was in fact permitted at some agricultural training sites in the countryside, where young Jews intent on emigrating to Palestine were allowed in some instances to receive training and work experience on "Aryan" farms. Zionist groups were often exempt from the periodic, temporary bans on meetings of Jewish organizations during the 1930s, while very few Zionist speakers were subject to the commonplace *Redeverbote* (bans on public speaking) that the police routinely applied to speakers at meetings of Jewish organizations.

Events in the Middle East in 1936 and 1937 raised questions in Berlin about the wisdom of a Jewish policy that did so much to promote Jewish emigration to Palestine. The Royal Commission under Lord Peel, appointed by the British government in November 1936, to investigate the causes of the Arab revolt in Palestine and to recommend solutions, generated speculation throughout Europe and the Middle East about the creation of two nominally independent states, one Jewish and the other Arab (Nicosia 2000, chap. 7). Although the Commission's findings and recommendations were not made public until July, the German Foreign Office was already considering the implications of an independent Jewish state as early as 9 January 1937. On that date, Walther Hinrichs of *Referat Deutschland* warned the State Secretary's office that the Peel Commission would likely recommend an independent Jewish state in part of Palestine; he criticized past Foreign Office policy of ignoring the implications of an emigration policy that promoted the movement of German Jews to Palestine, and concluded with a warning about the strategic and ideological dangers of a Jewish state:

> Therefore it should be noted that a Jewish state in Palestine would strengthen Jewish influence in the world to unimaginable levels. Just as Moscow is the central authority for the Comintern, Jerusalem would become the base for a Jewish world organization that, like Moscow, would be in a position to carry out its work with diplomatic means. (PA: 9 January 1937)

The regime had found the existence of a Jewish "National Home" under British authority convenient, but would reject with unanimity the creation of even a nominally independent and very small Jewish state in Palestine. Party circles feared the establishment of an independent power base – Rosenberg's "Jewish Vatican" or "Jewish Comintern," while Foreign Ministry officials opposed adding a new state to the coalition of states hostile to the new Germany. Foreign Minister von Neurath expressed the Foreign Ministry's opposition to the idea of an independent Jewish state in Palestine on 1 June 1937, about a month before the publication of the Peel partition plan, with the words:

[...] for a state in Palestine would not absorb world Jewry, but would establish in the process a legal power base for international Jewry, something like the Vatican state for political Catholicism or Moscow for the Comintern. (Nicosia 2000, 121)

Following the publication of the Peel Commission recommendations on 7 July 1937, a debate ensued among government and party agencies over the implications of domestic Jewish policy on German foreign policy. Specifically, there was growing concern that the policy of promoting Zionism in Germany and Jewish emigration to Palestine with the transfer of some Jewish assets via Haavara had significantly enhanced Zionist efforts to build an independent Jewish state. But by the end of the year, German fears about a Jewish state had disappeared. The specific recommendations of the Peel Commission to create two nominally independent states in Palestine – one Arab and one Jewish – were rejected by the Arabs and the Jews, and then dropped by the British. In the view of the German government, the question had become irrelevant. In November, 1938, a Foreign Ministry memorandum concluded:

Since the partition plan has been rejected by the British government itself, and there exists no possibility that it will be brought up again, we need no longer fear that [Jewish] emigration from Germany will promote a Jewish state in Palestine. (PA: 12 November 1938)

In fact, the debate over emigration and foreign policy had been resolved in early 1938 when Hitler directed that Jewish emigration be pursued by whatever means necessary, including the continued use of Zionism and Palestine. A note from the *Aussenhandelsamt* (Foreign Trade Office) of the *Auslandsorganisation* (Overseas Organization) to the director of the AO in the Foreign Office on 1 February 1938 advised:

In a decision reached just a short time ago, the *Führer*, on the advice of *Reichsleiter* Rosenberg, has decided that Jewish emigration from Germany should continue to be promoted by all possible means, and this is to be accomplished in the first instance by directing it to Palestine. (PA: 1 February 1938; BA: 28 February 1938)

Hitler's intervention in the debate over emigration policy and Palestine, along with the general radicalization of Nazi Jewish policy at the end of 1937 and the beginning of 1938, is probably best understood against the background of what one historian has called "Hitlers linking of war plans and racial policy" (*Hitlers Verknüpfung von Kriegsplanung und Rassenpolitik*) (Adam 1972, 159). There can be no doubt that specific policies and actions regarding the Jews were usually conditioned by the timing and requirements of foreign policy and war. At the beginning of 1938, there were still some 400,000 Jews in Germany, along with some 200,000 in a soon to be annexed Austria. The radicalization of Nazi Jewish policy in 1938, which, besides continuing the promotion of Jewish emigration to Palestine, also entailed new measures involving the elimination of the Jews from the German economy, their forced deportation from the *Reich* by brutal and arbitrary means, stepped-up violence culminating in the *Kristallnacht* pogrom, and other anti-Jewish measures, must therefore be understood within the larger context of the regime's efforts to prepare for war in 1938 and 1939.

The annexation of Austria in March 1938, provided the SS with the opportunity to formulate its own emigration procedures for Austria alone. All pretense of systematic and orderly emigration procedures was dropped in favor of rapid, brutal, and forced deportation (BA: no date). By the end of October 1938, Adolf Eichmann's *Zentralstelle für jüdische Auswanderung* (Central Office for Jewish Emigration) in Vienna had forced more than 50,000 Austrian Jews to leave the country, a number that was significantly more than had emigrated from the *Altreich* (Germany excluding an annexed Austria) for the entire year (BA: 21 October 1938). Shortly after the *Kristallnacht* pogrom of 9-10 November 1938, authority over Jewish emigration policy throughout Greater Germany was transferred via Hermann Göring to the SS. In January 1939, Reinhard Heydrich established the *Reichszentrale für jüdische Auswanderung* (Reich Central Office for Jewish Emigration) in Berlin. It was modeled after Eichmann's operation in Vienna, which, along with a similar office set up in Prague in March 1939, were attached to the Berlin *Reichszentrale* as branches. Its task was reiterated in a memorandum from Hermann Göring to the Interior Ministry on 24 January 1939: "The emigration of Jews from Germany is to be promoted with all available means" (LA: 24 January 1939). The SS continued previous policies of promoting the emigration/deportation of Jews to Palestine through the first year and a half of the war. The Zionist Association for Germany (*Zionistische Vereinigung für Deutschland*) and the revisionist State Zionist Organization (*Staatszionistische Organisation*), along with most other remaining Jewish organizations, were dissolved either just before or just after the *Kristallnacht* pogrom. However, the Palestine Office (*Palästinaamt*) of the Jewish Agency for Palestine continued to operate in Berlin in the headquarters of the defunct Zionist Organization for Germany at 10 Meineckestrasse through May 1941, although it was not able to secure the emigration of Jews from Germany to Palestine much past the end of 1940 (BA-P: 10 October 1940, 13 March 1941, 9 May 1941). Moreover, the

Gestapo and the SD were also indirectly involved in the "illegal" immigration of Jews into Palestine (Ball-Kaduri 1975, 388-92; Höhne 1967, 318). Agents of the *Mossad*, with the tacit approval of the Nazis, maintained offices in Berlin and Vienna to organize the illegal transport of Jews via Yugoslavia, Italy, Rumania and Bulgaria, past the British immigration quotas and blockade, to Palestine. As one former *Mossad* agent involved in organizing the illegal migration of Jews from Germany to Palestine in 1938 and 1939 observed in his memoirs:

> In pre-war Germany these operations were neither illegal nor secret. The Gestapo office directly across the street from our own knew exactly where we were and what we were doing. The illegality began only at the shores of Palestine with the British blockade. (Avriel: 1975, 28)

Nazi encouragement of Zionism and Jewish emigration to Palestine was by no means an endorsement of Zionist ideology and aims. Like some of their nineteenth century predecessors, the Nazis did not consider Zionism a positive force in Jewish life, and certainly rejected the goal of an independent Jewish state in Palestine. An SD report of 20 October 1936, clearly summarized a National Socialist approach to Zionism that had been consistent since the pronouncements on Zionism by Hitler and Rosenberg during the early days of the movement. After reiterating the utilitarian nature of that approach, the report warned about the true nature of Zionism in the following way:

> Moreover, the very reserved position of the ZVfD in Germany vis-à-vis the authorities does not alter the sharp opposition of the World Zionist Organization to the National Socialist state[...]If the ZVfD, as an existing Jewish organization inside the boundaries of the *Reich*, has behaved in a reserved manner, the reason for this is not to be found in a friendly disposition toward the state, but in the realization that every Jewish organization, regardless of what kind, must be a 100% opponent of National Socialism. (BA: 20 October 1936)

Moreover, the relatively small size of Palestine, the regime's conviction that all Jews were enemies of Germany, and its vehement opposition to the Zionist objective of an independent Jewish state, meant that the Nazis could never conceive of Zionism and Palestine as the ultimate solution to the "Jewish Question". It was a question that was evolving for the regime as Germany's "living space" began to expand in 1938 and 1939 with the annexation of Austria, the destruction of Czechoslovakia, and the development of plans to invade and destroy Poland. The transformation of Germany's "problem" of removing about half a million Jews from Germany to one of removing millions of Jews from Germany's new "living space" in Europe would require radically different policies. Emigration to Palestine might help to eliminate Jewish life in Germany, but it could not solve the larger Jewish "problem" that would be the inevitable result of the conquest of Europe.

Encouragement of Zionism was part of a larger, "eliminationist" solution to the Jewish question in Germany before 1941, namely Jewish emigration and deportation. However, Hitler's plans for expansion in central and Eastern Europe in 1938 and 1939, and war as a probable consequence, meant the "eliminationist" requirements of Nazi leaders would have to develop other applications. On 25 January 1939, one day after the Reich Central Office for Jewish Emigration (*Reichszentrale für jüdische Auswanderung*) was officially established in Berlin to excellerate the process of deporting Jews from Greater Germany, an internal memorandum was circulated in the German Foreign Ministry asserting that Palestine would never be able to absorb more than a fraction of the Jews of Europe. It concluded:

> In reality there exists a larger German interest in maintaining the fragmentation of Jewry. For the Jewish question will not be solved for Germany even when not a single member of the Jewish race remains on German soil. In fact, developments in recent years have taught us that international Jewry will always be the perennial opponent of National Socialist Germany. The Jewish question is, therefore, at the same time one of the most important problems for German foreign policy. (ADAP: No. 664)

This view reflected the growing realization on the part of some government and party agencies that Germany's Jewish question was no longer merely a matter of removing half a million Jews from Germany. With the beginning of German expansion in Europe already under way, and the prospect of huge German conquests and ultimately the incorporation of millions of European Jews into a new, German-dominated Europe, radical new approaches to a Jewish question of very different dimensions would be necessary. Hitler himself alluded to the European dimensions of the Jewish question and a new racial order in Europe a few days later in his famous speech to the *Reichstag* (Domarus 1965, 1057). Certainly Palestine remained in the eyes of the SS a suitable destination for German Jews through 1939 and 1940 (PA: 5 April 1939; BLHA: 8 May 1940). However, Reinhard Heydrich's letter to German Foreign Minister von Ribbentrop of 24 June 1940, in the wake of the German victory over France, pointed to the need for a larger, territorial "final solution" to the Jewish question in Europe as a whole. After noting that his *Reichszentrale* in Berlin had achieved the removal from Greater Germany of more than 200,000 Jews since January 1939, Heydrich spoke in terms of radically different measures to cope with the much larger number of Jews under German control. He continued to think about resolving the Jewish question in "territorial" terms, of transferring Jews to some other territory or territories away from Germany and Europe, as had been the intent of Nazi Jewish policy before the war. By the summer of 1940, however, with a war in progress and a substantial portion of European Jewry under German control, and previous "territorial" approaches no longer feasible, he began to ponder a single, "final solution" for European Jewry as a whole. He wrote: "The total problem – it already concerns around $3^{1}/_4$ million Jews in the territories currently under German authority – can no longer be resolved through emigration. A "territorial" Final Solution is therefore necessary" (PA: 24 June 1940).

The Lublin and Madagascar schemes were considered briefly in 1939 and 1940 by the SS, the German Foreign Ministry, and to some extent by Hitler himself, but the realities of the war and the enormity of the "problem" quickly rendered those options unworkable. The Lublin plan of the fall/winter 1939-1940 called for the concentration of hundreds of thousands of Jews from the *Reich* and from parts of western Poland that were incorporated into the *Reich* to be concentrated on a *Judenreservat* (Jewish reservation) that was to be set up near Lublin in eastern Poland. The Madagascar plan of 1940 in particular represented an even more dramatic radicalization in Nazi Jewish policy, one that combined the previous territorial approach of deportation to specific territories with a new willingness to entertain the idea of genocide. It embodied the transfer of millions of European Jews to a "Jewish reservation" on the French-controlled island of Madagascar off the southeast coast of Africa where they would live under the most primitive and appalling conditions until most simply died as a result (Browning 1992, 13-20). Presumably the Lublin idea in 1939-1940 would have had similar consequences for the victims.

Since the Madagascar Plan would have required the defeat of both France and Great Britain, it was quickly forgotten in the fall of 1940 when Germany failed to knock Britain out of the war, and Hitler rather quickly turned his attention to the Soviet Union. However, both the Lublin and Madagascar plans would appear to represent the link between the policies of elimination through emigration/deportation of the 1930s and elimination through mass murder, for they included elements of both. By the end of the fall of 1940, Nazi Germany's Jewish Question no longer involved the removal from Germany of half a million German Jews; German conquests and Nazi plans to reorganize Europe had transformed it into one that encompassed the removal of millions of Jews from Europe. The process of eliminating European Jewry through territorial resettlement in eastern Poland or Madagascar in 1939 and 1940, as that of eliminating German

Jewry by emigration and deportation to Palestine and other destination countries outside of Europe between 1933 and 1939, was quickly overtaken by events. The rapid expansion of German *Lebensraum* in the East, coupled with Hitler's failure to bring the war in the west to a successful conclusion, rendered both obsolete. The conquest of much of Europe from 1939 to 1941 and the prospect of millions of additional Jews coming under German control in the invasion and conquest of the Soviet Union left the regime with extermination as the only feasible way of removing the Jews from Europe (Browning 1985, 10-16).

It is useful to consider the nature of German Antisemitism through the lens of Antisemitic attitudes and policies toward Zionism, a Jewish ideology and movement that offered Antisemites a mechanism through which they might easily satisfy their desire to eliminate Jewish life in Germany. Antisemitism in Germany was never an immutable ideology, with precisely the same meaning and application for everyone, at all times and in all circumstances. Indeed, Daniel Goldhagen's term "eliminationist Antisemitism" is a misnomer, for the elimination of Jewish life in Germany was something that might be achieved for some Antisemites at certain times through assimilation, for others through emigration or deportation, and still others, ultimately, by extermination. The means were certainly different, but the end, the elimination of Jewish life in Germany and then Europe, would have been achieved in any case.

Saul Friedländer's theory of "redemptive Antisemitism" among Hitler and others in the Nazi leadership is instructive in this context (Friedländer 1997, chap.3). Antisemites in Germany generally held the Jews responsible for Germany's problems, if not for the problems of the entire world. Most considered the emigration or expulsion of the Jews as Germany's only chance for redemption, while others came to believe that the extermination of the Jews would ultimately bring redemption. Friedländer considers German Antisemitism within the context of the interaction of ideological fanaticism and pragmatic calculation, combining periodically with uncontrolled rage that was generally characteristic of Hitler's approach to the Jewish question since the early years of the Nazi movement. Those unchanging components of Hitler's view of the world and the role of the Jews in it manifested themselves in different ways at different times, with words and actions often triggered by events over which he had little control. For example, the sweeping and unimagined German victories between 1939 and 1941 were the likely catalysts in Hitler's mind for the radicalization of Nazi Jewish policy that led ultimately to the Final Solution (Browning 1992, 121). For Hitler and for others, elimination of the Jews was essential for the survival of the German

Volksgemeinschaft; it was a constant in the quest for German redemption. The use of Zionism and Jewish emigration to Palestine before World War II, among other approaches, to achieve that redemption should be seen as a reflection of the often erratic and contradictory nature of German Antisemitism, and, in particular, the improvisational character of its application.

Finally, there is no evidence that the centrality of emigration and deportation in Nazi Jewish policy before World War II, which included the promotion of Jewish emigration to Paslestine, embodied in any way the ultimate intention to commit genocide. Indeed, there is not the slightest indication in the vast documentation on Nazi Jewish policy during the 1930s that the Nazi regime thought about the larger, European dimension of its Jewish question until early 1939 when its preparations for war and conquest were well under way (Schleunes 1970). Nor does the evidence indicate that the regime pursued its policies toward the Jews during the 1930s with the resolution of a larger, European Jewish question in mind. The preference for Jewish emigration from Germany to Palestine, and to other destinations outside of Europe, would in fact seem to preclude any prewar intent to plan for the systematic extermination of the Jews of Europe. It appears likely that the German conquest of most of Europe during the first two years of World War II, coupled with the unfeasibility of resolving the European Jewish question using means employed before the war in Germany, resulted in a rapid and radical evolution to the Final Solution.

Literature Cited

Unpublished Archival Sources

BA (Bundesarchiv Berlin): R/58-955, Bericht "Die Zionistische Weltorganisation", II/120, 20 October 1936.

BA: Sammlung Schumacher 240/I, Gestapo Würzburg, 28 February 1938.

BA: R/58-1253, Der Sicherheitsdienst des RFSS und des SS-Oberabschnittes/ Donau, no date.

BA: R/58-1253, Zentralstelle für jüdische Auswanderung (Wien) an II/112, 21 October 1938.

BA-P (Bundesarchiv Potsdam): 75c Re 1-47, Palästinaamt der Jewish Agency for Palestine an die Geheime Staatspolizei-Leitstelle Berlin, 10 October 1940, 13 March 1941, and 9 May 1941.

BLHA (Brandenburgisches Landeshauptarchiv Potsdam): Rep. 41 Bötzow-34, Geheime Staaspolizei, Staatspolizeistelle Potsdam, Rundschreiben, Br.Nr. 2323/40 II B, 8 May 1940.

GLA (Generallandesarchiv Karlsruhe): 357-29914. Geheimes Staatspolizeiamt/ Baden an das Bezirksamt Karlsruhe, Nr. 13040, 15 September 1933.

LA (Landesarchiv/Berlin): Rep. 57, Nr.375, Der Beauftragte für den Vierjahresplan an den Herrn Reichsminister des Innern, 24 January 1939.

NStA (Niedersächsisches Staatsarchiv/Wolfenbüttel): 12A Neu 13, Staatsinnen-ministerium 16059 Juden. Württ. Politische Polizei an das Reichsministerium des Innern/Berlin, Nr. 3/1376/33 a, 4 September 1933.

PA (Politisches Archiv des Auswärtigen Amts Bonn): Sonderreferat-W. Finanzwesen 16, Bd. 2. Runderlass des Reichswirtschaftsministeriums, 54/33, 28 August 1933.

PA: Referat-D. Po5 NE adh7, Bd.1. Bericht über die Lage der jüdischen Flüchtlinge aus Deutschland in den verschiedenen Ländern, September 1933.

PA: Inland II A/B. 83-21, Bd.1. "Die Entwicklung der Judenfrage in Deutschland und ihre Rückwirkung im Ausland" von Vicco von Bülow-Schwante, no date.

PA: Inland II A/B, 83-21a, Bd.1a, Aufzeichnung des Referat Deutschlands (Hinrichs), 9 January 1937.

PA: Büro des Reichsaussenministers-Palästina, Deutsches General-Konsulat Jerusalem an AA, 22 March 1937.

PA: Inland II A/B, 83-24a, Bd.1. Aussenhandelsamt der AO der NSDAP an den Leiter der AO im Auswärtigen Amt, Ag. 13/1, 1 February 1938.

PA: Pol.Abt. VII, Politik 36-Palästina/Judenfrage, Aufzeichnung des Referat Deutschlands, 21 November 1938.

PA: Inland II A/B, 83-24a, Bd.1, Der Reichsführer-SS u. Chef der Deutschen Polizei an das Auswärtige Amt, S-PP (II B) Nr. 5888/38, 5 April 1939.

PA: Inland II/G, 86-29B, Der Chef der Sicherheitspolizei und des SD (Heydrich) an den Herrn Reichsaussenminister, IV D 4 – 1574/40, 24 June 1940.

USHMM (United States Holocaust Memorial Museum, Washington, D.C.): 11.001M.01, 2-146, Geheimes Staatspolizeiamt, Berlin an die Staatspolizeistelle in Frankfurt/Oder, II F 259/198, 23 November 1933.

USHMM: 11.001M.01, 17-18, "Juden: Politische Gliederung in Zionisten und Assimilanten", II 1 B 2, 25 June 1935.

USHMM:11.001M.01, 7-506, "Welche Fragen und Aufgaben ergeben sich für den SD bei der Bekämpfung des Judentums," 4 April 1937.

Published Sources

Adam, Uwe Dietrich. 1972. *Judenpolitik im Dritten Reich*. Düsseldorf: Droste Verlag.

Adler, H.G. 1960. *Die Juden in Deutschland von der Aufklärung bis zum National-sozialismus*. München: Kosel Verlag.

ADAP (*Akten zur Deutschen Auswärtigen Politik 1918-1945*): Serie D, Bd.V, Nr.664.

Avriel, Ehud. 1975. *Open the Gates*. New York: Atheneum.

Ball-Kaduri, Kurt Jacob. 1975. Illegale Judenauswanderung aus Deutschland nach Palästina 1939-1940: Planung Durchführung und Internationale Zusammenhänge. *Jahrbuch des Instituts für deutsche Geschichte* 4: 387-421.

Browning, Christopher. 1985. *Fateful Months: Essays on the Emergence of the Final Solution*. New York: Holmes and Meier.

Browning, Christopher. 1992. *The Path to Genocide: Essays on Launching the Final Solution*. Cambridge: Cambridge University Press.

Chamberlain, Houston Stewart. 1938. *Die Grundlagen des neunzehnten Jahrhunderts*. 2 Bde. 23. Aufl. München: F. Bruckmann K.G.

Domarus, Max (ed.). 1965. *Hitler: Reden und Proklamationen*. Vol. 2/I. München: Süddeutscher Verlag.

Doron, Joachim. 1983. Classical Zionism and Modern Antisemitism: Parallels and Influences, 1883-1914. *Studies in Zionism* 3: 169-204.

Dühring, Eugen. 1892. *Die Judenfrage als Frage der Rassenschädlichkeit für Existenz, Sitte und Kultur der Völker*. 4. Aufl. Berlin: Reuther und Reichard.

Feilchenfeld, Werner, Ludwig Pinner, and Dolf Michaelis. 1972. *Haavara Transfer nach Palästina und Einwanderung deutscher Juden 1933-1939*. Schriftenreihe wissenschaftlicher Abhandlungen des Leo Baeck Instituts 26. Tübingen: J.C.B. Mohr/Paul Siebert.

Frey, Thomas [Theodor Fritsch]. 1893. *Antisemiten-Katechismus. Eine Zusammenstellung des wichtigsten Materials zum Verständnis der Judenfrage*. 25. Aufl. Leipzig: H. Beyer.

Friedländer, Saul. 1997. *Nazi Germany and the Jews: The Years of Persecution, 1933-1939*. New York: HarperCollins.

Friedman, Isaiah. 1977. *Germany, Turkey, and Zionism 1897-1918*. Oxford: Oxford University Press.

Frymann, Daniel [Heinrich Class]. 1913. *Wenn ich der Kaiser wär'... Politische Wahrheiten und Notwendigkeiten*. Leipzig: Dietrich.

Goldhagen, Daniel. 1996. *Hitler's Willing Executioners: Ordinary Germans and the Holocaust*. New York: A. Knopf.

Graetz, Heinrich. (no date) *Volkstümliche Geschichte der Juden*. Bd.3. Berlin-Wien: K. Löwit Verlag.

Hertzberg, Arthur. 1990. *The French Enlightenment and the Jews*. New York: Columbia University Press.

Hitler, Adolf. 1941. *Mein Kampf*. New York: Reynal and Hitchcock.

Höhne, Heinz. 1967. *Der Orden unter dem Totenkopf: Die Geschichte der SS*. Gütersloh: Magnus Verlag.

Katz, Jacob. 1980. *From Prejudice to Destruction: Anti-Semitism, 1700-1933*. Cambridge, Massachussetts: Harvard University Press.

Lagarde, Paul de. 1887. *Juden und Indogermanen. Eine Studie nach dem Leben.* Göttingen: Dietrich.

Marr, Wilhelm. 1879. *Der Sieg des Judenthums über das Germanenthum. Vom nicht confessionellen Standpunkt aus betrachtet.* Bern: R. Costenoble.

Mommsen, Hans. 1962. Dokumentation: Der nationalsozialistische Polizeistaat und die Judenverfolgung vor 1938. *Vierteljahrshefte für Zeitgeschichte* 10: 68-87.

Mosse, George. 1978. *Toward the Final Solution: A History of European Racism.* New York: Harper and Row.

Nicosia, Francis. 1991. The End of Emancipation and the Illusion of Preferential Treatment: German Zionism, 1933-1938. *Leo Baeck Institute Yearbook* 36: 243-265.

Nicosia, Francis. 1992. Zionism and Palestine in Anti-Semitic Thought in Imperial Germany. *Studies in Zionism* 13: 115-131.

Nicosia, Francis. 2000. *The Third Reich and the Palestine Question.* New Brunswick, New Jersey: Transaction Publishers.

Niewyk, Donald. 1990. Solving the "Jewish Problem": Continuity and Change in German Antisemitism, 1871-1945. *Leo Baeck Institute Yearbook* 35: 335-370.

Phelps, Reginald. 1963. Hitler als Parteiredner im Jahre 1920. *Vierteljahrshefte für Zeitgeschichte* 11: 288-331.

Phelps, Reginald. 1968. Hitlers grundlegende Rede über den Antisemitismus. *Vierteljahrshefte für Zeitgeschichte* 16: 399-420.

Poliakov, Leon. 1971. *The Aryan Myth: The History of Racist and Nationalist Ideas in Europe.* New York: Basic Books.

Rose, Paul Lawrence. 1990. *Revolutionary Antisemitism in Germany: From Kant to Wagner.* Princeton, New Jersey: Princeton University Press.

Rosenberg, Alfred. 1922. *Der staatsfeindliche Zionismus.* Hamburg: Deutschvölkische Verlagsanstalt.

Rubenstein, Richard L. and John K. Roth. 1987. *Approaches to Auschwitz: The Holocaust and Its Legacy.* Atlanta, Georgia: John Knox.

Safrian, Hans. 1993. *Die Eichmann-Männer.* Wien: Europaverlag.

Schleunes, Karl. 1970. *The Twisted Road to Auschwitz: Nazi Policy Toward German Jews, 1933-1939.* Urbana, Illinois: University of Illinois Press.

Das Schwarze Korps, 14 May 1935, and 26 September 1935.

Treitschke, Heinrich von. 1975. *History of Germany in the Nineteenth Century.* Chicago: University of Chicago Press.

Vital, David. 1987. *Zionism: The Crucial Phase.* Oxford: Oxford University Press.

Wahrmund, Adolf. 1887. *Das Gesetz des Nomadenthums und die heutige Judenherrschaft.* Berlin: Reuther und Reichard.

Wildt, Michael (ed.). 1995. *Die Judenpolitik des SD, 1935-1938: Eine Dokumentation.* München: Oldenbourg.

Wildt, Michael. 1998. Before the "Final Solution": The Judenpolitik of the SD, 1935-1938. *Leo Baeck Institute Yearbook* 43: 241-269.

Woltmann, Ludwig. 1903. *Politische Anthropologie. Eine Untersuchung über den Einfluss der Decendenztheorie auf die Lehre von der politischen Entwicklung der Völker.* Eisenach und Leipzig: Thüringische Verlags-Anstalt.

Zimmermann, Moshe. 1986. *Wilhelm Marr: The Patriarch of Anti-Semitism.* New York: Oxford University Press.

Finland's Jews and the Final Solution

Robert D. Rachlin

On 20 January 1942 near Berlin, the explicit program for the annihilation of Europe's Jews was established at the Wannsee Conference, presided over by SS-Obergruppenführer Reinhard Heydrich. Finland's Jews, estimated in the *Protocol* as 2,300, were included in the plan. Despite the presence of the Wehrmacht and Gestapo in Finland from 1941 to 1944, not a single Finnish Jew was deported or seriously molested by the Finnish or German authorities.

Finland's record was not unspotted. On 18 August 1938, sixty Jewish asylum-seeking refugees arrived in Helsinki aboard the S/S Ariadne from Stettin and were denied entry. On 6 November 1942, twenty-seven foreign refugees, including seven, possibly eight, Jews, were expelled by Finnish officials via the German freighter *S/S Hohenhörn*, anchored in the Gulf of Finland at Helsinki. Elina Suominen (1979) has related this sorry event.

This essay explores the position of the Jews of Finland during the Second World War in the context of pre-war history and events that occurred during the war, in particular, the visit of Reichsführer-SS Heinrich Himmler to Finland in 1942. The author proposes tentative answers to the question: Why were Finland's Jews spared when Jews in other countries occupied by or allied with Germany were not?

Chief credit for scholarship about this aspect of Finnish history belongs to Hannu Rautkallio, whose *Finland and the Holocaust: The Rescue of Finland's Jews* (1987) is the only book-length study of the wartime Jews of Finland in English. This is an adaptation of his *Ne Kahdeksan* (The Eight) (1985). His *Suomen juutalaisten aseveljeys* (Finland's Jewish Comrades in Arms) (1989) details the military participation of the Jewish community in Finland's war effort against the Soviet Union. The author knows of no other book-length studies of this facet of Finland's war years. Students of this period in Finland must draw heavily on Rautkallio's archival research.

Background of the Finnish Jewish Community

From the Middle Ages Finland was part of the Kingdom of Sweden. Finland became a grand duchy of Russia in 1809 with Sweden's defeat in the Napoleonic Wars. Sweden admitted Jews in 1782, but restricted residence to four cities. Discharged Czarist soldiers constituted the first significant Jewish settlement in Finland in the 1860s. In 1858, Russia allowed soldiers to settle with their families wherever their military service ended. These "cantonists" were the nucleus of the present-day Finnish Jewish community. They dwelled in Finland under temporary license and severe restrictions. The Russian government issued a decree in 1889 that specifically addressed the presence of the Jews in Finland. Certain named Jews were to be allowed to remain there at the sufferance of the government, but only in Helsinki, Tampere, and Turku (S. R. Cohen 1968, 130). To this day, most Finnish Jews live in one of these three cities. Their occupations were strictly limited. They supported themselves chiefly as dealers in second-hand clothes. These economic restrictions applied to all ex-cantonists, not just Jews. A military decree issued in 1858 allowed ex-soldiers settled in Finland "to earn a living by selling home-made handicrafts, bread, berries, cigarettes, second-hand clothes, and other inexpensive textile products" (Harviainen n.d.). Children were allowed to remain in Finland only so long as they lived with their parents and were unmarried.

There appears to have been no restraint of religious worship. Jews held services at the island fortress of Sveaborg (Finnish: Suomenlinna) outside Helsinki, and the authorities granted the Jews permission in 1865 to build a synagogue (S. R. Cohen 1968, 130). This grant contrasted with the Russian policy to discourage the Jews from settling in Finland and isolate them from full engagement with the life of the native inhabitants of the country. It suggests that the antipathy to the Jews, which erupted into violence at one time or another in most areas of Europe, existed in considerably milder form in Finland, indeed in Scandinavia generally. Perhaps in light of this fact, one of the architects of the Final Solution expressed doubts that these measures would be easily manageable in Scandinavia: "Unterstaatssekretär [Martin] Luther teilte hierzu mit, daß bei tiefgehender Behandlung dieses Problems in einigen Ländern, so in den nordischen Staaten, Schwierigkeiten auftauchen werden, und es sich daher empfiehlt, diese Länder vorerst noch zurückzustellen" ("Assistant Secretary of State Luther notes in this regard that in some countries, such as the Nordic states, thorough treatment of this problem will be met with difficulties; it is therefore recommended to defer action in these countries.") (Wannsee 1982, 9-10).

In 1918, with Finnish independence, Jews were accorded full rights of citizenship. By an act of Parliament concerning "Mosaic Confessors," promulgated 12 January 1918, Jews were for the first time allowed to adopt Finnish citizenship. In the 1920s and 1930s, the Jewish population of Finland peaked at about 2,000. Finnish Holocaust scholar Harviainen (n.d.) reports that in 1939 the Jewish population was about 1,700. The number of Jews appears to have declined thereafter, although in the Wannsee Protocol, in which the program of extermination known as the Endlösung – the Final Solution – was decided upon, the number was given as 2,300. Acculturation was gradual. In the first years of settlement, Jews spoke mainly Yiddish or Russian. Finnish Jews gradually adopted first Swedish, then Finnish. Finland has two official languages: Finnish and Swedish. Finnish is the native language of about ninety-four percent of the population and Swedish of about six percent The Jews settled chiefly in the south and southwest where Swedish linguistic and cultural influence was strong. To this day, many Jews in Finland still speak Swedish as the language of choice. Yiddish, sadly, has largely disappeared.

Jewish Participation in Finland's Wars

In 1939, the Soviet Union demanded that Finland cede territory to protect Leningrad from land and sea attack. Finland refused. On 30 November 1939, three months after conclusion of the German-Soviet Nonagression Pact, Soviet troops invaded Finland. The "Winter War" began with stunning victories by the outnumbered Finns, but Russian superiority in men and arms soon turned the tide in favor of the aggressors, forcing Finland, after a few months' fighting, to sue for peace. The price of peace was major territorial concessions to the U.S.S.R., including western Karelia, which remains part of Russia.

After Norway's capitulation to Germany in June 1940, both Sweden and Finland acceded to Germany's request that its troops be permitted transit. With troops garrisoned on Finnish soil, Germany, on 22 June 1941, attacked the Soviet Union. Both Germany and Finland were prepared for what was for Germany the initiation, and for Finland the resumption, of hostilities against the U.S.S.R. Finland's "Continuation War" against the U.S.S.R. ended with an armistice signed on 19 September 1944, a unilateral imposition of extraordinarily harsh terms by the Soviet victors. The "negotiations" between the Finnish delegation and the Soviet Union are set out in Thede Palm and Georg Enckell, *The Finnish-Soviet Armistice Negotiations of 1944* (Stockholm: Almqvist & Wiksell, 1971).

Of the two thousand-or-so Jews of all ages in Finland in 1939, three hundred men were sent to the front. Many did not return. A 1995 statement by the Jewish War Veterans of Finland puts the number of Jewish dead at twenty-three more than one percent of the entire Finnish Jewish community (Livson and Matso 1995). Jewish soldiers and officers fought alongside Waffen-SS troops and had frequent and often cordial contact with them. Jewish medical officers treated wounded Germans. One Jewish major in the medical corps, Leo Skurnik, risked his life transferring an entire SS field hospital under enemy fire to a safer location (Rautkallio 1989, 201). He, one other Jewish officer, Salomon Klaas, and Dina Poljakov, a nurse, were awarded the German Iron Cross, which all refused to accept.

Near the front lines in Eastern Karelia, where German troops had arrived to reinforce the Finns, a small synagogue was actually established. Known as "Scholka's shul" – "Scholka" was the nickname of a soldier, Isak Smolar – the small, round hut with a chimney pipe protruding through a high conical roof, was the site of regular Sabbath services, complete with a Torah scroll for the weekly reading. Nearby German soldiers did not interfere, and some reportedly showed respect for the worship (Rautkallio 1989, 202).

Participation in hostilities alongside Germans was not a simple matter for the Jewish soldiers, who surely knew of Nazi racial policies and were increasingly aware of the extent and barbarity of Nazi measures against the Jews of Germany and occupied territories. News of the exterminations was widely disseminated as early as 1942 in Sweden (Koblik 1988, 146), despite Hitler's frequent outbursts of anger at press criticisms. At least two newspapers in Sweden, *Göteborgs Handelstidning* and the extreme anti-Hitler *Trots Allt!* persistently published reports of German atrocities. Similar concerns about the press existed in Finland, where the Swedish-language press appears to have taken the lead in exposing Nazi brutality. Pressures from Germany against critical newspaper accounts in Finland increased in 1944, as the tide of war turned against the Third Reich. In April 1944, Hitler imposed an arms embargo against his Finnish "comrades-in-arms" in the wake of Finnish press criticism of German evacuation of the collection and installations of Tartu University in Estonia (Erfurth 1979, 137). Two months later, *Svenska Pressen* was suppressed for three months for giving offense to the Germans (Erfurth 1979, 143). Upton (1965, 98) argues that despite "occasional brief items" about anti-Jewish measures in Europe, there was no comment or discussion. He concludes that Finns "could have formed no adequate picture of what was happening to European Jewry [...]. In short, nothing that might be offensive to Germany could appear." This view is unconvincing, in light of the reports that appeared in Sweden as well as in Finland. As early as 1938,

Helsingin Sanomat, the leading Finnish-language daily in Helsinki, reported on 7 September 1939 German efforts to banish Jews from Germany. Rautkallio (1987, 49-51) cites several Finnish press reports that prove awareness in Finland of Nazi anti-Jewish policies.

A 1997 Finnish video documentary *Daavid* includes many interviews with Jewish ex-military personnel. Their fear of Germany was overshadowed by a passionate purpose to preserve Finnish independence and retake the lands wrested from Finland by Stalin in the Winter War. The motivation of Finnish Jews fighting beside Germans is summed up in English by the Jewish War Veterans of Finland: "The very special fact in this whole matter was that whoever conquered Finland the Jews would be the losers. Their only hope was that Finland stays [sic] independent and that was worth fighting for" (Livson and Matso 1995). Marshal C. G. Mannerheim, commander-in-chief of Finland's armed forces during the Winter War and Continuation War, paid tribute to the fallen Jewish soldiers by appearing, at his own request, at the synagogue in Helsinki on Independence Day, 6 December 1944. In a large room of the Helsinki synagogue there is a bronze statue of Mannerheim. Other mementos of Mannerheim, including a plaque, are visible in the synagogue, where Mannerheim's memory is revered.

Anti-Semitism in Finland

Finland, like other countries, has not been immune to anti-Semitism, although the sentiment never seems to have become widespread or ripened into violence. To some scholars, Finnish anti-Semitism is a subset of a prevailing national xenophobia. According to Karmela Liebkind, a professor of social psychology at the University of Helsinki, "Finland is a distinctly xenophobic country and has been so for centuries" (Liebkind 1998). Tapani Harviainen, professor of Semitic languages at the University of Helsinki, notes: "The fact seems to remain that in the young Republic all minorities suffered from prejudice and xenophobia to some extent but evenly distributed" (Harviainen n.d.). He adds this interesting observation, which recalls Nazi ideology identifying Jews with Bolshevism: "a significant number of the Soviet leaders and well-known Bolsheviks were Jews, and this fact easily led people to the following conclusion: because he is a Jew he must be a Bolshevik, and as such an enemy of Finland."

Rautkallio acknowledges the "latent anti-Semitism to which no nation is totally immune" (1987, 84), and mentions the airing of anti-Semitic views by *Ajan Suunta* (Trend of the Times), published by the extreme right-wing IKL (*Isänmaallinen Kansanliike* = Patriotic People's Movement) (49). IKL became adept at using code words whose meaning was clear. IKL members of Parliament submitted an interpellation about the arrival of Jewish refugees in Finland, complaining that it was unreasonable for Finland to become the homeland of refugees "whose kinsmen hold decisively influential positions in both the political and economic life of big nations" (cited in Rautkallio 1987, 79). In case the IKL's meaning escaped anyone, it demanded to know specifically how many refugees were Jews (80).

Early advocacy of Jewish civil rights was met in some quarters with hostility (Rautkallio 1987, 11). Abusive references to Jews erupted in the national legislature only a few years before the turn of the century (17). Anti-Semitism in Finland from the late nineteenth to the early twentieth century must be viewed in the context of Finland's status as a dependency of Czarist Russia. Czar Nicholas II was notorious for his hatred of Jews, and the fifty years preceding Finland's independence were also an era of violent pogroms in Russia proper.

Finnish attitudes toward minorities in general and Jews in particular can be more accurately assessed in the relatively aseptic environment of the present era, in which Finland is prosperous, independent, and at peace. According to the Institute for Jewish Policy Research, post-war anti-Semitism has had limited currency in Finland, with no reports of violence. IJPR's 1997 report on Finland reports that in 1975 a Finnish translation of *The Protocols of the Elders of Zion* and other anti-Semitic books were published in Turku. In 1993, the report continues, 138 tombstones in the Turku Jewish cemetery were desecrated, prompting strong condemnation by both the government and the media.

In the copious correspondence of the Helsinki Jewish Community, now maintained by the Finland National Archives, the author found a single piece of correspondence directed to the community suggestive of anti-Semitism: a one-page typed letter dated 1 February 1941 and signed "Der Wächter Amos" with three handwritten crosses beneath. The letter, addressed to the rabbi of the community, accused certain unnamed Jews of "offenses and violations" ("Verfehlungen und Vergwaltigungen") against Finnish girls, who allegedly reported the misdeeds to the "Frauenkommite [sic] der N.D.S.A.P. [sic]". The writer admonished the rabbi to warn his congregation against such crimes, threatening that "sonst geht es wie in Deutschland" ("otherwise things would be as in Germany"), and all Jews would have to pay for the acts of a few lechers. The singularity of this document among the hundreds of pieces of correspondence in the files of the Helsinki Jewish Community is evidence of the rarity of overt anti-Jewish feeling in Finland at the time.

Current Finnish attitudes toward minorities in general are reflected in the *Report on Finland*, issued in 1997 by the European Commission against Racism and Intolerance (ECRI). This report, which was written by Professor Liebkind, cited above, devotes special attention to the Roma/Gypsy and the ethnically and linguistically distinct Lapland Saami communities. The report encourages greater police training in discrimination issues, relaxation of strict language requirements for employment, and the need for greater public commitment to combat racism. Since the cut-off date for data underpinning this report, there has been an influx of Somali refugees to Finland. The author has received anecdotal reports of racial tensions in areas where these refugees have settled.

The overall impression is that Finland, while not free of anti-Semitism and ethnic/racial tensions, including anti-Semitism, does not experience them widely. Conversations with prominent members of the Helsinki Jewish community have convinced the author that anti-Semitism is not now, and has not been within living memory, a source of serious concern to Finnish Jews. Even the emergence of the Jewish community from a life of small trade to economic prominence has not been accompanied by a rise in animosity toward its members. The absence of strong, indigenous anti-Semitic impulses furnishes the beginning of an explanation for the safety of the wartime Jewish community in Finland. However, other factors must be taken into account.

Finnish Awareness of Nazi Atrocities

Aside from the press reports cited above, there is evidence that Finns were aware of the breadth and extent of Nazi measures against the Jews in Germany and German-occupied lands. Just which Finns were aware of what is not always clear. What *is* clear is that government officialdom was on notice of these actions as early as the fall of 1941, owing to a visit officer Olavi Viherluoto, an officer of Valpo, the Finnish State Police. Two months earlier, the German *Heeresgruppe Nord* drove the Red Army out of Estonia. Viherluoto was in Estonia to interrogate Estonian communists about trips they had made to Finland. While there, Viherluoto met with Gestapo personnel. Conversations touched on the Jewish Question. Viherluoto asked his German interlocutors about the noticeable absence of Jews in Estonia, but was met with evasions. The grim details were disclosed ultimately, not by Gestapo personnel, but by openly anti-Semitic Estonian police collaborators, who reveled in narrating what had occurred. Viherluoto's report to Valpo recited that the Estonians, including one Mikson, had told him there were hardly any more Jews in Estonia. "All the male Jews have been shot.

After the capture of Tartu, 333,600 Jews and Communists were shot [...].
Mikson, that is, related that the same morning I had last visited the central
prison they had taken 80 Jews in trucks into the woods, ordered them to
kneel down at the edge of a pit and shot them from behind" (Rautkallio
1987, 135).

Rautkallio, disposed to judge Finnish action and inaction benignly,
acknowledges (1987, 136) that Valpo knew of the atrocities by virtue of the
Viherluoto report, but concludes that Valpo viewed these events as an anom-
aly, more characteristic of Estonian virulence toward the Jews than representative of explicit German policy. At his post-war trial, Valpo chief Arno
Anthoni insisted that, although he had seen the report, he never read it. The
absence of documentary evidence of specific knowledge means little. It is
unlikely that Viherluoto, clearly affected by what he had learned, could have
refrained from orally relating the grisly details to his colleagues.

Less than a month after Viherluoto's Estonia trip, his boss Anthoni went
to Tallinn as guest of the Gestapo and met with local Gestapo chief Martin
Sandberger. This began the collaboration between Anthoni and the Gestapo
for the exchange of information about refugees and political prisoners.
Anthoni later denied that his interactions with Sandberger involved the
Jewish Question, but later events dispel any residual doubt about Anthoni's
knowledge of the Final Solution.

Anthoni's Collaboration with the Gestapo

The Wannsee Conference took place 20 January 1942. Thereafter, extermination of Europe's Jews was the express policy of the Third Reich. At
Heydrich's official invitation, Anthoni made his first trip to Berlin two and
one-half months after Wannsee. These meetings focused on "close collaboration between the State police organizations of the two countries"
(Rautkallio 1987, 153). Was the Jewish Question included in this "close collaboration"? Rautkallio notes that Heydrich himself was out of the country
at the time, implying that Heydrich's absence precluded consideration of the
Jewish Question. This inference is weakened by the presence of Gestapo
chief Heinrich Müller, whose sphere of activity certainly included the Final
Solution. Any doubt is further dispelled by the post-war evidence of
Friedrich Pantzinger, a high official of the German security police.
Pantzinger testified that the Gestapo demanded placement of all Jewish
Finnish citizens in German custody and described Anthoni as quite willing
to comply. Anthoni agreed that "the Jews should be surrendered to the

Gestapo" (Rautkallio 1987, 156-57). Müller was among the fifteen participants in the Wannsee Conference. With the deadly resolves of that meeting fresh in his mind, it is improbable that Müller ignored Finland's Jews during Anthoni's visits.

Nazi Demands

Did the Nazis demand the surrender of Finland's Jews? This is a central issue in what little scholarly debate exists about the status of the Finnish Jewish community during the war. Cohen and Svensson's article (1995, 70) has this headnote:

> This article discusses how the Finns turned over foreign Jews to Nazi Germany in November 1942. The article explores the possibility that the extradition was part of a much larger intended delivery of foreign and Finnish Jews into Nazi hands and provides an alternative interpretation to Hannu Rautkallio's *Finland and the Holocaust*, the only work on this subject in English.

Rautkallio had concluded that the Nazis "left Finland out of their *Endlösung* grand design" (1987, 259) and characterizes as a "myth that the SS leadership and Hitler himself had actually demanded the handing over of Finland's Jewish population" (257).

Cohen and Svensson dispute Rautkallio's contention that the Nazis put no pressure on Finland to abandon its Jews to them. It should be noted that William Cohen is the son of a survivor Dr. Walter Cohen, whose allegedly abrasive behavior while a refugee in Finland is extensively covered by Rautkallio (1987, 180-201). Cohen and Svensson cite a February 1943 communication from German Foreign Office Undersecretary Martin Luther, who, as noted above, was quoted in the Wannsee Protocol as worried about Scandinavian resistance to the Final Solution. Luther replied to concerns expressed by Berlin's minister in Helsinki, that Germany's Jewish policies were arousing Finnish public opinion. Luther replied, urging the envoy to remind the Finns that "the struggle against Bolshevism also represents in every regard a struggle against Jewry" (Cohen and Svensson 1995, 83, quoting from Browning 1978, 153). This is hardly tantamount to a demand for Finland's Jews, although it shows that Finland was not exempt from Germany's anti-Jewish policies. Rautkallio dismisses the exchange out of hand, saying that the minister "apparently imagined" that the SS and Himmler were exerting pressure on Finland with respect to its Jews and "was, of course, mistaken" (1987, 253).

Himmler Visits Finland

Reichsführer-SS Heinrich Himmler, with his control of the police mechanism, wielded power in the Third Reich second only to Hitler. Himmler's unswerving commitment to the Final Solution is beyond question. His willingness to negotiate the freedom of Jewish prisoners with the Allies through the Swedish Red Cross came about only as it became obvious to Himmler that the war was lost (Koblik 1988, 117-140). He visited Finland in late July and early August 1942, apparently at the urging of his masseur, Felix Kersten, a Finnish national.

Felix Kersten, an ethnic German, was born a Russian subject in Estonia in 1898 and became a Finnish national in 1920 after fighting in Finland's war of liberation from Russia. He studied manual therapy under a Chinese practitioner and rendered professional services to the titled and wealthy in Germany and the Netherlands. In 1939, a patient recommended him to Himmler, who suffered chronically from stomach cramps. Conventional medical treatment had been ineffective. Kersten, after five minutes of manual therapy, was able to relieve the pains and thereafter advanced to a position of frequent resort by Himmler and, if Kersten is to be credited, to that of confidant as well.

Kersten has been the focus of vigorous controversy. He contends in his memoirs that he exerted a decisive influence over Himmler with respect to the Jewish Question and claims credit for saving Finland's Jews. Kersten, according to Rautkallio, "has spun yarns as well as altering, adding, and eliminating facts" (1987, 164). Rautkallio's cynicism toward Kersten was not shared by the World Jewish Congress, which credited him with saving 3,500 Jewish lives. (Letter from General Secretary A. Leon Kubowitzki to Kersten, 4 December 1946, cited by Rautkallio 1987, 61, fn. 67). He received as well the endorsement of H. R. Trevor-Roper who considered it "well attested" that "thousands of Dutchmen, Germans, Jews and indeed others owe their survival to his intercession" (Kersten 1957, intro., 11). Among other claims, Kersten has asserted credit for saving the Netherlands from an alleged plan by Hitler to deport the entire population to Poland in a pique over riots in Amsterdam in February 1941 (Kersten 1957, 172-175). This claim is painstakingly examined and questioned by Dutch historian and journalist Louis De Jong who also attacks Trevor-Roper's account of Kersten's exploits (De Jong 1974).

Kersten's memoirs have been published in several languages. The author has examined the English, German and Swedish memoirs, entitled respectively, *The Kersten Memoirs*, *Totenkopf und Treue*, and *Samtal med Himmler*, as they pertain to Himmler's voyage to Finland and Kersten's claimed part in thwarting German designs on the Finnish Jewish population. (References hereinafter to "the English memoir," "the German memoir," and "the Swedish memoir" are to these three works respectively.) The three memoirs are not identical. An earlier English memoir appeared in 1947 in the United States entitled *The Memoirs of Doctor Felix Kersten*. The Swedish memoir was an edition derived from the 1947 book and was examined and corrected by Kersten. The English and German memoirs are essentially the same, except for the omission from the English edition of certain entire entries contained in the German. The Swedish memoir stands apart textually and, unlike the other two, is not in diary form. It quotes Himmler as saying that Hitler planned to deport the Finnish Jews to Maidanek. The other two versions make no mention of a specific destination. A typed report by Kersten on letterhead of the Netherlands Red Cross, entitled *Memorandum über meine Hilfstätigkeit in den Jahren 1940-45* and dated 12 June 1945 in Stockholm, is held by the Netherlands Institute for War Documentation. In a section entitled *Die Judenfrage in Finland [sic]* Kersten asserts that Himmler's trip to Finland was ordered by Hitler "*u.a.*" (among other things) to demand the delivery of Finland's Jews.

Himmler's appointment book, previously available to archive researchers, is now generally available, having been published in Germany in1999 as *Der Dienstkalendar Heinrich Himmlers 1941/42*. It includes, in addition to entries from Himmler's own calendar, extracts from the daily calendars of Himmler's personal secretary Rudolf Brandt and his military adjutant Werner Grothmann. Equipped with copious notes by its editors, the *Dienstkalendar* is an essential check on Kersten's narrative of the Finland trip. De Jong makes much of chronological errors in Kersten's accounts. Comparison of Kersten's narrative with Himmler's *Dienstkalendar* does in fact suggest some dating errors, although the Kersten's chronology is, in the main, consistent with Himmler's. Discrepancies between dates and times given by Kersten and those in the *Dienstkalendar* do not necessarily refute Kersten. Schedules are not always adhered to, and the *Dienstkalendar* is a plan, not a journal. On the other hand, there is no reason to suspect secondary motives in making entries in the *Dienstkalendar*. The same cannot be said with assurance about Kersten's own accounts, created after the war when the actions and motives of people close to Himmler would be under scrutiny.

According to Kersten's diary, Himmler's trip to Finland was undertaken partly to discuss the Jewish Question with high Finnish officials (Kersten 1957, 141). In what Rautkallio calls "another version" of the incident, Kersten refers to a conversation in which Himmler relates an order from Hitler to fly to Finland to demand surrender of the Jews (Rautkallio 1987,

160). This likely refers to the Stockholm *Memorandum*, as previously noted. According to Rautkallio, "Himmler wanted information on certain matters pertaining to the Finnish economy" (1987, 162). It is doubtful that the second most powerful man in Germany would make a field trip to Finland in the middle of the war to collect economic data. At the very least, the trip had a ceremonial purpose. Himmler was received by Prime Minister J. W. Rangell, President Risto Ryti, and Marshal Mannerheim. Waffen-SS General Karl Wolff, who accompanied Himmler on the trip to look after the provision of Finnish Waffen-SS units, was to receive an unspecified "high Finnish decoration" from President Ryti, while Himmler was to be awarded the Great Cross of the Finnish Freedom War by Marshal Mannerheim. These planned ceremonials are related in the German memoir, but not in the English.

Five days before arriving in Finland, Kersten reports, Himmler said that they were going to Finland to "talk over" the Jewish question with Ryti and Foreign Minister Rolf Johann Witting. Noting that Finland's bread stocks would only last another three weeks, Himmler said that the Finns would have to choose between hunger and delivering up their Jews. Kersten appealed to Himmler's sense of humanity and comradeship in arms with the Finns, to which Himmler rejoined: "Hier gibt es kein Wenn und kein Aber. Hier muß sich Finnland fügen" ("On this there can be no ifs and buts about this. Finland must give in on this.") (Kersten 1952, 172).

The Finland voyage began on 29 July 1942 with a flight from Reval (Tallinn). Himmler was scheduled to arrive in Helsinki at 9:30 a.m. with a reception by President Ryti at 12:30 p.m. (Himmler 1999, 502). In the German memoir, Kersten reports that they actually landed at 12:30 p.m. and that Himmler had suffered an attack of stomach pain en route, requiring treatment by Kersten, who took the opportunity to advise his master that it would be pointless to raise the Jewish question at the start and that he should confine himself first to getting acquainted. Kersten describes the Ryti reception as a lunch, following which Himmler went immediately to his hotel with his stomach pains.

That day or the next – the chronology is unclear – Kersten tells of a private conversation about German designs on the Finnish Jews that he had with Foreign Minister Witting. This alleged conversation is key to Kersten's claimed role in shielding Finland's Jews from deportation. In the English and German memoirs, under the respective headings "*Surrender of the Finnish Jews*" and "*Die Auslieferung der finnischen Juden*", no date is given. In the Swedish memoir, the conversation is said to have taken place immediately after the lunch with President Ryti, which would place it the day of

Himmler's and Kersten's arrival in Finland, 29 July. In both the English and German memoir, Kersten fixes the conversation at a time when Himmler was at his hotel and says it occurred without his knowledge. The German memoir has a footnote by Kersten that this section was taken from his concluding report to the Swedish government. The disparate provenance of this section of the memoir and its apparent derivation from a source other than Kersten's diary, may explain the absence of a date. It may also invite suspicion of some revisionism prompted by post-war memory cleansing. Kersten's efforts to secure Swedish citizenship were delayed for eight years owing in part to strong opinion against him in some quarters in that country (Koblik 1988, 120-121).

At all events, the conversation as set out in all three memoirs is essentially to the same effect. Kersten and Witting agreed that the Jewish problem was best handled by procrastination, without open opposition by the Finns. Kersten saw two possible avenues: (1) explain to Himmler that surrendering the Jews would require an act of Parliament, which Kersten asserted or believed, apparently erroneously, would not meet again in regular session for another three months; (2) emphasize that the Finns had no sympathy with measures against the Jews, especially where Jews had fought and died in the Winter War ("No Finn would understand how anyone could be willing to surrender the mothers and wives of such men;" Kersten 1957, 144), and that handing the Jews over to Germany would embitter public opinion in Finland. Kersten and Witting agreed that Finland should feign a willingness to call the Parliament into special session if necessary. The critical food shortage in Finland created a pressure point that Germany could bring to bear on Finland. Although not mentioned by Kersten, it would also have been obvious that Germany was dependent on Finland's co-belligerency with Germany in the prosecution of the war against the Soviet Union in Karelia, thereby affording Finland its own leverage.

The following day Kersten engaged in a ruse with Himmler. Himmler told Kersten he now planned to discuss the Jewish question with the Finnish Government. Kersten suggested that Himmler allow Kersten, as a Finn, to sound out opinion in a preliminary talk with Witting and Rangell. In light of these conversations, Himmler could decide on further action. Himmler agreed, and Kersten absented himself for sufficient time to permit such a conversation with Witting and Rangell – which of course did not take place – to be conducted. He then returned to Himmler, assuring him that both ministers shared his outlook in principle, but still "harboured doubts about the immediate technical procedure" (Kersten 1957, 145). Kersten then reports that Himmler at once telephoned Hitler and brought him up to date.

Hitler was supposedly satisfied and agreeable to putting the issue off until November, when the Parliament would meet again. If Kersten's subterfuge took place on 30 July, the day after arrival in Finland, the day was a busy one and one in which Himmler came into conflict with his Finnish hosts on yet another matter.

The *Dienstkalendar* (Grothmann's entry) shows that Himmler was to have a late breakfast at the German Embassy at 12:30 p.m., and leave for Mikkeli, where Marshal Mannerheim was headquartered, at 5:00 p.m. This would have left little time for the charade planned by Kersten. According to Kersten's entry for 30 July, Witting was present in the garden of the Embassy talking with Kersten, when Himmler suddenly joined them to talk about ocean exploration. In the middle of that conversation, Kersten writes, Himmler suddenly switched the topic to Sweden, proposing that Germany and Finland reach an understanding about Sweden to give Northern Sweden, where many Finns live, to Finland, with Germany to occupy and ultimately annex central and southern Sweden. Himmler said that Hitler believed he had made a mistake by not occupying Sweden at the same time as Norway. Witting reacted sharply to this proposal and made it clear that Finland had no interest in any plots against Swedish sovereignty, especially in view of the help Sweden had given Finland in the Winter War. Hitler's alleged designs against Sweden are not surprising for several reasons, among them, German dependence on Swedish ore, Hitler's irritation with criticism from the free Swedish press, Sweden's opposition to Finland's participation in the war against the Soviet Union, Sweden's neutrality, and its policy of granting refuge to Jews, including half of Norway's Jews (Koblik 1988, 22, 23, 32, 33, and *passim*). Sweden's neutrality was especially annoying to Hitler, as suggested by the Nazi slogan "wer nicht mit uns ist, ist gegen uns" ("who is not with us is against us"). Sweden's frantic efforts to avoid provoking Germany while, at the same time, official and unofficial voices were expressing dismay at German racial policies underscore Sweden's perilous position in the midst of the European conflict. Finland's alleged rebuff to Himmler's suggested initiative against Sweden is equally unsurprising in view of the historical ties between Finland and Sweden, as well as the large ethnic Swedish population within Finland. What *is* surprising, however, is Kersten's implication that a harsh word from a Finnish foreign minister was sufficient to cause Hitler to abandon plans to occupy Sweden. In fact, according to Kersten's narrative, Himmler, after hearing Witting's reaction, retreated behind an assertion that he had been expressing his private thoughts only, in effect distancing Hitler from them and asking Witting and Kersten to keep this conversation a secret among the three of them (Kersten

1957, 143). This account has been accepted by Ackermann (1970, 190-191), citing Kersten's *Totenkopf und Treue* without comment.

The historical accuracy of Kersten's account of the conversation between Himmler and Witting about Sweden must be questioned. Although Himmler was capable of going behind Hitler when Germany's defeat was imminent by attempting independent negotiations with the Allies, it is unlikely that, on the one hand, Himmler would have broached so delicate and radical a proposal as invasion of Sweden with the Finnish Foreign Minister absent Hitler's approval or, on the other hand, that the enterprise would so quickly have been abandoned. Kersten's dating of this alleged conversation as 30 July also seems to conflict with the timing of the ploy Kersten says he perpetrated on Himmler with respect to the fictional meeting with Witting and Rangell about the Jews. Since the account of that ruse appears to derive from a report to the Swedish government at a time when Kersten was exerting himself to obtain Swedish citizenship in the face of severe criticism from within that country, it would be naïve to receive it without reservation.

There is reason, independent of Kersten's evidence, to believe that the question of Finland's Jews surfaced at least once again during Himmler's visit. From the evening of 30 July to 2 August, Himmler's appointment book shows that he traveled to Mannerheim's headquarters in Mikkeli, thence north to Lapland where German units were stationed, then to Oulu, where he inspected a German infantry regiment, and finally south to the Hämeenlinna region, where, on the evening of 2 August, he traveled to the island of Petäys, about 120 kilometers north of Helsinki. On Petäys, Himmler occupied a summer house, apparently arranged by Kersten as a private hideaway. The *Dienstkalendar* (Grothmann's entry) discloses that on 4 August, Himmler traveled to another island where Prime Minister Rangell was staying. During a conversation with Rangell, Himmler is said to have raised the issue of Finland's Jews, to which Rangell reportedly replied: "Wir haben keine Judenfrage" (We have no Jewish question). Rangell's alleged declaration to Himmler, whether historical or not, is reported in many accounts of the period. A footnote in the *Dienstkalendar* (Himmler 1999, 506, n. 7) cites Himmler scholar Richard Brietman for the proposition that "Himmler sprach Rangell auf Finnlands Haltung zu den einheimischen Juden an und forderte deren Ausgrenzung, was Rangell mit Hinweis auf deren vollständige und unproblematische Assimilation ablehnte." ("Himmler approached Rangell about Finland's posture with respect to its indigenous Jews, insisting on their exclusion. Rangell referred to their complete and unproblematic assimilation and rejected the idea.") Brietman does not give a source for this statement, but Rautkallio (1987, 168, n. 106) ascribes it to a statement by Rangell himself, made during an interrogation in 1947 and an interview thirteen years later. Cohen and Svensson (1995, 75) and Rautkallio (1987, 166) quote a Valpo report that Himmler raised the Jewish issue with Rangell, but that the Valpo official who overheard this "could not hear Prime Minister Rangell's response."

Rautkallio reports that years later "some surprising features" connected with Himmler's trip were discovered, but that "so far it has not been possible to substantiate them" (168). The "surprising features" relate to an incident where some Finnish soldiers photographed the contents of Himmler's briefcase "with all its interesting papers" (168-69). Rautkallio gives no details and predicts that what he characterizes as a detective story "will probably remain a mere curiosity" (169).

A typescript bearing the name of Captain Veikko Sjöblom may cast some light on the "detective story." This typescript was given to the author by Harry Matso, general secretary of the Jewish War Veterans of Finland in Helsinki on 21 October 1998. An article on the same subject by the same author was published in the organ of the Federation of Finnish War Veterans, *Sotaveteraani* (The War Veteran), April 1994, p. 41, under the title "*Suomen vastavakoilu kaappasi Himmlerin salkun*" (Finnish counterintelligence snatches Himmler's briefcase"). Sjöblom, according to the typescript, served in Finnish counterintelligence. The typescript describes various activities during Himmler's visit as well as the briefcase escapade. It is unclear from the typescript which of the events there described Sjöblom witnessed and which he is repeating from hearsay. The context in which the briefcase episode is described suggests that Sjöblom participated in it: "The briefcase contained, not documents regarding SS-troops fighting on the Northern front, but information identifying 2,300 Finnish citizens of Jewish origin. This was immediately related to the President [Ryti], the Commander-in-Chief [Mannerheim], and the Prime Minister [Rangell]."

Taken at face value, the report supports an inference that Finland's Jews were on Himmler's agenda. On the other hand, the reference to "information identifying 2,300 Finnish citizens of Jewish origin" prompts skepticism: 2,300 is the precise figure given in the Wannsee Protocol for the population of Finnish Jews, a number that was almost certainly exaggerated by at least four hundred. According to Attorney Sari Laitinen of Minneapolis, who kindly translated this document for the author, the Finnish original she rendered in the quoted extract as "information" (*henkilötietod*) implies at least a basic level of detail, such as names and addresses. If there were fewer than 2,300 Jews in Finland, where would names and addresses for 2,300 have come from?

The typescript goes on to describe meetings between Himmler and Rangell and Himmler and Mannerheim. Sjöblom tells how Rangell took Himmler for a trip to Rangell's villa, presumably the island home near Petäys. During the trip, Himmler tried to initiate discussion of the Jewish Question, but Rangell quickly changed the subject. The conversation with Mannerheim on this subject is reported to have terminated more decisively. According to Sjöblom, Mannerheim replied firmly to Himmler's initiation of discussion about the Jews: "Not even one single Jewish soldier will be taken from my army to be turned over to Germany. That cannot happen except over my dead body."

Mannerheim's resolute response to Himmler is in character. According to a Valpo report cited by Rautkallio (1987, 163), the imperious marshal made an overpowering impression on Himmler. Indeed, there is evidence that Mannerheim was held in awe by Hitler himself, who flew to Finland earlier that year to congratulate Mannerheim on his seventy-fifth birthday (Erfurth 1979, 157). Whatever the exact words spoken on that occasion, Mannerheim's part in shielding Finland's Jews from Germany is widely acknowledged (Elazar 1984, 136; Encyc. Jud. 1971, 1298). Professor Liebkind told the author: "Finland is very often dependent on single individuals in crucial positions. . . .Such individuals – and no form of popular sentiment – was the only thing that rescued Finns [i.e., Finnish Jews] during the war. Mannerheim was one of those [...]" (Liebkind, 1998).

Raul Hilberg (1985, vol. 2, 447), quoting a communication from Adolf Eichmann to one von Thadden in the Foreign Office points out that as late as 5 July 1943, Eichmann set a deadline of 3 August 1943 for application of the Final Solution to ten laggard countries, including not only neutral Switzerland and Sweden, but also partner-in-arms Finland. Hilberg adds (fn. 87) that "Finland, an Axis partner, was the only European ally that was never pressured into deporting its Jews." While Germany may never have threatened Finland, it seems clear that German officials charged with implementing the Final Solution never abandoned Finland as a target. It remains to seek an explanation for the undeniable fact that, as Hilberg puts it (554) "the destruction process never did reach remote and independent Finland."

How were Finland's Jews Saved?

Simple explanations are tempting, but usually wrong. Many factors combined to exempt Finland's Jews from the Final Solution.

1. *Finland's status as a voluntary co-belligerent.* While Finland never embraced Nazi ideology or the whole of German war aims, it shared a common enemy: the Soviet Union. Finland was a vital element of Hitler's tacti-

cal designs on the U. S.S.R., controlling the land approaches to Leningrad from the north and bordering on the sea approach via the Gulf of Finland to the west. Although Finland's participation in the mutual war effort with Germany was limited to that region of the Eastern Front where Finnish territory was in play, participation was vigorous and enthusiastic. Hitler's admiration for Mannerheim, as well as the esteem in which Finnish soldiers were held by their German counterparts, may have moderated Nazi plots against Finland's Jews. As German liaison chief Waldemar Erfurth wrote: "The Finnish brother-in-arms were highly respected everywhere in Germany and their performance for the common cause honestly appreciated" (100). Erfurth noted that there was an impression in Germany that the Finns could get whatever they wanted from Hitler. It is not likely that Germany's complaisance toward the Finns rested so much on sentiment as on geopolitical necessity. As counterpoint, however, it must be remembered that in Italy, an avowed ally of Germany with respect to all its war aims, over 7,500 Jews were lost to the Final Solution.

2. *The small size of Finland's Jewish community.* According to Gideon Bolotowsky, chairman of the Central Council of Jewish Communities in Finland, Finland's Jews never reached "critical mass" sufficient to warrant German attention. Germany placed greater weight on maintaining a good working relationship with Finland than on an anti-Jewish initiative that would risk disrupting the military collaboration by arousing public and official Finnish opposition (Bolotowsky, 1998). But small size did not protect the Jews of Norway, thirteen hundred according to the Wannsee Protocol. About half of Norway's Jews perished.

3. *The free press.* Despite government anxiety about German anger at press reports, the Finnish press remained generally untrammeled during the war. Finns were told of German measures against the Jews. Frank press reports from Sweden were also widely read in Finland. In both Sweden and Finland, however, the government sought to moderate press reports critical of Germany.

4. *Opposition of Finnish leaders.* Two prominent members of the cabinet, K A. Fagerholm and Väinö Tanner – both leaders of the dominant Social Democratic Party – opposed measures against the Jews. They were joined by Prime Minister Rangell and Marshall Mannerheim. Less prominent Finns also played a part. Tanner, in his memoir of the Winter War (Tanner 1957, 136), relates how Santeri Jakobsson, mayor of Lauritsala, not far from the Karelian Isthmus, went to Sweden to rally support for the Jews. Tanner adds sympathetically: "The trip cost Jakobsson his official position in Lauritsala." As early as February 1939, Finnish and Swedish language newspapers in

Finland carried an open appeal to readers to furnish financial assistance to Jewish refugees. Bishop Aleksi Lehtonen of Tampere was one of the signers (Rautkallio 1987, 83). It should be added that, while Bolotowsky credits Tanner and Fagerholm, he is not convinced that Mannerheim deserves credit. Bolotowsky told the author that Abraham Stiller, wartime head of the Helsinki Jewish community, related to Bolotowsky how he (Stiller) went disguised as a clergyman to Mannerheim to seek help in protecting the Jews. Mannerheim replied, according to Stiller, that he had no influence in the matter.

5. *Swedish public opinion.* Sweden preserved its wartime neutrality by walking a thin line between overt opposition to German racial policies and avoiding provocation that might lead to a German attack. The same considerations moderated the activism of Sweden's state Lutheran Church, whose chief prelate, Archbishop Erling Eidem, was in a continual dilemma between strong antipathy to Nazi racial policies and patriotic resolve to refrain from compromising Sweden's delicate relationship with Germany (Koblik 1988, 79-115). Sweden supplied iron ore to Germany and had granted Germany transit rights for its troops traveling from occupied Norway to Finland. Certain elements of the Swedish press were outspoken, a fact that did not escape high German authority in Finland (Erfurth 1979, 153-54). There is evidence that opinion in Sweden may have restrained the Soviet Union both in its wartime and post-war policy toward Finland (Nevakivi 1994, 114 and fn. 81). Swedish public opinion may have moderated German, as well as Soviet, conduct in Finland

6. *Low profile of Finnish Jews.* Nazi propaganda trumpeting allegations of pervasive Jewish economic influence would have had little resonance in wartime Finland. The Jews of that era were mostly small businessmen with little effect on the Finnish economy (Bolotowsky 1988). In few European countries did the indigenous Jewish population play so small an economic and political rôle. Demonizing such an inconspicuous community would have been unconvincing.

7. *Rarity of overt anti-Semitism.* Anti-Semitism was a minor current in the flow of Finnish life. When Jewish refugees began to arrive in the late '30s, there were isolated eruptions of anti-Jewish sentiment among the urban intelligentsia. This may have flowed from worry about competition from among the refugees (Bolotowsky 1998). Whatever subterranean anti-Semitism existed in Finland was never enough to burst into overt action or popular calls for measures against the Jews.

8. *Jewish participation in Finland's wars.* The Finnish leadership resisted Nazi schemes against the Jews largely because Finns recognized and acknowl-

edged Jewish patriotism. Finland's wartime activities were grounded on a steadfast commitment to its territorial integrity. All other considerations were subordinate. Mannerheim's open homage to the Jewish community in 1944 shows that patriotism overcame any impulse to accommodate the ideology of Finland's co-belligerents. Finland could hardly be expected to view Jews who were loyally fighting and dying for their country as suspicious aliens. Nazi liturgy calculated to cast Jews in that rôle would have conflicted with the wartime experience of ordinary Finns. It must be added, however, that by the time of Mannerheim's visit to the synagogue, an armistice had been concluded between Finland and the U.S.S.R., a condition of which was Finnish cooperation in driving the remaining German troops out of Finland.

Rautkallio does not offer an explicit answer, although he implies that there were two reasons the Finnish Jews were spared: (1) Finland's commitment to Western democracy and individual rights, and (2) the military collaboration with Germany (1987, 169-70). The latter indisputably played a prominent part in the salvation of the country's Jews. But the commitment to democracy, while genuine, furnished uncertain support. France, the Netherlands, Belgium, and Norway all had democratic traditions whose longevity dwarfed that of Finland, independent and democratic for only twenty years. Democratic traditions did not shield French, Dutch, Belgian, and Norwegian Jews. In France, which arguably gave birth to the very notion of individual human and political rights, over sixty-four thousand Jews were delivered to their deaths. The Netherlands, a bastion of liberalism, saw over one hundred thousand murdered.

Finland erected few obstacles to full integration of its Jewish population. Yet, pre-war Germany, in which Jews largely assimilated for generations had figured prominently in business, the professions, scholarship, and the arts, had a history of official and semi-official anti-Semitic initiatives long pre-dating Hitler. Assimilation was flimsy armor against anti-Semitism.

When the evidence is examined impartially – to the extent that impartiality is possible in this context – it appears that the salvation of Finland's Jews rested not on generalized nobility of the Finnish people or on any single broad feature of Finnish culture. Rather, the accident of Finland's situation between two warring totalitarian powers, combined with Finland's decision to make Germany's cause her own to a strictly limited extent, together with a recognition by Finland's leaders of the participation of the Jews in that effort won Finnish Jews a reprieve that, happily, outlasted the Third Reich. Had Germany won the war, or even defeated the U.S.S.R., there is no reason whatever to suppose that Germany would have spared Finland's Jews the fate of their brothers and sisters in all other lands where the Third Reich held sway.

As Livson and Matso wrote: "whoever conquered Finland the Jews would be the losers." The Jews' safety lay ultimately in an independent Finland.

Note

The author acknowledges with thanks a generous grant from the Finlandia Foundation Trust which helped defray research costs. He also acknowledges with thanks the special assistance of the Finland National Archives and the Netherlands Institute for War Documentation.

Literature Cited

Ackermann, Josef. 1970. *Heinrich Himmler als Ideologe*. Göttingen: Musterschmidt.

Bolotowsky, Gideon. 1998. Interview with author. Helsinki, 18 October.

Browning, Christopher R. 1978. *The Final Solution and the German Foreign Office*. New York: Holmes & Meier.

Cohen, S. Ralph. "Scandinavia's Jewish Communities." *The American Scandinavian Review* 56, no. 2 (1968): 125-35.

Cohen, William B. and Svensson, Jörgen. 1995. "Finland and the Holocaust." *Holocaust and Genocide Studies* 9, no. 1: 70-92

De Jong, Louis. 1974. "Hat Felix Kersten das niederländische Volk gerettet?" trans. from the Dutch original ("Heeft Felix Kersten het Nederlandse volk gered?") by Marianne Holberg, in *Zwei Legenden aus dem Dritten Reich* (Stuttgart: Deutsche Verlags-Anstalt).

Elazar, Daniel J., Liberles, Adina Weiss, and Weiner, Simcha. 1984. *The Jewish Communities of Scandinavia*. Lanham, Maryland: University Press of America.

Encyclopaedia Judaica. 1971. "Finland." Jerusalem: MacMillan.

Erfurth, Waldemar. 1979. *The Last Finnish War*. Washington, D.C.: University Publications of America, Inc.

European Commission against Racism and Intolerance. 1997. "Report on Finland." Strasbourg.

Harviainen, Tapani. "The Jews of Finland and World War II." Typescript, n.d.

Hilberg, Raul. 1985. *The Destruction of the European Jews*. Rev. ed. New York: Holmes & Meier.

Himmler, Heinrich. 1999. *Der Dienstkalendar Heinrich Himmlers 1941/42*. ed. Peter Witte et al. Hamburg: Christians.

Institute for Jewish Policy Research and American Jewish Committee. "Finland." *Antisemitism World Report 1997*.

Kersten, Felix. 1945. *Memorandum über meine Hilfstätigkeit in den Jahren 1940-45*. Typescript. (Stockholm) (in possession of the Netherlands Institute for War Documentation, Amsterdam).

Kersten, Felix. 1947. *Samtal med Himmler*. Stockholm: LJUS.

Kersten, Felix. 1952. *Totenkopf und Treue*. Hamburg: Robert Mölich.

Kersten, Felix. 1957. *The Kersten Memoirs*. Intro. H. R. Trevor-Roper. New York: MacMillan.

Koblik, Steven. 1988. *The Stones Cry Out: Sweden's Response to the Persecution of the Jews, 1933-1945*. New York: Holocaust Library.

Liebkind, Karmela. 1998. Personal e-mail to author. 19 January.

Livson, Aron and Matso, Harry. 1995. "Jewish War Veterans of Finland." One-page typescript.

Nevakivi, Jukka. 1994. "A Decisive Armistice 1944-1947: Why was Finland not Sovietized?" *Scandinavian Journal of History* 19, no. 2: 91-115.

Rautkallio, Hannu. 1987. *Finland and the Holocaust: The Rescue of Finland's Jews*. Trans. Paul Sjöblom. New York: Holocaust Library.

Rautkallio, Hannu. 1989. *Suomen juutalaisten aseveljeys* (The Finnish-Jewish Brotherhood-in-Arms; summary in English). Helsinki: Tammi.

Sjöblom, Veikko. "Suomen vastavakoilu valokopioi Himmlerin salkun asiakirjat – Marskalkka torjui vaatimuksen juutalaisten luovuttamisesta" (Finland's counter-intelligence photocopied documents in Himmler's briefcase – Marshal rejected demand to turn over Jews). Unpublished and undated typescript.

Suominen, Elina. 1979. *Kuoleman laiva S/S/ Hohenhörn* (The Death Ship S/S/ Hohenhörn). Helsinki: Söderström.

Tanner, Väinö. 1957. *The Winter War*. trans. Stanford, California: Stanford University Press.

Upton, Anthony F. 1965. *Finland in Crisis*. Ithaca, New York: Cornell University Press.

Wannsee Protocol. 1982. *The Holocaust*, 22 vols. New York: Garland.

Fact, Fiction, Truth, Lies

The Rights of Imagination and the Rights of History in Four Holocaust Accounts

David Scrase

In the 1990s the world of Holocaust survivors, scholars, and Holocaust autobiography was shaken by numerous scandals. Several individuals, four of whom I wish to examine here, were exposed as less than completely honest in their writings that centered on the Holocaust or on their own lives during the Holocaust. Three of these authors wrote in German: Wolfgang Koeppen (1906-1996), Stephan Hermlin (1915-1997), and Binjamin Wilkomirski (1941-); the fourth – Jerzy Kosinski (1933-1991) in English. All but Wilkomirski were established writers. An examination of these four authors, who are all so different yet who all faced similar accusations in regard to their use of the Holocaust and to matters autobiographical, reveals the scandals as, in essence, overblown. Yet, the persistent accusations against the authors raise larger questions about the relationship between the Holocaust and that category of writing we call by various names, including autobiography, memoir, and autobiographical fiction.

The scandal involving Wolfgang Koeppen began quietly in 1992 but really dates back to the immediate post-war years. In 1948 a book appeared with the title *Notes From the Underground [Aufzeichnungen aus einem Erdloch]*. Its author was given as Jakob Littner. *Notes From the Underground* was published in Munich by Herbert Kluger (1895-1962), who had just founded a publishing house that he ran from his two-room apartment. The book describes how Jakob Littner, an assimilated Jewish stamp-dealer in Munich, sought to escape deportation, but was continually overtaken by the Germans as he moved from one Central European city to the next. After eking out a wretched living in the ghetto of Zbaracz in the Ukraine, he, together with others, was forced underground, literally. Hiding in subterranean holes, the small group was finally liberated by the Red Army in March 1944.

Although the book attracted the attention of none other than Gerald Reitlinger, a pioneer in Holocaust writing, whose reaction was very positive (Reitlinger 1953, 271), it did not enjoy any great success and was soon forgotten. A facsimile reprint of this 1948 work came out in 1985, published by Kupfergraben. This too showed no immediate signs of being successful. By the end of the 1980s it was no longer available.

In the 1950s Koeppen had published three novels, which, as a trilogy casting a critical eye on the development of the new Federal Republic of Germany, had established his reputation as a major post-war writer. More novels, eagerly awaited by both readers and critics did not, however, materialize. Works were occasionally announced as in progress, with titles even (e.g. *Ein Maskenball, Tasso,* and *Das Schiff*), but none was published. Journalists and critics began to speak about "the Koeppen syndrome" – i.e., the drying-up of a major talent. Koeppen's publisher, Suhrkamp, did its best to extract a new work from him, and when, in the late 1980s, the head of Suhrkamp, Siegfried Unseld, somehow learned of Koeppen's role in the Littner work, a new publication of the book under Koeppen's name seemed ideal. Suhrkamp accordingly acquired the rights to "Jakob Littner's" book, removed it from the market and made plans to bring out the exact same book but under the authorship of Wolfgang Koeppen.

The Suhrkamp Verlag was at this time in the process of taking over and resuscitating the Jüdischer Verlag, which had recently shut down operations. Unseld felt that no better book could be found to re-establish Germany's Jewish publishing house than the *Notes* under the authorship of the legendary Wolfgang Koeppen – "legendary" because of his distinguished writing *and* the long years of relative silence since 1957, when his last major work had appeared. Koeppen agreed, but only to a posthumous publication, apparently foreseeing copyright if not moral difficulties (Fiedler 1999, 104; Zachau 1999, 116 et seq.). Somehow, Unseld was able to change the aging author's mind.

The second reprint of the book duly appeared as the first volume in the new Suhrkamp subsidiary, the Jüdischer Verlag, in 1992. Its author was clearly given as Wolfgang Koeppen, and the new title was *Jacob Littners Notes from the Underground [Jakob Littners Aufzeichnungen aus einem Erdloch]*. From Koeppen's brief Foreword, dated 1991, we learn some of the circumstances surrounding the 1948 publication. The publisher, Herbert Kluger, had met a Jewish stamp-dealer, Jakob Littner, who had miraculously survived the Holocaust in Galicia. At the end of the war, he had returned to his native Munich, where he had related his experiences to Kluger in the hope that an established writer might use his story to produce a publishable text. Kluger invited Koeppen to be that writer. The survivor, about to emigrate to the United States, was offering two CARE packages per month as remuneration. Forty years old, the author of two forgotten novels that had appeared in 1934 and 1935 but who had written nothing for over ten years and who remained more or less unknown, Koeppen had no other marketable skills, no other source of livelihood. He accepted. For reasons about which we can only conjecture, he kept his name from the title page and did not reveal his part in the preparation of the manuscript until forty-four years later.

The 1992 printing of the book under Koeppen's name was an immediate success and was reviewed in all the major newspapers and journals – for the most part positively. There were, however, certain questions that were posed again and again: Why did Koeppen hide his authorship of this work for so long? A corollary to this question was a nagging curiosity about the source. If Koeppen's source was the publisher's notes, taken down as Littner described his experiences, (this was the gist of the Foreword), how comprehensive were they? The other question posed by most critics concerned the last words of the Foreword: "I was eating food from American cans and describing the sufferings of a German Jew. *It turned into my story*" [my emphasis. "Ich aß amerikanische Konserven und schrieb die Leidensgeschichte eines deutschen Juden. Da wurde es meine Geschichte" (Koeppen 1992, 6)].

Initially, attention was directed at this statement rather than at the assertion that Littner had merely provided a few pages of factual information such as dates and place names, which was at first largely accepted. Recently, however, it was ascertained that Jakob Littner had provided Koeppen with a 183-page typescript, titled *My Journey through the Night. A Document of Racial Hatred. An Account of My Experiences [Mein Weg durch die Nacht. Ein Dokument des Rassenhasses. Erlebnisbericht]*. Koeppen had used this account as a very substantial basis for his text. The question thus changed from how much Koeppen was indebted to Littner to whether the changes and additions he made sufficed for him legitimately to claim authorship. Letters were exchanged, questions posed, interviews conducted, and any suspicions that, perhaps, this book was Littner's and not Koeppen's, were couched carefully, in general terms, and in muted tones: "And now it turns out to be Koeppen's story, and nobody knows whether the author has been particularly good at research or invention, or whether he had more than just a few notes of the publisher's at his disposal" [Nun ist es Koeppens Geschichte, und niemand

weiß, ob der Autor gut recherchiert oder gut erfunden hat, oder ob ihm doch
mehr als ein paar Notizen des Verlegers vorgelegen haben (Wiesner 1992,
vi)]. In the *Spiegel*, the anonymous writer said "Apparently the pseudonym
Jakob Littner was intended to lend the work the desired aura of authenticity [...]. There is a whiff of dishonesty about the description of the work's genesis" ["Offenbar sollte das Pseudonym Jakob Littner dem Werk den gewün-
schten Schein von Authentizität verschaffen [...]. Ein Hauch von Unred-
lichkeit liegt über der Entstehungsgeschichte dieses Romans"] (*Der Spiegel*
1992, 232).

In 1995 Professor Reinhard Zachau, of the University of the South in
Sewanee, Tennessee, applying himself systematically and with insatiable
curiosity to Koeppen's book and its reception, found his suspicions growing
to such an extent that he resolved to attain clarity by whatever means necessary. Franz Josef Görtz had already in 1992 ascertained that Jakob Littner
was a real person – there was doubt about this the moment Koeppen was
named as the author. Zachau first traced Littner's steps as an immigrant to
the U.S. and attempted to locate relatives who could supply the information
needed to settle the authorship question once and for all. He found out
when Littner arrived and where, in New York City, he had lived. The trail
seemed for a while to end there, for he found no relatives and neighbors to
provide him with any information. But he began to write to all the Littners
whose addresses he could find and, after some eighty letters and about one
year of fruitless research, he finally heard from a woman who gave him the
name Kurt Nathan Grübler, a nephew of Jakob Littner. Grübler had in his
possession the 183-page typescript of Littner's own account, and this typescript had, as it soon became clear, served Koeppen as his basic text (Zachau
1999, 117-119). By the time Zachau was ready to confront Koeppen with
clear questions, it was too late: Koeppen had died.

Both Reinhard Zachau and Roland Ulrich of the Wolfgang Koeppen
archives have compared the Koeppen text with the original Littner account
on which it is based. Littner's German original had not at that time been
published in Germany.[1] It was, however, published in an English translation
by Kurt Grübler in 2000. There are, furthermore, three sections of Littner's
text reproduced, in the original German, in the journal *Colloquia
Germanica*.[2] It is, therefore, possible to make some general comments about
the two versions with a view to establishing the credibility of Koeppen's
statement "It became my book."

Koeppen has deleted a considerable amount of detail, including, for
example, the names and the specific details of the many people with whom
Littner interacted. He probably did so in the interests of clarity – readers are

often confused or frustrated by a great multitude of characters. He has, however, added statements and clarifications, or phrases that emphasize a point. He has often expanded or embellished the sober presentation of actions that characterize Littner's account. Allowing for the fact that, when German is translated into English, the English version tends to be as much as twenty percent longer, it is possible to state that Littner's text, as we know it in the English version, is somewhat longer than Koeppen's. On balance then, it seems that Koeppen has deleted considerably more than he has added.

Comparing a few pages of each text Roland Ulrich describes how the two versions differ. Koeppen generalizes where Littner presents detail; Koeppen makes syntactical changes – especially where Littner has terse and incomplete grammatical structures. Koeppen specifies the time when things happen, especially the beginning of each new day when new decrees are issued. Littner often omits temporal specifics. Koeppen writes in the present tense, whereas Littner, writing retrospectively in 1945, uses the past tense. Koeppen intensifies the language of German control, domination, and exploitation, thus emphasizing the perilous plight of the Jews. Koeppen tends to bring order to the unfolding of events, which, in Littner's version, seem to occur without any discernible order.

Ulrich speaks of a "version that is almost identical to the original" ("einem kaum veränderten Original"), but then proves, through his examples – and this accords with the findings of my own limited examination – that Koeppen's text is indeed a new text; it has become Koeppen's story.[3] All in all, it seems to me, the differences suffice for one to conclude that the account has, in terms of the writing, become Koeppen's story, as he insists in the Foreword. On the other hand, Littner's account is essential, is used by Koeppen in its entirety, and is all-pervading in Koeppen's version. Although it was probably wrong to use *only* Littner's name as author of the work when it first came out in 1948, it is certainly wrong to *omit* his name in the identical 1992 version. Both authors should have been acknowledged – and probably in no rank order. More importantly, Koeppen had no right to mislead the public about the extent of his source, as he did continually once he had assumed authorship. Above all, the publisher, Jüdischer Verlag/ Suhrkamp, has been inexcusably lax in sharing information, as well as in what one might call "damage control." Reinhard Zachau points out that Suhrkamp has never truly answered the letters from Littner's stepson, Richard Korngold, who raised the question of plagiarism in 1993, just after the book's publication (Zachau 1999, 131). Had the Jüdischer Verlag and Koeppen together acknowledged the full extent of the source and had they given Littner full credit for his story, there would have been no controversy

and Koeppen's statement at the end of the Foreword might still have sound-
ed credible. After all, authors are bound to immerse themselves in any story
they write. "Madame Bovary? C'est moi!" said Gustave Flaubert.

There were, however, other reasons why Koeppen associated himself with
Littner's story to such a degree. Littner's own title for his work had been *My
Journey Through the Night. A Document of Racial Hatred. An Account of My
Experiences [Meine Reise durch die Nacht. Ein Dokument des Rassenhasses.
Erlebnisbericht]*. Koeppen had ignored this title, calling the work instead *Notes
from the Underground*. He thus called up the shades of Dostoevsky, whose
Notes from the Underground in the German version is *Aufzeichnungen aus dem
Kellerloch*. Certainly Koeppen, who was of the generation of Existentialism
and the Absurd, and who had included Kierkegaard and Dostoevsky as
diarists in his essay "The Diary and the Modern Author ["Das Tagebuch und
der moderne Autor"] chose his title carefully, intending his reader to make the
obvious connections. But there was another reason for feeling comfortable
with his chosen title, and this reason also allowed him to associate himself still
more strongly with Littner's book, and with Littner's fate.

Koeppen had left Germany in 1935 for Holland, where he intended to
stay for the duration of National Socialism. He returned to Germany, however, in late 1938, and settled again in Berlin and made a precarious living
writing screenplays for Dfa. (Not one of the screenplays ever reached the
screen.) As the war progressed, and more and more older men were drafted,
as the bombs began to rain down on Berlin ever more persistently, the paci-
fist Koeppen went to Munich and eventually went underground in
Starnberg. Here he lived in a cellar, existing for a while on raw potatoes
(Wiesner 1992, vi). His situation was clearly not so dire as Littner's, but
Koeppen was able to empathize strongly.

Yet, even if all these factors combined to make him look upon the story
of Littner as "his story," even if his text fell short of plagiarism, there is no
doubt that his behavior, as well as that of his publisher, was, in absolute
terms, morally reprehensible. Koeppen was guilty of the sin of hiding, of not
acknowledging the full extent of his source. Plagiarism is too strong a word
to describe his appropriation of Littner's text. His biggest mistake was, perhaps, to remain silent when he might have spoken.

In 1996 a German journalist, Karl Corino, spent a semester in the United
States as a guest professor at Washington University, St. Louis, where he
taught a course on East German Literature. His readings and research
involved, among others, the esteemed writer Stephan Hermlin, author of the
widely acclaimed *Evening Light* (1979) and *Places of Destiny* (1985), who

enjoyed the status of "grand old man" of East German literature. Both works, which deal extensively with episodes from Hermlin's life during the Third Reich, were generally read as autobiography, even though that designation was missing from the title pages.

In his role as head of the literature section of the Hessian Radio, Corino was also engaged in preparing an obituary of Hermlin, who, in his eighties and in ill health, was expected to die soon. Corino's research revealed discrepancies regarding aspects of Hermlin's biography and cast doubt on, in particular, Hermlin's participation in the German resistance to National Socialism in the 1930s and in the Spanish Civil War, and on his movements as a Jew underground in occupied France. A bitter controversy erupted, which was hardly stilled by the writer's death in the midst of the polemic.

The case of Stephan Hermlin is, however, radically different from that of Koeppen in that plagiarism was never charged. Indeed, there is no other author or text involved. But there is a striking similarity in the two cases. Hermlin, too, remained silent for years, as he became an esteemed writer whose biography was placed in reference works. He might have spoken up, for example, to clarify and correct the discrepancies in these many entries. According to these reference works, Hermlin grew up privileged, in a wealthy Jewish family in Berlin. His mother was from England. His father was a German-born businessman, musician, and art-collector who was incarcerated after *Kristallnacht*. Their fate after November 1938 remains unclear, but one might assume that his father, at least, perished. Hermlin became a member of the Communist Youth in 1931, was active in resistance circles in the first three years of the Third Reich, then left Germany. After being in Egypt, Palestine, England, and Spain, he participated in some way in the Spanish Civil War on the Loyalist side, then, after the outbreak of the war, served as a "prestataire" (i.e., foreign auxiliary) in the French forces until the capitulation. He then went underground in France until he was able to flee to Switzerland in 1944. At the end of the war he returned to Frankfurt am Main, and, in 1947, settled in East Berlin.

Emerging from the various reference works are inconsistencies and questions about important phases in Hermlin's life. What, precisely, were his movements between 1936 and the outbreak of war? What, if any, was his participation in the Spanish Civil War? What did he do in occupied France from 1940 until his flight to Switzerland? When exactly did he flee to Switzerland? These questions lead to larger ones. Who is responsible for the accuracy of biographical information, especially when such information has the possibility of shedding greater insight into important historical events? Are persons of public renown ultimately responsible for representations of their lives? And can we expect a poet's autobiography to be absolutely factually correct – especially where recent history is concerned? These immediate questions about Hermlin's life were the ones that occupied Karl Corino as he worked on Hermlin's obituary; both these immediate questions and the larger ones are those that concern me here.

In the course of checking dates and precise facts Corino located the statement Hermlin made in writing for the U.S. occupational authorities as he applied for a residence and work permit for the American Zone in 1946. He immediately discovered numerous inaccuracies. For example, Hermlin had stated in his "Military Government of Germany *Fragebogen*" that he had received his school-leaving certificate ("*Abitur*") in 1933 and had then studied at the University of Berlin from 1933-36. In fact, Hermlin never finished high school ("Gymnasium") and never enrolled at any university. Hermlin also stated that he had been incarcerated in the Sachsenhausen concentration camp from January to March 1934. In fact he was never in a concentration camp in Germany (although he did spend some time in an internment camp in occupied France), and, moreover, Sachsenhausen was not established until 1936.

Corino's careful enquiries in his search for factual information for his obituary now became a full-time crusade, almost a witch-hunt. By treating Hermlin's works *Evening Light* and *Places of Destiny*, together with many of Hermlin's essays, as autobiographical writing, Corino emphasized discrepancy and error in his conclusions. His mother was not English, but from Galicia. His father was not quite the rich businessman projected in Hermlin's writings, but had been bankrupted in the 1920s. Hermlin's parents had emigrated to England in 1939, where they both later died – Hermlin's mother became a British citizen during this time. Hermlin's brother Fredy had died while transporting bombers in Canada, not while in a spitfire on a mission over the North Sea. Corino located a younger sister of Hermlin's, living in Israel, whom Hermlin had never mentioned in his writings. Embittered by this neglect, she was only too happy to provide Corino with information damning to Hermlin.

Corino went public with all this information, unleashing a tremendous war of words with the battle-lines roughly drawn along the old ideological divide between East and West Germany. The ailing Hermlin was himself drawn into this battle and accused his accuser of lying. Shortly after, in 1997, Hermlin died. Corino had meanwhile (1996) published a book on, as the subtitle runs, "The Legends of Stephan Hermlin" (*Die Legenden des Stephan Hermlin*), titled *On the Outside Marble, Inside Plaster-of-Paris (Außen Marmor, innen Gips)*. In due course, the wide-spread support Corino initially enjoyed crumbled somewhat as people began to question whether Hermlin had purposely created a legend for himself and, if he had, whether it was important in assessing the work for which he was esteemed, his stories, essays, and lyrical writings. Were not many of the "lies" tucked away in bureaucratic archives, away from public scrutiny? Many began to suspect that Corino's motives in exposing Hermlin were, indeed, largely political, and part of the tensions rife in the new Federal Republic of Germany after the fall of the Wall and the demise of the GDR. One astute warrior in the battle surrounding Hermlin was Hans Marquardt, the East German publisher of Hermlin's *Evening Light*. In his article in *Neues Deutschland*, headed "Corino's Piece in the German-German Cultural War," Marquardt related how Hermlin had privately told him during the lengthy period while he was writing the work that "it was both [biographical fact *and* fiction], as is always the case in prose that aspires to art" (Marquardt 1996, 11).

Defenders pointed out continually that nowhere did Hermlin call his writings true autobiography. Moreover, they said, a German Jew seeking to return to his occupied country after years of leading a double existence might be forgiven for providing misinformation that he thought might persuade the occupational government to admit him and approve employment. It was, they said, a purely bureaucratic matter, and not part of the public record.

Now that the dust has settled, it is possible to see the unfortunate affair in the following terms: Hermlin, a lifelong socialist, used most of his writings to promote socialism. If he used his own biography in these writings, as he most assuredly did, and if this was prose raised to art (as he described *Evening Light*), why should he not exaggerate, distort, and augment the data of his life in such a way as to help his cause? And is lying in an official questionnaire, in the confusion that was Europe in the immediate post-war years, so reprehensible, when the lies stem from a victim trying to re-establish himself as opposed to, say, a perpetrator trying to rehabilitate himself? Is it not poetic truth that one expects of a poet rather than literal facts?

Clearly it would have been better had Hermlin not lied to the authorities, but the distortion of one's personal life in works of fiction is a writer's prerogative, so long as general facts are not contradicted. As in the case of Wolfgang Koeppen, it is Hermlin's silence over a period of years that leads to problems. Faced with words in black and white, though written by others, which he knew to be inaccurate or, at best, confusing, he could have, and should have, provided information to have them corrected. But the same kind of author's pride that led Koeppen to speak of Littner's narrative as "his" story may well have led Hermlin to shrug his shoulders at the compilers' mistakes. His own writings are a different matter. He never designated them as autobiographical and, therefore, was at liberty to write whatever he wished.

The Painted Bird by the Polish-American writer Jerzy Kosinski describes the horrendous experiences of a small boy during World War II. Taken for a Jew or a gypsy, the boy is subjected to terrible cruelty and torture by the various Polish peasants he encounters as he wanders from village to village seeking security and comfort. While marketed as a novel, the work was generally accepted as a thinly disguised autobiography and Kosinski did nothing to dispel this notion. Indeed, in conversations he often alluded to the work as his autobiography. Although no stranger to controversy Kosinski seems not to have been attacked initially regarding the novel's authenticity as autobiography. It was quickly translated into many languages but not initially into Polish. It became hugely popular in Germany, won a major literary prize in France, and was widely adopted into university courses and reading lists. It was not until its relatively late translation into Polish in 1989, almost a quarter of a century after its American publication, that serious questions regarding its authenticity as autobiography were raised. The prominent Polish journalist Joanna Siedlicka traced people who had known the Kosinskis, made other investigations, and finally revealed that Kosinski's life, far from being one of separation from his parents, continually on the run, and exposed to bestial torment and exploitation, was one of relative ease and security. Her findings divided critics, scholars, and readers starkly in both Poland and the United States. Kosinski committed suicide in 1991, but probably not as a result of the scandal. Since the publication of Siedlicka's findings in *The New Yorker* in 1994 Kosinski's reputation has been permanently stained.

Jerzy Kosinski's situation resembles Hermlin's, but with significant differences. Kosinski wrote a novel, which may or may not have been autobiographical. True, he always admitted, insisted even, that it was. Friends of Kosinski's told of having heard episodes of *The Painted Bird* recounted by him as events from his own life *before* the publication of the novel. But Kosinski was also known both to exaggerate and to hedge a little when pressed. In his "Notes by the Author," appended to the German edition of the work, Kosinski attempted to explain "that the book described a set of circumstances lived in one language and 'unfrozen' by its expression in another."

Shortly after the novel appeared in the United States, but more than twenty years before its publication in Polish in Kosinski's native country, a number of Polish journalists, with official communist party support, attempted to "correct" the book's negative image of Poles and Poland as anti-

Semitic. That particular image had clearly reached Poland, even if the book had not. The articles and commentaries were, however, poorly documented and clearly erroneous.

These same Polish articles were later of aid to Joanna Siedlicka, who, after the book appeared in Polish, also attempted to salvage Polish honor whilst denigrating the Polish émigré writer. In them she found the names of people interviewed during the 1960s, whom she was now able to interview again with regard to specifics in the novel. Because she now had the Polish version of the book, her research was more focussed, her attacks better directed (Sloan 1994, 49-50). She ascertained that the young Kosinski did not experience the events he later described in his novel and that he had, in fact, been able to survive the war and the occupation in relative comfort. In her quest to retrieve Poland's honor, Siedlicka had, in effect, proven the book to be fiction – it is a novel just as it had always been described on the title page. En route to this conclusion, it is revealed again and again that Kosinski was "a fantastic liar," as Agnieska Osiecka said (Sloan 1994, 46), an "uneven man," as an acquaintance put it, and "an absolute mythomaniac," as the journalist Mira Michalowska said (Sloan 1994, 53).

In the United States, Kosinski was known as a bit of a character not only in literary circles but also on the New York social scene and in the realm of popular culture. That he should exaggerate, and assume identities that were larger than life, should not surprise us. Ultimately, however, the scandal tarnished Kosinski's reputation permanently, both in the U.S. and, especially, in Poland, where Poles found it impossible to accept the picture Kosinski gave of his native land. James Park Sloan ends his perceptive article on Kosinski with the words:

> Maybe it is only the historian's task to reassert the annoying complexity of events against the satisfying simplicity of a story line. If the novelist trimmed his experiences to accord with a personal myth, the narrative that resulted fell on receptive ears. Certainly it was a myth that the world, demanding purity and innocence of its victims, was all too ready to appropriate. Now all must profess to be shocked – shocked – that a practitioner of the liar's profession, a man who survived the war by living a lie, told lies. (Sloan 1994, 53)

Every writer lies, Sloan is saying. There is a poetic truth that is not only acceptable, but is constantly the goal of the writer. When Kosinski insisted that, yes, *The Painted Bird* was autobiographical, he was viewing the life of the small boy as representative of his own life as an outsider in his native land. In this regard the fictional "autobiographies" by Kosinski and Hermlin contain "lies" that are excusable. The only difference is that whereas Koeppen and Hermlin both remained silent when silence meant covering up the truth or allowing a lie to continue, Kosinski was constitutionally incapable of remaining silent. His only mistake, if mistake it was, was to say too much.

Binjamin Wilkomirski, a musician living in Switzerland, is the undisputed author of *Fragments: Memories of a Wartime Childhood [Bruchstücke: Aus einer Kindheit 1939-48]*. He is the only one of our four authors who is still living, and the only one who was not an established writer. There is no doubt that *Fragments* was published as an autobiographical account of the early childhood years of a Holocaust survivor. The memories presented therein were seemingly "retrieved" through psychotherapy, as a note appended to the narrative suggests. The book was an instant success, and Wilkomirski was feted on both sides of the Atlantic, receiving numerous prizes. He was also in constant demand as a speaker.

It was not long, however, before doubts about the work's authenticity arose. A prime doubter and critic was a Swiss compatriot, Daniel Ganzfried, who is the son of a Holocaust survivor. For a time Wilkomirski enjoyed the support of his publishers and of prominent Jewish groups. But gradually Ganzfried's research, as well as the voices of other detractors, won out. It is now clear that Wilkomirski is, in fact, not a Jewish Holocaust survivor, but Bruno Grosjean, a Swiss born in 1941 and adopted, after years of being their foster-child, by Kurt and Martha Dössekker in the 1950s. His book has now been removed from the market.

At high school in Switzerland two of Dössekker's teachers showed an interest in the Holocaust and encouraged the young boy's own growing interest in that subject. He is known to have told various friends that he was of Polish origin, and that he had come to Switzerland as a very young child (Lappin 1999, 32 and 59). As a young man he gradually began to take on a Jewish identity. As an adolescent he recounted to friends some of the stories that later made up *Fragments* and then, much later told the same stories to his partner Verena Piller. Piller encouraged Dössekker to write these stories down, partly for therapeutic reasons, since he suffered ill-health and constant bad dreams. Two inheritances, a small one from his birth-mother Yvonne Grosjean and another from the estate of his adoptive parents, the Dössekkers, enabled him to set up a library and archive of Judaica and Holocaust materials. He also began to travel, making site-visits to camps and cities in Poland, especially, and to Israel. Gradually he made contact with survivors and others with expertise about the camps and, in particular, Jewish children in the Holocaust.

By the 1990s, Dössekker, who had as early as 1979 conceived of the notion that he might actually be named Wilkomirski (Lappin 1999, 41), was ready to market his book under the name Binjamin Wilkomirski. The enthusiasm with which it was greeted, the prizes and awards, the interviews, the films, and the plaudits are all well known. The suspicions, the doubts, and the gradually emerging facts are equally well known. The first person to express such doubts publicly was Daniel Ganzfried. Ironically, Ganzfried had been asked to interview Wilkomirski by the Swiss magazine *Passages* for an issue devoted to "creativity" in individuals who excelled in an area different from their prime area of expertise. Wilkomirski, as a professional musician and, now, the author of a book on the Holocaust, was just such a "creative" person; Ganzfried, as the son of a Holocaust survivor and the recent author of a "novel" about his father's experiences, was ideally suited as the interviewer. He duly conducted the interview and concluded that Wilkomirski's account was not credible. He then, with some passion, made further investigations. But *Passages* would not accept what he ultimately wrote, and so he offered it to the *Weltwoche*, a major Swiss cultural weekly. *Weltwoche* printed it in August and September of 1998.

Meanwhile others in the United States had become skeptical, including Raul Hilberg, who found too many falsehoods in the account. Whenever, during his travels, Wilkomirski was asked whether the book was fiction, he always insisted that it was autobiographical. During the summer of 1998, the writer Mark Pendergrast, who had just published a book critical of "recovered memory," also voiced grave doubts about the book as factual autobiography. He read the Afterword as tantamount to admitting that the text relied on "recovered memory." Gradually, more people began to call the book a fraud. Articles in 1999 by Philip Gourevitch in *The New Yorker*, and Elena Lappin in *Granta* made it very clear that Wilkomirski was Dössekker and that, if *Fragments* described the life of any child, it certainly was not the life of the young Dössekker – or, by the same token, of "Binjamin Wilkomirski," since they were one and the same person.

By early 1999, at which time the book was still available in both German and English, it was clear to most people that *Fragments* as autobiography was fraudulent. Wilkomirski's agent, Agentur Liepman AG of Zurich, commissioned the Swiss historian Stefan Mächler to investigate the authenticity of the book. Mächler, whose special interests encompass anti-Semitism, political asylum, and refugees in Switzerland, duly fulfilled this commission, and the book, *The Case of Wilkomirski [Der Fall Wilkomirski]* appeared in 2000.[4] The detailed investigation, with photographs, takes up some 327 pages. Toward the end, in a chapter headed "The Truth of the Biography," Mächler lists sixteen points where Wilkomirski's story is demonstrably false. Upon presenting his findings to Wilkomirski's agent, to his publishers, to his partner Verena Piller, and to Wilkomirski himself before the book was published, Mächler was immediately vindicated when the agent abjured all rights to the text, and the publishers removed the work from circulation. For his part, Wilkomirski reacted strongly, accusing Mächler of misunderstanding matters, of insulting him, of denigrating him. But clarity had finally been established. What remains is a need to draw conclusions.

Why do some writers attempt to mislead their readers? Or, to look at the issue from a writer's perspective: How much latitude do authors legitimately enjoy in regard to omission, addition, invention, distortion, or the use of falsehoods?

With regard to Wolfgang Koeppen the question, as we have seen, is not why he accepted the commission to rewrite Jakob Littner's account: he was artistically sterile at the time, had urgent need of the CARE packages, and empathized with Littner's wartime situation. Why he omitted his own name when it might have appeared as joint author is less explicable, but it is conceivable that at that time, 1948, he felt that the text was Littner's, or that he did not want the kind of shared recognition that would come to him as a joint author. Why did Koeppen accede to Unseld's (Suhrkamp's) request that the publishing house be allowed to re-print the account in 1992 under his own name? Out of vanity? Probably not. It is more conceivable that Koeppen was now of the opinion that the modified text was indeed his (as he wrote in the Foreword). Furthermore, Littner was by now certainly dead, and, in any case, Littner had reacted to the book when it first came out in Koeppen's form back in 1948 by saying that he could not find himself or see his situation in the version that Koeppen wrote (Falcke 1992, 7; see also Zachau 1999, 116). It can hardly be that Koeppen (and his publishers) feared possible copyright difficulties because if that were the case they would surely have included Littner's name. An important point is that he had not written anything substantial for nearly four decades. It is likely that he, an old man, bowed to persistent pressure from his publisher and agreed against his better judgment to an immediate publication. Why did he never reveal the full extent of his source – a 183-page typescript? He probably assumed that this typescript, which had never surfaced in forty and more years, was lost, or no longer in existence. Why complicate things by now revealing its existence? If these tentative answers are true, then a very real question arises as to the honesty of his actions, a question that is difficult to dismiss. It is hard to find any explanation to exonerate Koeppen from his culpable behavior regarding his source.

With regard to Stephen Hermlin there are two distinct areas of concern.

On the one hand there are his so-called autobiographical writings that do not always accord precisely with the facts. But these writings were never labeled as autobiography, and Hermlin did not tout them as such. What emerged from *Evening Light*, in particular, was less Hermlin's life than an exemplary life of someone who left the comforts of bourgeois culture for communism and somehow, as a Jew and a communist, survived the Holocaust that swallowed up so many of the foreign Jews who were in France. It is a beautifully written work of literature, with passages of great lyrical beauty. Is its factual truth important, or unimportant? To paraphrase Hermlin himself, an author needs to be able to create from his own experiences *and* use his imagination for literature to reach the height of art.

But what about the lies contained in Hermlin's account to the American occupation authority? It is possible to understand why, in 1946, he said he was in Sachsenhausen, and why he gave himself some academic qualifications as he sought to live in a country and work for its Frankfurt radio station in the literature section. These statements are false and Hermlin knew it, but the questionnaire was never intended for publication and would never have come to light had not Corino painstakingly sought it out. The fact that he allowed inaccuracies perpetrated by lexicographers and editors in the prominent reference works to pass without correction or comment, that he stood by silently when others attributed actions to him that were not true, is also reprehensible – even if we agree that such mistakes were those of the compilers. Hermlin was not a big liar. He was a manipulator of the truth. As a literary artist, he was able to get away with it for most of his life, but in 1996 truth came out. Hermlin's reputation was permanently damaged by these actions.

Jerzy Kosinski, like Hermlin, also wrote a work widely construed as autobiographical. He did not remain silent, but continually agreed with those who alluded to *The Painted Bird* as his autobiography. It was not; it did not accord with the facts of his life. Kosinski was, however, generally known as a witty, effervescent, erratic, and boastful raconteur. One believed what he said at one's peril. Did he wittingly try to mislead? I think not. In his introduction to the second edition of the novel, dated 1976, Kosinski clearly states that the work is fiction and not autobiography, but says that he "knew fiction could present lives as they are truly lived (Jerzy Kosinski 1976, xi).

Binjamin Wilkomirski is unique among the four. He went for the big lie. It was Joseph Goebbels who said: "The bigger and more monstrous the lie, the bigger the chance that it will be believed, for it will become unimaginable that anyone would have dared to invent a lie of such proportions." It was a statement Wilkomirski knew – although he attributed it, wrongly, to

Himmler (Lappin 1999, 42). In the end event, of course, this lie failed. Given the role therapy (in one form or another) played in *Fragments*, given Wilkomirski's precarious physical and mental health, it is fairly clear that Wilkomirski, or Dössekker as we must also call him, invented a parallel life for himself to swallow up his own wretched situation in a bigoted Swiss milieu: illegitimate, poor, removed from all contact with his mother, institutionalized in orphanages, tossed from foster parent to foster parent, ultimately adopted by a couple who wanted a doctor dynasty rather than a balanced and loving son. This is well described by Elena Lappin, who used the linguist Paul Postal's image of the man with two heads, one of which is always invisible, to explain her reading of Dössekker as a man with a divided personality (Lappin 1994, 28 et. seq.). Stefan Mächler sums up in much the same way at the end of his book about the Wilkomirski case (Mächler 2000, 287 et seq.). Wilkomirski is a very disturbed person who still believes his lie. As such, one might be more inclined to pity him than condemn him.

We tend to understand the words "autobiography" and "memoir" as identical and to use them interchangeably. In fact, there is an essential difference between the two, and one that is not without importance in this study. Autobiography is a western phenomenon and dates from St. Augustine's *Confessions*. It reached a peak in the early nineteenth century and declined in the second half of the nineteenth century (Fraser 1984, 15-16). In the twentieth century, and especially since the end of World War II, however, it has increased in popularity, an increase that has been augmented by the considerable output of autobiographically based fiction. This great increase in popularity in more recent years is due not least to changes in social attitudes. The contemporary reader is ready for, and attracted to, greater openness on the part of the writer.

Autobiography proper is the life of a person who is not yet integrated into society, not yet a truly social being. It is the story of such a person's development, maturation, education, and growth into society. As Bernd Neumann says, the autobiography is a description of "the life of a person who is not yet socialized, it is the history of his growth and his education, of his growth to a position in society" (Neumann 1970, 25). A memoir, on the other hand, comprises the reminiscences of those who merely record events pertinent or tangential to their lives but not essential to their development. The autobiography is accordingly more concerned with inner events and developments; the memoir depicts external events touching upon one's life. The autobiography can tolerate distortions and even falsehoods in a way the memoir cannot. Littner's account is not an autobiography in this sense of the word; it is a memoir, which helps to explain why he did not like the changes Koeppen made. For Littner these changes appeared as inaccuracies.

Given this essential difference between an autobiography and a memoir, Hermlin's *Evening Light* may now be seen as an autobiography. It does, indeed, portray Hermlin's life in terms of its development, in terms of Hermlin's growth and integration into society. Corino's judgment, caught up in his argument about facts, misses the point.

Jerzy Kosinski's *The Painted Bird* is a novel. It is fictional. And yet the trials faced by a young outsider in a bestial world parallel those of a Jew in an anti-Semitic world. The fact that the Kosinski family was sheltered by Christians does not remove or even reduce Polish anti-Semitism, neither does the fact that the Kosinskis were well off and seldom separated change their alienated situation within Polish society. Despite the novel's terrible realism, it does not profess to give real events. The plucking out of eyeballs from their sockets, for example, stands as an image of cruelty, not as a real event, typical of the Polish peasantry.[5] The Polish reaction was as much directed at such images as to Kosinski's critique of Polish anti-Semitism. Given the above definition of an autobiography, it is quite possible to see the work, too, as an autobiography. The speechlessness of the young boy at the end of the novel, which has been proven *not* to have afflicted young Kosinski, takes on new significance. It is not meant to be read literally, but is meant to convey how a victim of violent discrimination feels and how difficult it is to communicate that feeling.

Paradoxically, Wilkomirski's book could, like Kosinski's, be acceptable as autobiography if it were instead labeled fiction. But then the author would have needed to emphasise the Swiss episodes somehow and lead the reader to the real life in the autobiography, namely the life of Bruno Grosjean/ Dössekker. But, as we have seen, it is not Wilkomirski's or Dössekker's life that is related in *Fragments*. As it is, nowhere does the account allow the reader to glimpse the sad situation of the Swiss Dössekker through what happened to the Latvian (or Pole) Wilkomirski in the Third Reich – even though Switzerland plays a role in the work itself. It is one thing to write a novel and allude to it as an autobiography. It is another to write an autobiography, which you insist is fact, that is without any clearly visible symbolic value.

Few people raise questions about the historical veracity of fiction, so long as what they read seems credible, or has a clear purpose (e.g. symbolic) beyond the propagation of actual fact. They are in essence willing to accept a lie. In fact, the writer's craft encompasses, ipso facto, the use of the lie – as is clear from the words by James Park Sloan quoted above. The word, in essence, cannot be the thing. The account of the story cannot be the event itself. Some of the writer's exasperation at the general lack of awareness of this fact comes through in Hermlin's statement that the writer's craft or art automatically merges fact and fiction. As long as we bear this in mind and accept it, much of the criticism directed at Hermlin and Kosinski in particular dissolves into insignificance.

In a perceptive essay with the title "The Rights of History and the Rights of Imagination" in her book *Quarrel and Quandary*, Cynthia Ozick points out that the rights of imagination are not identical with the rights of history. Writers always write with "intention," even though that intention might not be clear, either to us or, even, to themselves. If a writer intends to bridge the gap between history and imagination by writing a fictional work based in history, then, says Ozick, fictional autonomy ceases to exist and the rights of history win out:

> It would seem, though, that when a novel comes to us with the claim that it is directed consciously toward history, that the divide between history and the imagination is being purposefully bridged, that *the bridging is the very point*, and that the design of the novel is to put human flesh on historical notation, then the argument for fictional autonomy collapses, and the rights of history can begin to urge their own force. (Ozick 2000, 116)

Intention played a major role in all four works under scrutiny. In the case of Stephan Hermlin, he clearly intended to show an exemplary development of an individual toward a life within socialism. The facts of the Third Reich as experienced by him were not the main point. He was not writing a story "to put human flesh on historical notation," as Ozick puts it, but instead was using history to clothe a person and show that person's growth and maturation.

With Jerzy Kosinski the situation is similar. Kosinski was expressing his own feelings and experiences vicariously through a nameless child in a nameless country whose fictional experiences are described in the novel. Kosinski was not writing a work that professed to be a history of Polish peasant life in the 1940s.

Wolfgang Koeppen's situation is different. Although some critics who have been able to read both the German account by Littner and that by Koeppen have alluded to the way in which Koeppen has stressed the presence and behavior of the "good" Germans in his version, no one has objected to any real falsification of Littner's experiences as a Jew trying to survive in German-occupied Europe. Obviously Koeppen could not be accused of falsifying his own biography either. Instead, any accusations directed at him must center on his refusal to say all he knew about his source. These accusations can not be refuted.

As far as we can tell, Bruno Dössekker really believed he was Binjamin Wilkomirski and set out to write down the deep "memories" of his time in the camps as they came to him through psychotherapy. In this case he did not set out to deceive, and his account can not strictly be called fraudulent. Yet, in terms of Cynthia Ozick's views on the rights of history/imagination, and if we accept as accurate Wilkomirski's statement that his book is historically valid, then it has to be said that the rights of history should, in the case of *Fragments*, prevail. In this case, however, it is the rights of imagination that have won out. In a sense Wilkomirski is defrauding Dössekker.

Did any of these writers write with the intention of deceiving their readers? Almost certainly not. Wilkomirski still believes that what he wrote is fact and can hardly be deemed fraudulent. Hermlin and Kosinski were both writing imaginatively, so that history's rights were subordinate. In terms of the actual written works Koeppen was also working with imagination – although, of course, his source material was history and not fiction.

Why all the fuss, then? It is because the topic in question is the Holocaust. The Holocaust has assumed a role of enormous importance in the last several decades. Sensitivities have been aroused as trials took place, as universities arranged courses, as symposia and conferences were organized, museums opened, and memorials erected. Survivors, who until only recently had often kept silent about their experiences, now have come forward, writing books, giving talks, going on tour. Survivors were viewed not only with pity or admiration, but with awe, and were all but sanctified. The 1978 TV mini-series "Holocaust," Claude Lanzmann's film "Shoah," Steven Spielberg's "Schindler's List" – all helped make the word "Holocaust" generally known. More recently the question of monetary compensation for victims and the revelations of the culpable activities of the Swiss banks in the 1930s and 1940s have raised the American consciousness of the Holocaust still more.

At the same time, the voices of denial were raised, and extreme right-wing groups sought to fan the smoldering pockets of anti-Semitism into consuming flames. The *facts*, as they emerged in all their gruesome enormity and then in the more detailed and more precisely directed selectivity of individual events, and the specific events (the Auschwitz trials, the trial of the "butcher of Lyons," Maurice Papon, Dr. Hermann Gross etc.) took on greater significance and became the prime instrument with which to oppose denial. Survivor accounts, as well as visual images in films and museums, provided the "human face" but they had to accord with the facts. Such accounts necessarily allowed the rights of history to prevail.

Small wonder, then, that readers looked for the fraudulent accounts, fake stories, the lies, all of which took on major significance. They were seen to bolster the efforts of deniers. They were an insult to survivors and sullied the memories of these sanctified few. If this was all the case for the United States, it was doubly true for Europe, where new generations from the post-Holocaust era began to ask ever-increasingly blunt questions about the past, about the participation of their parents' and grandparents' generations. Europe, after all, had been the site not only of the events themselves, but also of the major post-war activities and problems resulting from those events. We need think only of the displaced persons, the division into East and West and the Cold War, the trials, the continuing searches for perpetrators, the presence of collaborators, the questions about the role of the churches, the Waldheim affair, the *Wehrmacht* exhibition, the electoral successes of right-wing groups, continuing anti-foreigner activities (which often took the form of anti-Semitism), and, not least, the central position of two perpetrator nations (Germany and Austria) as they attempted to put the past behind them and be accepted, responsible figures in a constantly re-configuring Europe.

It is for this reason that our writers have been so vehemently attacked. Koeppen was accused of insensitivity toward the Jewish victim whose story he took, and of profiting from it in a cold and calculating manner. Hermlin was taken to task for similar insensitivity toward concentration camp inmates by placing himself in Sachsenhausen in the questionnaire for the American occupational authorities. Kosinski was, according to his Polish critics, lying about his compatriots and whipping up sympathy for himself by "lying" about his war-time experiences. Wilkomirski reached the height of effrontery and insensitivity by masquerading as a survivor, as a Jew, and was accused of betraying the trust that victims have come to expect. This trust was exploited to the fullest degree by Dössekker's choice of persona – a very young child in all its innocence.

All have their defenders. Koeppen was a writer who was merely doing what all writers do: appropriating material and making it his own. In a recent, perceptive article on that case by Thomas Wirtz, a highlight runs "*No Koeppen Scandal*" (Wirtz 1999, 47). Hermlin was caught between East and West – as his detractor, Karl Corino, also soon found himself to be. Kosinski was a novelist and perhaps mentally disturbed. And Wilkomirski/Dössekker was revealed as a victim, not of the Holocaust, but of the shortcomings of the social welfare system in Switzerland in the 1940s and 1950s. His victim status is so extreme, the argument might run, that his mental stability has been irreparably harmed. In short, it is argued, he is mentally ill and he cannot be held fully responsible for his actions.

Current events, social context, newly discovered information – all play major roles in the emotional, often outraged, way people have viewed these fairly recent "scandals." At the same time, major works of history have come forth at regular intervals, beginning with Raul Hilberg's *The Destruction of the European Jews*. Survivors have emerged from their silence late in life to bear witness.

All this has meant that the limits on what is permissible in depicting the past have become more stringent. One invents at one's peril in the sensitive world of the Holocaust. Where the Holocaust is central it is best to be open, to distinguish between fact and fiction, to accede to the rights of history, and not wander too far into the realm of the parable, myth or symbol, especially if one professes to be writing "autobiography." Today, to ignore the dangers involved is to run the risk of indignant cries of "lies" as, in the end, all our writers discovered.

Notes

[1] The original Littner text with essays by Zachau and Ulrich is scheduled to be published in Germany by Metropol in the summer of 2001.

[2] A copy of the original typescript is to be found in the U.S. Holocaust Memorial Museum in Washington, D.C.

[3] In a brief, sober, and revealing article in the *Frankfurter Allgemeine Zeitung*, Thomas Wirtz alludes sharply to what he calls Roland Ulrich's "decisive ambiguity" [Roland Ulrich kommt zu einem vergleichenden Urteil, das an entschiedener Uneindeutigkeit nichts zu sehen läßt] (Wirtz 1999, 47).

[4] *Der Fall Wilkomirski* is scheduled to be published in English by Knopf in 2001 and will include the complete text of *Fragments*.

[5] It is, however, interesting to note that this very image appears in the account of the Polish massacre of Jews in Jedwabne in July 1941 (see Gross 2001, 64).

Literature Cited

Corino, Karl. 1996. *Außen Marmor, innen Gips. Die Legenden des Stephan Hermlin*. Düsseldorf: Econ.

Der Spiegel. 1992. Zeuge der Verachtung (16 March), 228-232.

Falke, Eberhard. 1992. Literarisches Carepaket. *Die Zeit* (8 May, sec. *Literatur*), 7.

Fiedler, Theodore. 1999. "...eine sehr komplizierte Rechtslage wegen der Urheberrechte." *Colloquia Germanica* 32: 103-104.

Fraser, Catherine C. 1984. *Problems in a New Medium. Autobiographies by Three Artists*. New York: Peter Lang.

Gourevitch, Philip. 1999. The Memory Thief. *The New Yorker* (14 June), 48-68.

Gross, Jan Thomasz. 2001. Neighbors. *The New Yorker* (12 March), 64-77.

Hermlin, Stephan. 1979. *Abendlicht*. Berlin: Klaus Wagenbach.

Hermlin, Stephan. 1985. *Bestimmungsorte. Fünf Erzählungen*. Berlin: Klaus Wagenbach.

Hermlin, Stephan. 1995. *In den Kämpfen dieser Zeit*. Berlin: Klaus Wagenbach.

Koeppen, Wolfgang. 1992. *Jakob Littners Aufzeichnungen aus einem Erdloch*. Frankfurt am Main: Jüdischer Verlag im Suhrkamp Verlag.

Kosinski, Jerzy. 1976. *The Painted Bird*. New York: Grove Press.

Lappin, Elena. 1999. The Man with Two Heads. *Granta* 66: 7-65.

Littner, Jakob. 1948. *Aufzeichnungen aus einem Erdloch*. Munich: Herbert Kluger.

Littner, Jakob. 2000. *Journey through the Night*. Trans. & ed. Kurt Nathan Grübler. New York: Continuum.

Littner, Jakob. 1999. Mein Weg durch die Nacht. Ein Dokument des Rassenhasses. Erlebnisbericht aufgezeichnet von J. Littner [Drei Auszüge]. *Colloquia Germanica* 32: 105-113.

Mächler, Stefan. 2000. *Der Fall Wilkomirski. Über die Wahrheit einer Biographie*. Zurich: Pendo.

Marquardt, Hans. 1996. Das Corino-Dossier im deutsch-deutschen Kulturkampf. *Neues Deutschland* 14 October, sec. Feuilleton p. 11.

Neumann, Bernd. 1970. *Identität und Rollenzwang: Zur Theorie der Autobiographie*. Frankfurt am Main: Athenäum.

Ozick, Cynthia. 2000. *Quarrel & Quandary. Essays*. New York: Alfred A. Knopf.

Pendergrast, Mark. 1999. Recovered Memories and the Holocaust: On Binjamin Wilkomirski's *Fragments. The Bulletin of The Center for Holocaust Studies at the University of Vermont*, 3(2): 1-6.

Reitlinger, Gerald. 1953. *The Final Solution: The Attempt to Eliminate the Jews of Europe*. New York: The Beechhurst Press.

Sloan, James Park.1994. Kosinski's War. *The New Yorker* (10 October), 46-53.

Ulrich, Roland. 1999. Vom Report zum Roman. Zur Textwelt von Wolfgang Koeppens Roman *Jakob Littners Aufzeichnungen aus einem Erdloch. Colloquia Germanica* 32: 135-150.

Wiesner, Herbert. 1992. Das Ghetto hieß Zbaraz, Galizien. *Süddeutsche Zeitung* (26 March), VI.

Wilkomirski, Binjamin. 1995. *Bruchstücke. Aus einer Kindheit 1939-1948*. Frankfurt am Main: Jüdischer Verlag im Suhrkamp Verlag.

Wilkomirski, Binjamin. 1996. *Fragments*. Trans. Carol Brown Janeway. New York: Schocken Books.

Wirtz, Thomas. 1999. Unbeschadet. *Frankfurter Allgemeine Zeitung* (6 September), 47.

Zachau, Reinhard. 1999. Das Originalmanuskript zu Wolfgang Koeppens *Jakob Littners Aufzeichnungen aus einem Erdloch. Colloquia Germanica* 32: 115-133.

Teaching the Holocaust with a Human Rights Framework

David A. Shiman

On the first day of the new school year, all the teachers in one private school received the following note from their principal:

> Dear Teacher:
> I am a survivor of a concentration camp. My eyes saw what no man should witness.
> Gas chambers built by learned engineers.
> Children poisoned by educated physicians.
> Infants killed by trained nurses.
> Women and babies shot and burned by high school and college graduates.
> So, I am suspicious of education.
> My request is: Help your students become human. Your efforts must never produce learned monsters, skilled psychopaths, educated Eichmanns.
> Reading, writing, arithmetic are important only if they serve to make our children more humane. (Ginott 1972, 317)

Studying the Holocaust is an intellectual activity, of course, but it is also a moral challenge. Courses offered within liberal arts programs at universities often strive to operate within an environment of disengaged scholarship. While a case can be made for such an approach, those of us involved in the preparation of teachers or who work directly with children in schools must engage the moral as well as the intellectual dimension of Holocaust education.

Living in a democracy and an increasingly interdependent world requires that we be constantly on guard against the emergence of a social climate accepting of human rights violations; the seeds of genocide are planted long before the ultimate acts are evident. Schools have an important role to play by helping to construct and maintain a social climate in which it is difficult, if not impossible, for governments and other institutions to propose and implement policies that violate human rights, both at home and abroad. Systematic study of the Holocaust and other genocides teaches that we must be prepared to act against injustice and be willing to assume responsibility for the well-being of our fellow humans.

Human Rights, as articulated in the United Nations' Universal Declaration of Human Rights and other documents, provides a framework to employ when analyzing historical events (Guyette and Shiman 1998), examining the actions of governments and citizens in their contemporary world, and developing plans for student action projects. This essay develops this framework and discusses the relationship between the Holocaust, other genocides and human rights. In addition, it offers suggestions to educators for designing classroom instruction around themes that support a broadly defined vision of democratic citizenship, with human rights at its core. Most examples in this chapter are drawn from the Holocaust. However, teachers can employ the themes generated to examine other genocides, such as those of the Hereros in South West Africa in the early 1900s, Armenians in the Ottoman Empire during the period 1915-1923, Cambodians under the Khmer Rouge Regime in the 1970s, Bosnians in the former Yugoslavia in the 1990s, Tutsi in Rwanda in the 1990s, and Native Americans in the United States during the past several centuries.

Defining the Holocaust, Genocide, and Human Rights

The United States Holocaust Memorial Museum defines the Holocaust as:

> The state-sponsored, systematic persecution and annihilation of European Jewry by Nazi Germany and its collaborators between 1933 and 1945. Jews were the primary victims; six million were murdered. Jews, the handicapped and Poles were also targeted for destruction or decimation for racial, ethnic, or national reasons. (United States Holocaust Memorial Museum 1994, 3)

The Holocaust is a specific genocide, one of many that have transpired in history. The scholar Raphael Lemkin originally coined the term "genocide" in 1943 in his book *Axis Rule in Occupied Europe*. The United Nations adopted the following definition of genocide:

> Any of the following acts committed with intent to destroy, in whole or in part, a national, ethnic, racial or religious group, as such: (a) killing members of the group; (b) causing serious bodily or mental harm to members of the group; (c) deliberately inflicting on the group conditions of life calculated to bring about its physical destruction in whole or in part; (d) imposing mea-

sures intended to prevent births within the group; (e) forcibly transferring children of the group to another group. (United Nations' Convention on the Prevention and Punishment of the Crime of Genocide, 1948)

Although there is scholarly debate regarding the scope and inclusiveness of this definition, there is general agreement that the Holocaust was a genocide of unparalleled scale during the twentieth century.

Worldwide revulsion to the crimes of the Holocaust served as a major impetus for the adoption by the UN of documents declaring certain rights to be universal human rights. The Preamble to the Universal Declaration of Human Rights captures this sentiment with the following phrase: "disregard and contempt for human rights have resulted in barbarous acts which have outraged the conscience of mankind"(United Nations' Universal Declaration of Human Rights 1948). From the emergence of Nazi rule in Germany in 1933, to the liberation of the Nazi camp system by the victorious Allied armies in 1944-45, Nazi Germany had abrogated rights guaranteed to both its own citizens and those Europeans who fell under its rule through the use of state-sponsored terror and violence. That "assault on human rights," aptly labeled by the British historian Ian Kershaw (1995), combined with the League of Nations' failure to stem Fascist aggression in the 1930s, strengthened the Allied powers' determination to develop a more stable and peaceful world order after World War II. To do so, they sought to create a system of international law and regulation that would eliminate the violations of human rights embodied in the Holocaust and other genocides.

Heightening this concern were the post-war trials of Nazi and Japanese war criminals, the most famous of which occurred in Nuremberg, Germany in 1945-46. Evidence presented in subsequent trials held in European countries sustained the concern that future generations would need to be vigilant and responsible in their protection of human rights.

The significance of the Nuremberg Trials was their establishment of a charter that included precedent-setting standards for the conduct of both individuals and governments. The four crimes enumerated in the charter of the International Military Tribunal – crimes against peace, war crimes, crimes against humanity, and conspiracy to commit those crimes – served as the basis for indictments against leaders, organizers, instigators, accomplices and perpetrators. Unlike comparable events at the end of past wars, the rule of law, not summary justice or ill-conceived efforts at prompt retribution, served as the guiding principle for the conduct of the trials of the twenty-four major criminals and those tried elsewhere in Europe.

The Universal Declaration of Human Rights (UDHR), adopted unanimously on December 10, 1948, by the UN General Assembly, was the first major step to establish a set of human rights standards. These were to serve as a legal structure and a moral code to hold governments accountable for the ways in which they might violate or deny the human rights of those living within their borders.

This Declaration asserted in its Preamble that "[...]the recognition of the inherent dignity and of the equal and inalienable rights of all members of the human family is the foundation of freedom, justice and peace in the world" (United Nations' Universal Declaration of Human Rights 1948, Preamble). The Declaration contains thirty articles that address basic political, civil, social, economic, and cultural rights. Among others, these include: rights to life, speech, religion, equality before the law, asylum, food, shelter, nationality, assembly, social security, and education. The UDHR asserts these to be fundamental and inalienable rights to which everyone is entitled, regardless of who they are and where they happen to have been borne. The General Assembly of the United Nations proclaimed the UDHR was to serve as a "common standard of achievement for all people and all nations" (United Nations' Universal Declaration of Human Rights 1948, Preamble), as a moral measure of the behavior of governments toward their people.

The creators of the Universal Declaration wanted human rights to have the force of international law. Elaborating the rights guarantees stated in the UDHR are the International Covenant on Civil and Political Rights (and the Optional Protocol) and the International Covenant on Economic, Social, and Cultural Rights, both of which were drafted and opened for signature by UN member states in the 1960s. These binding international treaties seek to establish clear guidelines and monitoring procedures for measuring the progress of the world community in safeguarding human rights. These two International Covenants, together with the UDHR, are known as the International Bill of Rights.

The United Nations' Convention for the Prevention and Punishment of the Crime of Genocide was also adopted in 1948. It attempted to hold individuals and governments accountable for massive human rights violations and criminal acts. The United Nations General Assembly began the process of drafting this convention in 1946, and, after much debate concerning the definition of victim groups (particularly concerning the term "political group"), adopted the convention on December 9th, the day before the adoption of the UDHR. Inspired by the Nuremburg trials and in the spirit of the Genocide Convention, the UN Security Council in 1994 established the International Criminal Tribunals concerning the former Yugoslavia and Rwanda. Although not specifically considering genocide, the Tribunals do strive to hold individuals accountable for "crimes against humanity" and "war crimes." It is one of the first instances of the world community attempting to monitor the conduct of individuals and governments regarding human rights, as intended by the framers of the Genocide Convention and the Charter of the International Military Tribunal at Nuremberg (Ferencz 1996).

A Rationale for Teaching Human Rights

The Universal Declaration of Human Rights (UDHR) offers one of the earliest rationales for teaching human rights, proclaiming "that every individual and every organ of society [...] shall strive by teaching and education to promote respect for these rights and freedoms and by progressive measures [...] to ensure their universal and effective recognition" (United Nations' Universal Declaration of Human Rights 1948). Human rights, however, was slow to develop as an instructional area in the United States or anywhere else in the world. However, by the mid-1980s, some curriculum had been published (Shiman 1985; Pettman 1986) and a few states, particularly California and New York, had incorporated human rights education into curriculum policy guidelines. By the 1990s, Amnesty International had launched a global effort to advance human rights education in schools and communities. In 1994, the United Nations approved the Decade for Human Rights Education 1995-2004 and its ambitious goal of having human rights education programs in every nation in the world. Since then, there has been a proliferation of efforts all over the world to promote education for human rights in both school and community settings. (For detailed information on the growth of human rights education, visit the following web sites: Human Rights Education Associates <www.hrea.org>, Human Rights Resource Center, University of Minnesota <www.umn.edu/humanrts>, and People's Decade for Human Rights Education <www.pdhre.org>).

The mission for human rights education that has emerged over the past decades embodies five overlapping dimensions:

1. *inform and instruct* about human rights and the responsibilities which accompany them;
2. *empower* individuals and groups with the knowledge, skills and attitudes necessary to realize a more just global society;
3. *mobilize* individuals and groups to work on behalf of those needing support;
4. *protect* against future human rights abuses; and
5. *reconstruct* society in accordance with the principles of justice, caring and human dignity. (Flowers and Shiman 1997, 174)

Human rights education strives to graft advocacy and action dimensions to a more traditional academic conception of education. It seeks to fuse the moral and the intellectual.

Human rights education requires that students examine perspectives other than their own and recognize that human rights problems occur not only in foreign lands but also within their own country and community. Teachers educating for human rights challenge their students to become more competent at understanding the complex world before them and to see themselves as citizens in a global community. This instruction in human rights calls on students to develop greater empathy for the suffering of their neighbors and to be "courageous enough to act on behalf of the common good" (Wood 1992, 81).

Rationales for Teaching the Holocaust

There are four major rationales for teaching the Holocaust found in policy documents of state departments of education and in curriculum created by the United States Holocaust Memorial Museum and Facing History and Ourselves. These are: a) to explain the present through the study of the past, focusing on historical inquiry and debate and employing aspects of the Holocaust to "symbolize the problems and dilemmas of the contemporary world;" b) to understand human behavior and society, employing an interdisciplinary approach incorporating literature, psychiatry/psychology as well as the traditional social studies disciplines to examine themes such as the nature of prejudice, stereotyping, and scapegoating; c) to develop civic virtue for participation in a democracy (Friedlander 1979); and d) to prepare youth for global citizenship by focusing on the universal attributes of the Holocaust and other genocides and their implications for behavior of future adult citizens.

Curriculum built on these rationales complements an instructional framework based on human rights. Such a framework concentrates on the progressive violation of human rights that culminated with the ultimate violation for more than six million people. It also extends learning to include the analyses of present conditions and the development of student human rights action projects. Most rationales for studying the Holocaust discussed below stop short of promoting curriculum to enable students to act on an emergent sense of moral responsibility.

Among the states, New Jersey was a pioneer in Holocaust education. Its 1983 curriculum resource guide stated:

> The quest for a world society based upon justice and human dignity will be hindered and delayed until people recognize and move actively to eliminate

those factors which create a climate in which genocide in any form can occur. Knowledge and awareness of those factors will lead to that elimination. The factors are most clearly seen in a study of the Nazi Holocaust. (Flaim and Reynolds, 1983, V)

Using the Holocaust as an historical case study, teachers can help students become aware of the extent to which suffering was the outgrowth of individual and group decisions made in a totalitarian society whose goals were antithetical to the protection of individual rights and the safeguarding of human dignity. The 1995 revision of New Jersey's earlier curriculum guide entitled *The Betrayal of Mankind: The Holocaust and Genocide* expanded the focus to include a wide range of genocides. It also reaffirms "the responsibility of each individual to prevent another Holocaust or genocide" (State of New Jersey 1995, L).

The State of Florida published a resource manual on Holocaust education in 1998 that drew heavily on the work of the United States Holocaust Memorial Museum. State statute mandates instruction in the history of the Holocaust. It declares that such instruction:

> Leads to an investigation of human behavior, an understanding of the ramification (sic) of prejudice, racism, and stereotyping, and an examination of what it means to be a responsible and respectful person, for the purposes of encouraging tolerance of diversity in a pluralistic society and for nurturing and protecting democratic values and institutions. (State of Florida 1998, xix)

In a similar vein, Ohio's 1994 curriculum guide promotes a Holocaust education program that would "enable students to become knowledgeable, sensitive, and responsive to the consequences of apathy" (Rabinsky and Danks 1994, 2). Educators using this guide emphasize that virtuous citizens are actively committed to the defense of the rights of others and recognize the direct relationship between the triumph of tyranny and the failure of citizens to act in defense of fundamental human rights. Keeping in mind that bystanders outnumbered perpetrators, victims and rescuers in every society where Nazi Germany implemented genocidal policies, the Ohio guide encourages youth to assume the moral responsibility to sustain fundamental rights and freedoms (Rabinsky and Danks 1994).

The California history-social science framework brings human rights, the Holocaust, and genocide together with powerful and compelling rationale.

> There is no more urgent task for educators in the field of history and social science than to teach students about the importance of human rights and to analyze with them the actual instances in which genocide – the ultimate violation of human rights – has been committed. We study the atrocities of the

past not only to preserve their significance as historical events but also to help identify ways to prevent the atrocities from ever happening again. (State of California 1987, 1)

Its broadly defined rationale for the study of these issues is placed in a global context. It articulates a commitment to the goals of human rights education presented earlier in this chapter: information/instruction, empowerment, mobilization, protection, and reconstruction. The California guide also connects human rights to the survival of a democratic state.

> History demonstrates that the strongest protection for the rights of minorities and individuals is to be found in a democratic system of government where due process and equal rights are guaranteed to all and where citizens have an informed commitment to the improvement and preservation of a just and democratic society. The goal of the history-social science curriculum is to educate today's young people so that they know the history of human rights and of the efforts to protect these rights and so that they understand the democratic process, respect the rights of others and willingly accept their obligations as citizens. (State of California 1987, 5)

To protect the rights of minorities and individuals, young people need to be knowledgeable about the history of human rights, with the Holocaust being viewed as a central case study of just how fragile the survival of democracy really is. Young people can apply their understanding of that history and become empowered as citizens to respect the rights of others. That requires a broad perspective on the problem of human rights, one not limited to the history of the United States but encompassing issues of human rights throughout world history.

Besides California, Connecticut also created a curricular bridge between teaching the Holocaust and human rights. Connecticut published a resource guide entitled *Human Rights: The Struggle for Freedom, Dignity, and Equality* in 1987 that focussed principally on the Holocaust experience, placing it within the larger context of human rights. This guide even advocates student action. Its final chapter, entitled "Taking Action," calls on teachers to "encourage students to act on their beliefs about issues by becoming involved in a human rights organization or activity" (State of Connecticut 1987, 57).

Among the many organizations promoting the study of the Holocaust, the United States Holocaust Memorial Museum (website www.ushmm.org) and Facing History and Ourselves (website: www.facing.org) are two of the most influential ones. Both incorporate the rationales presented at the beginning of this section, but neither approaches study of the Holocaust with a specific focus on human rights. The Holocaust Museum does not advocate for student activism in its curriculum materials, but its rationale talks of citizens in a democracy learning "to identify the danger signs and to know when to react" (United States Holocaust Memorial Museum 1994, 2). The Museum's Committee on Conscience does, however, work to stimulate worldwide action to halt "actions of genocide and related crimes against humanity around the world" (see website: www.ushmm.org/conscience). Facing History takes a more activist stance in its rationale: to "develop an educational model that helps students move from thought to judgment to participation as they confront the moral questions inherent in a study of violence, racism, antisemitism, and bigotry" (Facing History and Ourselves 1994, xxiii). Students are encouraged to examine their own attitudes and behaviors in light of insights gained through the study of the Holocaust.

The rationales summarized on the preceding pages tend to be a bit cautious when it comes to encouraging teachers to promote student activism as an outcome of their instruction about the Holocaust. Given the conservative nature of schooling, this is not surprising. However, it is an opportunity that should not be lost; studying the Holocaust prepares students to become human rights monitors and advocates for those oppressed.

Human Rights Education through the Study of the Holocaust: Themes for Instruction

Studying the Holocaust informs and empowers efforts to construct a humane and just world: the overarching goal of human rights education. Within this human rights framework, the Holocaust is examined not as a unique case but as one with more universal attributes and legacies. It offers categories for historical study as well as for monitoring human rights conditions at home and elsewhere.

To do so, requires the development of the following capacities that encompass both reactive and proactive efforts on behalf of human rights:

1. Analyze social conditions that nurture human rights violations and those that impede such violations;
2. Identify social conditions that make the realization of human right guarantees difficult if not impossible to realize;
3. Identify and publicize human rights violations or assaults on human rights in society;
4. Propose actions to redress human rights violations and protect against future violations;
5. Organize and act on behalf of human rights, both as individuals and as part of groups.

Teachers are able to make connections to a human rights framework and help their students develop these capacities through the examination of the four Holocaust themes discussed below. Careful study of these themes will enable students to understand betterhow decisions made by victims, perpetrators, bystanders, and rescuers facilitated the implementation of genocide or the struggle against it (Hilberg 1992).

Theme #1: Constructing the Other

The devaluation and dehumanization of targeted groups has been a characteristic of almost all instances of genocide and many violations of human rights in the twentieth century (Staub 1989, Kuper 1981, Keen 1986). The process of constructing "the other" in the minds of people is facilitated when certain social, cultural, economic, and political conditions exist. Among these conditions are difficult economic times, dominance of totalitarian political institutions and a popular tendency to defer to authority, development of ethnic cleavages in society where minority groups are vulnerable, and widespread public feelings of being "under siege" or of having been humiliated. Within such contexts, the labeling of minority groups as "others" enables the dominant groups to implement and justify policies and practices that violate the human rights of minority groups. In many societies, schools, youth organizations, the arts, religious institutions and the mass media have been important instruments for the development and dissemination of the images of the devalued "other."

During the Holocaust, Nazi Germany built upon a foundation of centuries old anti-Semitism in Europe and articulated a world view dominated by a form of racial anti-Semitism that had no place for those they deemed "unworthy of life." By denying Jews full participation in the community, stripping them of citizenship, and systematically reinforcing negative stereotypes of Jews embedded in the popular consciousness, the Third Reich marginalized Jews as a targeted group within German society and extended that policy to occupied Europe during World War II. Employing a definition of "the Jew" which prohibited their inclusion within a racially pure Germany or Europe, Nazi Germany sought to free both perpetrators and bystanders from moral qualms about their participation in the treatment of the "other." The Third Reich extended similar policies to disabled people, Jehovah's Witnesses, homosexuals, and the Sinti/Romani, viewing them as outside the boundaries of a racially pure continent. There are many examples of how human beings were transformed from outcasts to corpses.

Through the study of the Holocaust, we can generate important questions about processes and consequences related to constructing "others" in societies around the world, including our own. We may adapt those offered below to historical research or to monitor human rights conditions today:

- What groups are devalued and portrayed as dehumanized "others?"
- How are they described? What sorts of stereotypes?
- What group(s) play a dominant role in creating this "other?"
- What part do the following play in promoting this conception of the "other:" government, schools and textbooks, religion, language usage, popular media, cartoons and jokes, science, literature?
- What economic, political, and social conditions are related to the tendency to construct and discriminate against a particular "other?"
- What policies are implemented that violate the human rights of the "other?"
- Who benefits and who suffers as a result of these policies?
- What groups challenge the portrayal and treatment of the "other," and with what success? What actions do they take?

These questions, derived from the study of the Holocaust, bring students to consider what needs to be done to halt the human rights violations and what they might do to address the problems they have identified.

Theme #2: Rationalizing Injustice

Study of the construction and characterization of the "other" leads to consideration of the ways in which violations of their rights and even their physical destruction were rationalized. In most cases, longstanding and pervasive societal tensions and cleavages based on race, ethnicity, and religion provide the structural basis for highly destructive conflict (Kuper 68). Often, those in privileged positions within societal hierarchies of power and influence "view their privilege as in the natural order of things, and the social arrangements that maintain it as just"(Staub 1989, 235). The racial ideology of Nazi Germany legitimized Aryan superiority at the expense of targeted groups that were characterized through stereotyping in the mass media, education, and other government initiatives as threats to the future survival of the Aryan race. Once such rationalizations were accepted or viewed with indifference by the majority of the population, it was a small step for the state to initiate policies to destroy the targeted groups, whose very existence was seen as a threat to the survival of the majority.

There is a "just world hypothesis" at work here that allows people, particularly those in the dominant groups, to believe that one gets what one deserves. Once the victim is blamed for his/her plight, then the privileged can more easily accept the sufferings of "others" without feelings of remorse or guilt and can endorse or ignore their destruction without intervening to save them (Staub 1989, 82, Ryan 1971). Poliakov's point is well taken: "If only a minority hated the Jew to the point of wanting to kill him, the majority that was not fundamentally anti-Semitic could stand by and let the Jew be killed because of the general disrespect in which he was held" (Poliakov 1979, 8).

Besides exploiting this type of deep-seated prejudice, the legitimization for treatment of "others" in Nazi Germany was interwoven with the government's assertion of its national purpose and lofty goals. Hitler had declared in *Mein Kampf:*

> What we must fight for is to safeguard the existence and reproduction of our race and our people, the sustenance of our children and the purity of our blood, the freedom and independence of the fatherland, so that our people may mature for the fulfillment of the mission allotted it by the creator of the universe. (quoted in Dawidowicz 1975, 44)

This appeal for the resurrection of Germany justified human rights violations of all sorts, from denial of work to the denial of life, coopting the bystander and impelling the perpetrator. Acquiescence and participation in exploitative, destructive policies were easier when perceived as serving the national good and when, as was the case in Germany, the devaluation and dehumanization of the victimized groups had deep roots in national history.

Examination of the responses to Nazi genocidal policies in different areas of occupied Europe offers important material for study. Why did over 80 percent of the Jews in France, Poland, and Holland perish, whereas in Italy and Denmark over 80 percent of the Jews survived? What took place in France and Holland that appears to have facilitated the rationalization of injustice and its extension into mass murder? What other processes occurred in Italy and Denmark that facilitated the survival of Jews? Careful study of the variations in responses to patterns of injustice during the Holocaust can shed light on the extent to which democratic values and other cultural norms limited the power of Nazi Germany's dehumanizing policies and practices in certain states. Doing so can help to affirm a commitment to democratic values and human dignity.

Theme #3: Incremental Evil: Erosion of Human Rights

After World War II, a German professor described the process of "incremental evil" in the following manner:

> If the last and worst act of the whole [Nazi] regime had come immediately after the first and smallest, thousands, yes millions, would have been sufficiently shocked [...] But of course this isn't the way it happens. In between come all the hundreds of little steps, some of them imperceptible, each of them preparing you not to be shocked by the next. Step C is not so much worse than Step B, and, if you did not make a stand at Step B, why should

you at Step C? And so on to Step D. (Facing History and Ourselves 1994, xiv)

Instruction about the Holocaust should strive to make students aware of the need to be on guard against policies that violate human rights. By examining the anti-Semitic legislation in Germany between 1933 and 1941, students will understand the *step by step* approach taken by the Nazis in order to make anti-Semitism more palatable to the majority in Germany, to make Jews more cooperative, and to avoid foreign reactions (Zornberg 1995, 45). By doing so, students will be better prepared to recognize "first steps" and to combat "small" human rights violations.

When applying learning derived from the study of the Holocaust, teachers can involve students in examining human rights conditions in the post World War II world. By employing a list of human rights derived from the Universal Declaration and the Covenants discussed earlier, students can assess conditions in their own country and identify actions to be taken.

Of course, not all human rights violations are steps toward genocide. To make too tight a fit between specific violations and the possibility of genocide might encourage our students to dismiss as farfetched the conditions being considered. Nevertheless, the damage being done to those whose rights are being violated is very real. Students who have studied the Holocaust might be better situated to recognize the importance of acting on their behalf.

Theme #4: Courage and Resistance to Patterns of Oppression

Although only a small percentage of the population in occupied Europe actually took steps to resist Nazi policies of genocide and offer assistance to targeted victim groups, stories of these individuals shed light on important qualities of defenders of human rights. Findings from a research study based on interviews with over 600 rescuers of Jews during the Holocaust suggest that those who risked their lives to save members of targeted groups were more likely than nonrescuers to exhibit "the tendency to assume commitments and responsibilities towards other people" (Oliner and Oliner 1988). The researchers concluded that rescuers were more likely to have strong attachments to the people in their immediate environment (family and Jewish friends) and to ideals that forged linkages to the wider world (broad social commitments and egalitarianism) (Oliner and Oliner 1988).

The study of the Holocaust abounds with examples that highlight such commitments and assertion of responsibilities. For example, Le Chambon-sur-Lignon, a French Huguenot community in southern France sheltered and facilitated the rescue of over 5,000 Jewish youths during the Holocaust. Led by the Protestant minister André Trocme, the network of small villages in this French mountain region shared a commitment to providing shelter and refuge for Jews. It was a commitment based not only on a belief in the common humanity and dignity of all people, but also on a determination to sustain the values and moral principles that were at the core of community life. In another example, the Italian military sheltered Jews from German deportations during the period 1940-43 in areas administered by the Italian military in France, Yugoslavia, Greece, and North Africa. Their actions represented a mixture of Italian national pride, a disregard for Italian Fascist ideology, the rejection of biological racism as a world view, and the continuity of core value commitments emphasizing support for the persecuted and universal concern for those in need. Protection of Jews by Italian military and diplomatic officials continued until the September 1943 armistice with the Allies. This armistice precipitated the Nazi occupation of central and northern Italy, resulting in the deportation and eventual killing of over 8,000 Italian and foreign Jews living on Italian soil. Even during German occupation, Italians of all backgrounds, with the exception of a small minority of Italian anti-Semites who worked for the Fascist puppet government from November 1943 to the end of World War II, actively harbored Jews and resisted the efforts of Nazi Germany to exterminate them (Fernekes 1996; Steinberg 1990).

There are also the well-publicized stories of the Swedish diplomat Raoul Wallenberg, the German industrialist Oskar Schindler, and the pilots of the Danish fishing boats whose courage and ingenuity saved thousands of Jews. In addition, there are the less renowned stories of the "Righteous Gentiles" who sheltered, hid, and otherwise protected Jews from extermination in countries all over Europe. They have been honored at Yad Vashem, the memorial to the Holocaust located outside of Jerusalem (Hellman 1980). Finally, there are the stories of those who resisted. Resistance took many forms. The United States Holocaust Memorial Museum guidelines for teaching the Holocaust refer to armed revolt, partisan activism ranging from smuggling supplies to armed engagement, acts of willful disobedience such as practicing one's religion and cultural traditions in defiance of the rules, creating art, music, and poetry with the confines of the camps, and simply maintaining the will to live in the face of abject brutality (United States Holocaust Memorial Museum 1994, 5). There are stories here that complement those about the multitudes who went to their death without rising up in their own defense – a complex occurrence that eludes simple explanations.

Students need to encounter these types of stories as well as those of human rights violations imposed by the state and its supporters. Combining these stories with instructional strategies that incorporate moral decision making, collaborative learning, and discussion of ethical concerns supports some of the major tenets of human rights education, notably those of responsibility and caring. In this way, educators can contribute to the development of informed and empathic learners who might act on behalf of others when the need arises.

Instructional Approaches to Strengthen Human Rights and Oppose Genocidal Policies

If young people are to draw on their understanding of the Holocaust to become advocates for human rights, teachers need to incorporate certain principles into their instruction. First, understanding of context is critical. The complexity of historical or contemporary cases involving human rights and/or genocide must be acknowledged so that students and teachers develop conclusions that are grounded in accurate knowledge about each case. In the study of specific cases of resistance and rescue during the Holocaust, it would be improper to make comparisons between countries such as Italy, Poland, and Denmark, without recognizing the important variations in the policies of Nazi Germany during the period of occupation. Whereas Denmark was able to retain its own king and governmental structure from 1940 through September 1943, Poland was subdivided into regions and placed under direct German control from September 1939 until its liberation by the Soviet military in 1944-45. The nature of the occupation in Poland was far more harsh and severe than in Denmark, a factor that must be recognized and accounted for when considering the nature of resistance in both societies. Similarly, human rights violations carried out by the Third Reich against Jews and other targeted groups in Germany prior to 1939 must be viewed within the context of a climate of international disinterest and unwillingness to take action against state-sponsored violence, which permitted Hitler and the Nazis essentially to have a free hand in oppressing their victims. It would be informative for students to compare and contrast the influence of international concern and condemnation at that era with contemporary efforts in halting and/or punishing genocidal behavior by states. Today wholesale persecution and attempted genocide of entire cultures are condemned and resisted by international organizations, nongovernmental organizations, and independent states. Evaluating these anti-genocide efforts in light of the actions of the governments in Cambodia, Rwanda, and Bosnia would, no doubt, help to identify effective responses and those that need to be changed.

Second, reducing the distance between the learner and the objects of study should be a central focus of human rights and genocide education. Examination of the personal dilemmas faced by targeted groups and individuals, whether they be from the Holocaust (Jews, Sinti/Romani, Jehovah's Witnesses, or others) or individual prisoners of conscience or other victims of persecution from the past or present, establishes a direct connection between the learner and the object of study. It is conceptually difficult for learners to understand the scale of genocidal policies when they are rendered as statistical abstractions; thus teachers should translate statistics into people by facilitating the study of personal lives and stories, notably through the use of memoirs, autobiographies, fiction, testimony, and other means. By focusing on the values, beliefs, and decisions made by ordinary people (including oppressors, victims, activists, and bystanders), students see that the struggle for human rights is truly the outcome of everyday decisions, often made in difficult circumstances but always linked to contextual factors and long-standing value commitments.

Third, learners should be trained in social action strategies to apply their understanding of concepts and content from human rights and genocide cases to contemporary and future life situations. Although Nazi Holocaust policies ceased in 1945, the legacy of the tragedy continues to have major repercussions in contemporary society, ranging from investigations into compensation for the diversion of expropriated funds and property by neutral nations to the influence of the Nuremberg trials on the creation of a permanent international criminal court by the United Nations. Given opportunities for establishing linkages between the Holocaust and contemporary affairs, students should be encouraged to make careful and grounded judgments about the Holocaust's legacy for human rights work. One such opportunity is the development of public forums in which students can share their insights with adults in their own communities or electronically through the Internet with communities worldwide.

Recognizing that the concept of universal human rights is far better known in 1998 than in 1948 when the UDHR was introduced to the UN General Assembly, students can return to the violations of human rights faced in Nazi Germany and investigate if those types of violations are prevalent and pervasive in their own world. To what degree has citizen action led to changes in the defense and support of human rights since the end of World War II? In what ways are the ideals of the UDHR being realized in the United States and other societies? By examining the real or perceived dissonance between the ideals of universal human rights and the practices of governments today, students can identify conditions in need of change and offer suggestions for action to improve the quality of life of people in communities, near and far.

Conclusion: Encouraging Dispositions of Caring and Responsibility

In concluding, let us return to the theme of moral responsibility in an interdependent world that launched this essay. The following poem, created from a statement attributed to Pastor Martin Niemoller, starkly poses the consequences of apathy and the failure to assume moral responsibility for one's fellow citizens.

> First they came first for the socialists,
> and I did not speak out
> because I was not a socialist.
> Then they came for the trade unionists,
> and I did not speak out
> because I was not a trade unionist.
> Then they came for the Jews,
> and I did not speak out
> because I was not a Jew.
> Then they came for me,
> and there was no one was left to speak for me. (Niemoller 1986)

Responsibility and caring are core themes in human rights education programs, as well as being essential dispositions for global citizenship. The letter to teachers presented at the beginning of this essay, coupled with the indictment of apathy and indifference offered by Pastor Niemoller, challenge educators to create school communities that foster caring for others and engagement on their behalf (Noddings 1995).

As educators, we must challenge "we-they" dichotomies and the portrayal of the "other" that feed ethnocentrism and devalue human beings. In the spirit of multicultural and global education, Staub, who has analyzed the roots of genocide in various countries, argues for the need "to teach children about the shared humanity of all people" (Staub 1992, 405).

> In the educational realm, children can learn about the differences in customs, beliefs, and values of different groups of individuals while coming to appreciate commonalities in desires, yearnings, feelings of joy and sorrow, and physical and other needs. (Staub 1992, 405)

Such an orientation not only provides opportunity for all children to be recognized and valued but also connects them with others different from themselves. This is essential; however, it is only a small part of what is needed.

To challenge we-they dichotomies and ethnocentric thinking requires the development of a critical, though not hostile, stance toward authority consistent with democratic principles. Using the experience in Nazi Germany as a point of comparison, students should be encouraged to raise ethical/moral questions about local (school and community) and national policies and practices. They need to consider the legitimacy of the demands for obedience and begin to develop their own criteria, ethical and otherwise, for obeying.

Creating caring communities through the establishment of "cross-cutting relations" among society's subgroups (Staub 1989, 174) can be done within the classroom and through action learning projects within the community. Cooperating connects, and doing for/with others builds bridges between the "we" and "they." Rather than being just students of (and, by definition, bystanders to) social justice, students can identify projects that enable them to act on behalf of those whose human rights have been violated and those in danger of being violated. They might engage in action learning projects by working with Amnesty International's Urgent Action campaigns that are specifically designed for school children (see website <www.amnestyusa.org/education>), join a human rights campaign against hunger, homelessness or sweatshops, or initiate actions about prejudice and discrimination within their school and community. The list of opportunities is endless.

Schools can model a commitment to caring by incorporating community service into school graduation requirements. They might also make December 10th, the anniversary of the signing at the United Nations of the Universal Declaration of Human Rights, a day of celebration and an affirmation of commitment to justice. The day might include honoring students, teachers, and community members who acted on behalf of others, who did not stand by while rights were being violated, and who served as a conscience for the community. Communities of caring are constructed through mutual valuing and providing advocacy and protection for everyone's rights.

With institutional support, teachers can, as one educator wrote, "model caring behaviors, offer students opportunities to practice caring, support a widening circle of relationships in which caring is more likely to be meaningful, and regularly reward and affirm caring behavior" (Bosworth 1995, 693). The systematic development of caring, empathic environments in schools, combined with instruction about the Holocaust and other genocides using a human rights framework, can help young people develop the skills, attitudes, and knowledge to act decisively to protect and promote the human rights for all.

Note

I thank my colleague Bill Fernekes for permitting me to incorporate some of his contributions from an article we wrote together. See Shiman, David A. and William R. Fernekes. 1999. The Holocaust, Human Rights, and Democratic Citizenship Education. *Social Studies* 90:2, 53-62.

Literature Cited

Bosworth, K. 1995. Caring for Others and Being Cared for: Students Talk Caring in School. *Phi Delta Kappan* 76:9 (May): 686-693.

Chalk, Frank, and Kurt Jonassohn. 1990. *The History and Sociology of Genocide: Analyses and Case Studies*. New Haven, Connecticut: Yale University Press.

Dawidowicz, Lucy. 1975. *The War against the Jews 1933-1945*. New York: Penguin Books.

Facing History and Ourselves. 1994. *Holocaust and Human Behavior: Resource Book*. Brookline, Massachusetts: Facing History and Ourselves National Foundation.

Ferencz, Benjamin. 1996. War Crimes Trials – The Holocaust and the Rule of lLaw. In *Pursuit of justice: Examining the evidence of the Holocaust*. Washington, D.C.: United States Holocaust Memorial Museum.

Fernekes, William R. 1995. *Education against Prejudice: Presentation on Behalf of the United States Holocaust Memorial Museum* (paper presented at the Education against Prejudice Invitational Conference, Moscow, Russia, November 1995).

Fernekes, William R. 1996. *More Light than Darkness: the Foundations of Italian and Danish Responses to Nazi Genocidal Policies During World War II*. (unpublished manuscript).

Fernekes, William R. 2000. Education for Social Responsibility: the Holocaust, Human Rights, and Classroom Practice. In *The Holocaust's Ghost: Writings on Art, Politics, Law, and Education*. eds. F.C. Decoste, F.C. and Benjamin Schwartz, pp. 496-512. Calgary, Alberta: University of Alberta Press, 496-512

Flaim, R.F., and E.W. Reynolds. (eds.). 1983. *The Holocaust and Genocide: A Search for Conscience. A Curriculum Guide*. New York: Anti-Defamation League of B'nai B'rith.

Flowers Nancy, and David A. Shiman. 1997. Teacher Education and the Human Rights Vision. In *Human Rights Education for the Twenty-First Century*, ed. George J Andreopoulos, and Richard .P. Claude, pp. 161-175. Philadelphia: University of Pennsylvania Press.

Friedlander, Henry. 1979. Towards a Methodology of Teaching about the Holocaust. *Teachers College Record* 80(5): 519-542.

Ginott, Haim G. 1972. *Teacher and Child*, New York: Macmillan Company.

Guyette, Elise, and David A. Shiman. 1998. History and Human Rights: A Process for Analyzing Events, In *Human Rights, Here and Now*, ed. Nancy Flowers, pp. 75-78. Minneapolis, Minnesota: University of Minnesota Human Rights Center.

Hellman, Peter. 1980. *Avenue of the Righteous*. New York: Atheneum.

Hilberg, Raul (ed.). 1971. *Documents of Destruction: Germany and Jewry 1933-1954*. Chicago: Quadrangle Books.

Hilberg, Raul. 1992. *Perpetrators, Victims, Bystanders: The Jewish Catastrophe, 1933-1945*. New York: Harper Collins.

Keen, Sam. 1984. *Faces of the Enemy*. San Francisco: Harper and Row.

Kershaw, Ian 1995. The Extinction of Human Rights in Nazi Germany. In *Historical Change and Human Rights: The Oxford Amnesty Lectures 1994*, ed. O. Hufton, pp. 217-246 New York: Harper Collins Publishers.

Kuper, Leo. 1981. *Genocide*. New Haven, Connecticut: Yale University Press.

Nanda, Ved., J.R. Scarritt, and George W. Shepherd, Jr.(eds.). 1981. *Global Human Rights: Public Policies, Comparative Measures, and NGO Strategies*. Boulder, Colorado: Westview Press.

National Council for the Social Studies. 1985. *Human Rights* (theme Issue). Washington, D.C.: National Council for the Social Studies.

Niemoller, Martin. 1986. First they came for the socialists. In *Exile in the Fatherland, Martin Niemoller's Letters from Moabit Prison*. ed. Hubert G. Locke, Preface. Grand Rapids, Michigan: William B. Eerdman's Publishing.

Noddings, Nel. 1995. Teaching Themes of Caring. *Phi Delta Kappan* 76:9 (May), 675-679.

Oliner, Samuel P., and Pearl M. Oliner. 1988. *The Altruistic Personality – Rescuers of Jews in Nazi Europe*. New York: The Free Press.

Pettman, Ralph. 1986. *Teaching Human Rights: Grades 5-8*. Canberra, Australia: Australian Government Publishing Service.

Pettman, Ralph. 1986. *Teaching Human Rights: Pre-School and Grades 1-4*. Canberra, Australia: Australian Government Publishing Service.

Poliakov, Leon. 1979. *Harvest of Hate: The Nazi Program for the Destruction of the Jews of Europe*. New York: Holocaust Library.

Rabinsky, L. B., and C. Danks (eds.). 1994. *The Holocaust: Prejudice Unleashed*. Columbus, Ohio: Ohio Council on Holocaust Education.

Ryan, William. 1971. Blaming the Victim. New York: Pantheon Books.

Scrase, David, and Wolfgang Mieder (eds.). 1996. *The Holocaust: Introductory Essays*. Burlington, Vermont: University of Vermont's Center for Holocaust Studies.

Shiman, David A. 1985. *Teaching about Human Rights*. Denver, Colorado: Center for Teaching International Relations, University of Denver.

Shiman, David A. and William R. Fernekes. 1999. The Holocaust, Human Rights, and Democratic Citizenship Education. *Social Studies* 90(2): 53-62.

State of California. 1987. *Model Curriculum for Human Rights and Genocide*. Sacramento, California: California State Department of Education.

State of Connecticut. 1987. *Human Rights: The Struggle for Freedom, Dignity and Equality*. Hartford, Connecticut: Department of Education.

State of Florida. 1998. *Resource Manual on Holocaust Education*. Tallahassee, Florida: Department of Education.

State of New Jersey. 1995. *The Betrayal of Mankind: The Holocaust and Genocide, Curriculum Guide 7-12*. Trenton, New Jersey: New Jersey Commission on Holocaust Education.

State of Virginia. 1987. *Teaching the Past Describes Today...Tomorrow. Human Rights Education. Focus: Human Rights Education*. Richmond, Virginia: Virginia Department of Education.

Staub, Ervin. 1989. *The Roots of evil: The origins of genocide and other group violence*. New York: Cambridge University Press.

Staub, Ervin. 1992. The Origins of Caring, Helping, and Nonaggression: Parental Socialization, the Family System, Schools and Cultural Influence. In *Embracing the Other: Philosophical, Psychological, and Historical Perspectives on Altruism*, eds. Pearl M. Oliner, S. P. Oliner, L. Baron, L. A. Blum, and D. L. Krebs, pp. 390-412. New York: New York University Press.

Steinberg, Jonathan. 1990. *All of Nothing: The Axis and the Holocaust, 1941-1943*. London: Routledge.

United Nations. 1989. *ABC Teaching Human Rights: Practical Activities for Primary and Secondary Schools*. New York: United Nations.

United Nations. 1948. *Universal Declaration of Human Rights*. New York: United Nations.

United States Holocaust Memorial Museum. 1994. *Guidelines for Teaching about the Holocaust*, Washington, D.C.: United States Holocaust Memorial Museum.

Wood, G. 1992. *Schools that Work*. New York: Penguin Books.

Zornberg, Ira. 1995. *Classroom Strategies for Teaching about the Holocaust*. New York: Anti-Defamation League of B'nai B'rith.

A Jewish Response to Philosophical Questioning

Reflections on Emmanuel Levinas and the Holocaust

Richard I. Sugarman

Is it possible to study and teach the Holocaust from within the context of Jewish self-understanding? What would this mean? Even the most minimal positions of traditional Jewish understanding of God and human society were shaken by the ordeal of the Holocaust. Here I am speaking of the foundation of monotheism: the existence, benevolence, and perfection of a transcendent Divinity. These primary categories of Jewish theology were tested in the concrete, as never before, in the historical hour that divides Jewish history in two.

How are we to understand the responsibility for elevating "the witness" from an experiential to a philosophical category? This arduous philosophic task is one that Emmanuel Levinas (1906-1995) takes upon himself. Levinas recognized that his philosophic education, Talmudic training, and direct experience during the years of the Nazi horror presented him with an added responsibility to undertake the burden of such questioning. This essay is devoted to delineating the religious-philosophic stance of Levinas toward the Holocaust. This involves re-thinking some of the basic categories of traditional Western philosophy, categories foundational to European culture, and therefore to the study of the Humanities and its irreducible subject, the human being. Levinas raises the inescapable question of what the trial of the Holocaust means for Judaism, its understanding of itself, and the precarious place of the Jewish people among the nations.

Levinas writes on many levels. From among his vast literary *œuvre* there are only a few texts devoted exclusively to the Holocaust. However, from the mid-thirties until his last works, the haunting challenge presented by the phenomenon of the Holocaust is always a shadow on the margins of his philosophic and theological writing.

Emmanuel Levinas was born and raised in a traditional Jewish family in Kovno, Lithuania, for centuries a citadel of Talmudic learning until it was utterly destroyed by the Nazis. Levinas moved to France at the age of seventeen in order to study at the University of Strasbourg. He became a student of Husserl in the late twenties. Husserl, the founder of phenomenology, would devise a method of pure description of "meanings" that would transform philosophy into a rigorous science. During this same period (1928-29), Levinas attended the lectures of Martin Heidegger, Husserl's protégé before Heidegger embraced Hitlerism in 1933.

The meaning of Being itself as it unfolds as time and history, what all entities would hold in common, is the subject of Heidegger's pioneering work, *Being and Time* (1927). Levinas' early works are devoted to explicating the work of Husserl and exploring the modifications introduced by Heidegger. Levinas wrote translations of Husserl and articles devoted to phenomenology in the early thirties, thereby introducing the study of phenomenology to France. In the great debate between Ernst Cassirer and Heidegger at Davos in 1929, Heidegger requested that the young Levinas serve as his assistant. How stunning, then, the subsequent betrayal of morality by Heidegger.

Levinas occupies a unique position in the history of philosophy and Judaism, having studied and mastered the philosophy of Heidegger, whose name would become forever linked with the perpetrators of the Third Reich. In the mid-thirties Levinas accepted a position as a teacher for Israelite Universal Alliance. His interest in the Sacred texts of Judaism took a more philosophic turn with his reading of Franz Rosenzweig's *Star of Redemption* in 1934. As Richard Cohen notes in *Elevations*, Levinas' reading of Rosenzweig's philosophy of Judaism animates in Levinas the desire to renew previously submerged Hebraic wellsprings within philosophy (Cohen 1994). As early as 1935, Levinas authored a piece on the power and menace of "The Philosophy of Hiterlism" with subtle intimations of the relevance of Heidegger's ontological imperialism, where human beings would ultimately be reduced to the 'pure will' of the meaning of Being unfolding in history.

Levinas, the philosophical witness to the Holocaust, *par excellence*, was also a victim. During the Holocaust, Levinas survived for five years, from 1940 to 1945, in a camp designated for French Jewish prisoners of war near

Hannover. Only his wife and daughter survived with him. His entire family of origin, including his father, his mother, and his brothers were murdered in Lithuania.

Transforming philosophy in the direction of an irreducible ethics would become Levinas' post-war obsession. At the same time, he would devote himself to explicating what remained the unique vocation of Judaism in time of the nations.

Levinas' encounter with the Talmud would come much later. Beginning in 1947, he studied personally with a prestigious and rigorous Talmudic teacher, Morderchai Shoushanni. By this time Levinas was well known in continental philosophical circles. Only after his release from the German prisoner of war camp did Levinas begin to study, write, publicly lecture, and publish an ongoing series of philosophical readings of the Talmud, with special emphasis on the moral and religious guidance that the Talmud can provide on the contemporary world.

A Jewish Response to Philosophical Questioning

While Levinas writes on the Holocaust directly only in several essays in a vast corpus of philosophical writings spanning sixty years, he acknowledges in *Signature*, a trenchant autobiographical piece, that he thinks and writes in the "presentiment and memory of the Nazi horror." His best known piece on the Holocaust, "To Love the Torah More than God" (1979), opens a way for a radical philosophical questioning which arises in anticipation of a response that would not separate itself from the tenets of normative Judaism. At the same time, Levinas searches for an ethical foundation to philosophy. For Levinas, ethics – not ontology – emerges as "first philosophy."

What does this mean? Ultimately, no less than beginning the project of philosophy anew. His re-thinking of the tradition of the relation of ethics to ontology emerges in short texts, the first entitled *Existence and Existents*, begun "in the stalag." Here Levinas affirms that despite a philosophical debt to Heidegger, "it is necessary to leave the climate of that philosophy" (Levinas 1988, 15). The philosopher is responsible for his conduct even before he articulates a point of view. He is answerable to the other whose status as an "existent" always exceeds one's thematic appropriation of him. The other is ethically irreducible. His humanity may be expressed but is never exhausted by his function or significance for a system of linguistic signs or symbols. For example, before I encounter him (contra Buber), I am aware that he exceeds any possible relation that I may have with him. My sense of the other's mortality orients my sense of responding to the other in time. These themes emerge in Levinas' philosophically original work *Time and the*

Other, published in 1947, shortly after the appearance of *Existence and Existents* that same year.

Ethics, for Levinas, begins with this calling into question of my spontaneity by the other person. Explanation originates in expressing one's self to someone else. For Levinas, to reason is to justify oneself in the face of the other's questioning glance. In other words, I recognize the face of the other as registering my presence, position, and meaning. The meaning of discourse depends upon the expression of the face of the other. Otherwise there would be no possibility of distinguishing what is meant from what is said. Even dissimulation depends upon the capacity of a prior credibility and sincerity. This is one of the ways in which ethics is elevated by Levinas to the rank of "first philosophy." If we are condemned to think, that is to do philosophy, for better or worse, then prior to any "proof" there exists a moral responsibility that accompanies my responding to the other. For Levinas, the other comes before the self.

All these themes are adumbrated in Levinas' majestic work, *Totality and Infinity: An Essay on Exteriority* (1961) and elaborated in *Otherwise than Being: Beyond Essence* (1974), and in subsequent works, especially *Of God Who Comes to Mind* (1986). In these works and in the texts which distill his thinking until the very end of his life, one can see the traces of his remark from *Signature*: "All of this was written in the presentiment and memory of the Holocaust."

Levinas' way of reconceiving philosophy is all the more urgent in the aftermath of the Holocaust. Levinas is proposing a deconstruction of Being and a revaluing of the primacy of the other. The ethical demand that issues from the face of the other precedes claims made in the name of reason. It is through the face of the other that the Infinite makes itself visible in the finite, and conversely where the finite shows its fragility and expresses its shame before the Infinite. The mobile countenance of the other person interrupts the murderous impulse to violate the other. The promotion of ethics to the rank of "first philosophy" where freedom is finite, invested as responsibility which is infinite, bears witness to a time when the demotion of man is recognized as the most extreme inversion of Justice.

A Jewish Response: Between Question and Answer

There is a specifically Jewish dimension to the Holocaust that remains ineradicable. The Holocaust cannot escape its relation with the Jewish people, Jewish sources, the tradition that has guided the understanding of those sources, and the absence of all arresting answers despite or because of this tradition. Such a religious-theological approach to the Holocaust diverges from the ethical-philosophical in terms of its specificity. Still, while the words spoken are different, the language of philosophy, beginning with speaking with the other, solicits multiple interlocutors. Here there may be Jewish questioning in search of philosophical responses as well as the converse. In the language of traditional Judaism, a wise man is called a "Talmud Chachim," a student of wisdom. Here, we will take our clue from Levinas once again remembering that a philosopher is also one who is a lover of wisdom.

In order to engage in this peculiarly Jewish kind of enquiry, Levinas positions himself in the chain of traditional Jewish Theology by stretching one of its vital links. His governing premise is that questions can be asked within the context of the Torah through which God permits Himself to be questioned. Levinas first advances this position distinctively in his article "To Love the Torah More than God" (1979). Here, he returns to Biblical and Talmudic sources from which to take guidance for right conduct and understanding in the absence of theological certitude. Here, one finds echoes of the position of the eminent ninth century Jewish philosopher and sage, R. Saadia Gaon: "Our nation is a nation only by virtue of its Torah" (cited from Schwartz and Goldstein 1995, 256). Among the foundational precepts of the Torah is the affirmation that there is both justice and a Judge. Levinas' questioning emerges as part of a tradition which finds its first Biblical formulation in Genesis when Abraham receives an affirmative response to the question he asks: "Will not the Judge of all the earth do justly" (Gen. 18)? Where does one look, what does one do, when justice is not visible in the administration of human society? How much more urgent is this question when the absolute inversion of justice rules in an unprecedented manner.

Faith, prayer, trust, and hope were affirmed, denied, and ridiculed before, during and after the destruction of European Jewry during the Holocaust. One thinks of the prayer offered up by one of the survivors of a selection in Primo Levi's *Survival in Auschwitz*. Levi, the witness to this event, says "If I were God, I would have spit on his prayer" (Levi 1961, 152). Primo Levi has no use for such pious egoism. However understandable Levi's rejection, it leaves the phenomenon of prayer, the existence of God, and the reach of human responsibility unexplored. Conversely, there are examples where the lives of the victims were strengthened by what they regarded as the supreme test of their fidelity toward obligations of Jewish life, expressed in this most extreme ordeal. One of the most revealing examples was that of R. Elchanan Wasserman who, when taken out to be killed, remarked in the fashion of R.

Akiva that he was now fulfilling the "ultimate *mitzvah*," namely, to die *al kiddush Ha Shem*, that is, in a way that would sanctify the Divine name (Levi 1961, 208).

Before we can assess what is moral or immoral conduct, we must reckon with the opening question of Levinas' majestic work *Totality and Infinity*; "The question is whether or not we are duped by morality." Levinas spends the last fifty years of his life searching for ways to show that morality is inseparable from philosophy.

Unlike Job's friends, Levinas resists the temptation to explain the ways of Divinity to the victims and to suggest that where there is suffering, there must be sin. At the same time, he refuses to go the way of Rubenstein and other "death of God" theologians. Like Levi Yitzchak of Berditchev, he would interrogate the Almighty only on the basis of His own teaching and laws, the Torah. However, unlike Berditchev, Levinas does not work to reconcile creature with Creator. Rather he positions the Torah as fence against the madness that can issue from a direct contact with the Sacred. Jewish morality and right conduct find expression in the study and application of the laws of the Torah, even when Transendence is expressed as an absence.

From a philosophical point of view, Levinas is searching for the minimal conditions that must hold in order to show how it is that we do and can recognize the difference between perpetrators, victims, and bystanders. Levinas translates the language of the religious into the more universal language of philosophy. His distinctions must remain recognizable for atheists, believers, mystics, and agnostics alike. In this sense, his philosophical obsession is with understanding the conditions for the possibility of comprehending justice. The trace of the Transcendant is described through inter-human intrigue, for how can we speak meaningfully of human suffering, responsibility, and injustice unless these phenomena register as a presence or absence to human consciousness? Much of the thrust of Levinas' philosophic work is devoted to elaborating an ethical metaphysics that would serve to make these phenomena intelligible.

Levinas' work emphasizes the inseparability of morality and humanity. For Levinas, what was unique to the Holocaust was the crisis of morality itself. Part of his philosophic project consists in searching for those minimal conditions and categories that would make just ethical and religious discourse possible.

For the victims of the Nazi horror there existed a peculiar kind of loneliness in what appeared to be the disappearance of just institutions: "Who will say of the loneliness of those who thought themselves dying at the same time as Justice, at a time when the judgements between good and evil found no criterion but in the recesses of subjective conscience, no sign from without?"

(Levinas 1996, 119). How does one live in the absence of Justice, if one is able to survive at all? From a philosophical point of view, there is an inescapable recourse to what might appear an alibi: "The true life is absent." However, there is a decisive metaphysical difference between absence and non-existence, so long obscured in the history of philosophy. Awareness of this distinction offers scant consolation, but nonetheless permits a degree of intelligibility to emerge.

What is absent can reappear. My attachment to someone who is no longer is very different from one who never existed. My relation to the absent other tests my fidelity, my assumption of responsibility, and calls forth restraint and patience on my part. Here, Levinas' phenomenological approach begins with an investigation into some of the minimal conditions for a moral life. This will extend to the realm of the religious, for which ethics is itself an irreducible condition. The innocent one is recognizable in his agony only if the absence of justice presents itself to human consciousness. The catastrophe perpetrated on European Jewry is rendered tragic only when suffering appears as the inversion or postponement of meaning.

Tradition, unlike nostalgia, exists for the sake of the future while binding itself in the present to the past. Levinas' reading of the Sacred texts of Judaism makes the tradition of these texts come alive. The first self-consciously Jewish text linking persecution to anti-Semitism is found in the Scroll of Esther. Is it by accident, Levinas asks, whether the Book of Esther, the only text of the Bible to take place in the Diaspora, is also the only text that does not mention the name of God? Levinas presents his own gloss on the subject: "Among the nations! The opposite of the intimacy between God and Israel [...]. Here, in the Scroll of Esther there is persecution. [...] a book on anti-Semitism is intelligible only to Jews in their language and their writing!" Here, we might wish to ask Levinas the reason for what appears to be a hyperbolic claim. It has to do with the consciousness of the victim. "The suffering of anti-Semitic persecution can only be told in the language of the victim." However, his claim reaches further: "This suffering is not interchangeable through a series of signs." He refuses to see this suffering as a species of a type, "whatever the sociologists may say [...], even if all the other problems taken up in the Scriptures are inter-human and can be translated into all languages. Why? Is it perhaps because only the victims can fully register their own suffering and only they can grant pardon in their own names? [...] That cannot be translated into other languages! Is the word 'Holocaust' not too Greek to express the Passion?" He concludes his commentary by returning to the phenomenon of absence. "The name of God is not pronounced in the Scroll of Esther. But it is precisely there that His presence is expressed by His absence, beyond all nomination" (Levinas 1994, 45-46). Levinas implies that the absence expressed in the Book of Esther echoes in the condition of European Jews during the Holocaust.

If the language of the victims speaks for itself, it is not for itself alone that is answerable to others. In responding to his own question of the moral/religious legacy of the SHOAH, Levinas moves from the social, to the moral, to the religious dimensions of life. He precedes his pedagogical distillation by evoking the beginnings of the Book of Lamentations. In *Proper Names* he compares the abandonment of European Jewry during the Holocaust to the period of the destruction of the First Temple (586 BCE):

> Interregnum or the end of the Institutions, as if Being itself had been suspended. [...] not the least manifesto on the rights of Man [...]. Absence of any homeland, eviction from all French soil. Silence of every Church! Insecurity of all companionship. So these were the straits of the first chapter of *Lamentation*: None to comfort her! and to the complaint of the Yom Kippur ritual: "no high priests to offer sacrifices, nor any altar upon which to place to offer our holocausts." (Levinas 1996, 120)

Here, we see Levinas again linking the suffering of the Holocaust to ancient Biblical precedents. Once again he turns to traditional sources to illuminate the present, and in so doing binds the Jewish suffering to Judaism.

In Levinas' writings, however, there is an absence of unreflective theodicy, a bracketing of any discussion of spiritual blemishes as "causes" or the consolations that would come from rebuilding. Still, there are lessons to be learned. Even in memory, there is responsibility. In *God, Death, and Time*, Levinas elevates the phenomenon of "witnessing" to a philosophical category with active, moral responsibility. "Prior to all dialogue, the witness expresses his readiness to respond to and for the other within the formula 'Here am I' (Levinas 2000, 198). The "Here am I" implies a position from which I can extend myself in the direction of the future; memory survives in this futurity. At the same time it reverses the invisible subjectivity and potential tyranny of Gyges. I permit myself to stand in the accusative, the act of being seen without arrogating to myself the position of neutrality, or indifference, the myth of the privilege of the omnipresent spectator. Here, my responsibility knows no limits: "As a dedication of oneself, this witnessing is an opening of the self that expresses the surplus of exigency that expands as the exigency of responsibility is filled" (Levinas 2000, 198). Responsibility, then, expands with the knowledge gained by witnessing. In this sense, Levinas presses the argument that all knowledge takes on the transitive act of witnessing. The more one learns about the Holocaust, the more responsible one is for transmitting its moral lessons.

Levinas writes in *Proper Names* that there are at least three truths to be learned from the Holocaust that are "transmissible and necessary to a new generation" (Levinas 1996, 120). These include lessons that are addressed to everyone, and to Jews in particular. First, he warns against forgetting the fragility of living among the nations. He purposefully uses the charged word "assimilation" in this context to remind us of what we can and cannot do without. Here, he is speaking of assimilation as a culturally sedimented way of thinking and not simply as a matter of spatial proximity. Rather, this includes a kind of moral proximity. What does this mean? Levinas tries to clarify this matter in the second transmissible truth. "In crucial times when the perishability of so many values is revealed, all human dignity consists in believing in their return" (Levinas 1996, 121). He appears to be speaking of a kind of "believing" that can be tested in the realm of conduct:

> The highest duty, when 'all is permitted,' consists in feeling oneself responsible with regard to the values of peace. In not concluding, in a universe at war, that warlike virtues are the only sure ones; in not taking pleasure, during the tragic situation in the virile virtues of death and desperate murder. (Levinas 1996, 121)

Here, Levinas situates the Jewish condition proximate to the human condition. He then returns to his first lesson, while absorbing the second:

> But – the third truth – we must henceforth, in the inevitable resumption of civilization and assimilation, teach the new generation the necessary strength to remain strong in isolation, and all that a fragile consciousness is called upon to contain at such times. We must, reviving the memory of those who, non-Jews and Jews, without even knowing or seeing each other, found a way to behave amidst total chaos, as if the world had not fallen apart. (Levinas 1996, 121)

This is part of the responsibility inscribed by what we have characterized as the tradition of Jewish self-understanding.

Learning and Responsibility

If we are following the arguments put forward by Levinas, then there exists a Jewish way of responding to human suffering in the absence of visible justice that is relevant to everyone. From what Levinas has described, we learn that the position of the bystander is also that of "witness," and therefore charged with responsibility to ameliorate the suffering of the victim at the hands of the perpetrator. Otherwise, I would be forced to conclude that I am not necessarily my "brother's keeper." This is a position that is unacceptable to normative Judaism. Surely, I am not only permitted, but required by Jewish Law to preserve life at almost any cost. Such lives begin with but do not end with my own. Still, what can and should be done when there are so many brothers and sisters in whose number I may also be counted?

The morality inscribed in the Torah is enacted through laws. These laws are expressed concretely in actions that are accompanied by a burdensome range of details. Human freedom, then, genuinely expresses itself through the assumption of responsibility as measured by the Torah. This is not a mechanistic exercise or one that easily divides itself into parts. "Faith," here, is understood not as something "I have," but rather as fidelity to a way of life. It is in this sense that moral responsibility is the autonomy that renders human beings free and adult.

All of the *mitzvot* except for three may be suspended in order to save a life (*Pikuach Nefesh*), including one's own. The three that may not be abrogated are the practice of idolatry; the shedding of innocent blood; and gross acts of (sexual) immorality. It must be stressed that the distillate of the *mitzvah*, the "Halakah," is determined not simply from texts, but by *posekim* – "decisors" of the law. The limiting case in the prohibition against shedding innocent blood is that I may not actively take the life of someone else to save my own. In other words, if "a" orders "b" to kill "c" or "a" will kill "b," then "b" must resist his normal instinct for self-preservation. This is precisely the situation that the Nazi perpetrators created in order to reinforce the climate of all against all for the victims. These conditions imposed the most terrifying moral dilemma posed to the few remaining Rabbinical authorities in the ghettoes and death camps: Can I save my own life by taking the work permit of someone else? Were the Jewish Councils permitted to issue such cards knowing that saving one would mean the death of another? Is it permissible to save the few for the sake of the many? If so, which ones? These were precisely the kinds of questions asked by the Jews of Levinas' native Kovno to R. Ephraim Oshry, the sole surviving *posek* in Lithuania (see Oshry 1980). What kind of elevated moral sensibility is required even to ask such questions?

As a moral phenomenon, Levinas finds no justification for explaining away the sufferings of others in the name of any exterior ideal. "For an ethical sensibility, confirming, in the inhumanity of our time, its opposition to this inhumanity, the justification of the neighbor's pain is certainly the source of all immorality" (Levinas 1988, 99). If I wish to explain my own suffering to myself, then this may be edifying or cathartic or even morally transformative. Such self-accusation can be the beginning of a consciousness where I intercede for the other. What it must not become is another expression of moral preaching where I would superimpose a meaning on the suffering of the other. Summing up his position Levinas affirms: "*But it may be this risk that this is signified by the very fact that the Jewish condition is consti-*

tuted within humanity" (Levinas 1996, 122).

The reader cannot help but notice that the last word is always pending for Levinas. Conclusions tend to be responses awaiting new questions rather answers that would foreclose enquiry. Hence, the Talmudic position that learning Torah is itself an infinite task. Levinas works at establishing an ethical metaphysics where reason can never take the side of the perpetrator, let alone be employed to implement mass murder.

In the concluding words of his reflection "Nameless," a term used to describe the victims of the Holocaust, Levinas comments on the relation of Judaism to Humanity, the language of anti-Semitism, the disappearance of the Good in Being, and the importance of Jewish Law. Whatever binds Judaism to Humanity is a morality at risk, for the most part without institutions, tested by the force and power of history. It is through its teaching, its laws, "the four cubits of Halakah" (making reference to the Talmudic formula, "Since the day the Temple was destroyed, the Holy One, blessed be He, is only to be found in the four cubits of Halakah," *Berakot* 8a), that Judaism finds the transcendent echo of its historical voice. In other words, there is a morality inscribed in Jewish law to which I am obligated even in the absence of any external support or institution. My conduct is limited in advance by the one place where I find a sense of ethical security: the compass I find within the morality governing Jewish law. This is all we have left without relying on external institutions; the space that isn't anywhere: all that remains to those who are abandoned.

The phenomenon of "election" is here understood as an infinite responsibility for itself and answerable for all of humanity. For Levinas, this sense of infinite responsibility ultimately establishes the subject as fully human, and therefore, binding on every one. The surplus character of this responsibility is an essential part of the Jewish teaching. It is this refusal to abrogate responsibility that the language of anti-Semitism cannot tolerate. "Anti-Semitic language unlike any other is [...] an exterminating language that reveals to all Humanity, through the intermediary of a people chosen to hear it, a nihilistic evocation no other language could evoke" (Levinas 1996, 123). It is in this refusal of nihilism that Judaism is called upon to reaffirm its continuing attachment to ethical discourse even in the midst of inversion or postponement. Such ethical discourse is found in the common language of philosophy when answering to and for the other. Levinas' philosophy affirms that, for traditional Judaism, changes in the course of historical events, however cataclysmic, cannot alter foundational premises concerning the relation of God to humanity or the essential moral relations of human beings to one another.

Literature Cited

Cohen, Richard. 1994. *Elevations: The Highlighting of the Good in Rosenzweig and Levinas.* Chicago: University of Chicago Press.

Levi, Primo. 1961. *Survival in Auschwitz.* New York: MacMillan.

Levinas, Emmanuel. 1979. "To Love the Torah More than God." In *Judaism.* Trans. M.A. Stephenson and R. I. Sugarman with commentary by Richard I. Sugarman. New York: American Jewish College.

Levinas, Emmanuel. 1988. *Existence and Existents.* Trans. Alphonso Lingis. London: Kluwer Academic Publishers.

Levinas, Emmanuel. 1994. *In the Time of the Nations.* Trans. Michael B. Smith. Bloomington Indiana: Indiana University Press.

Levinas, Emmanuel. 1996. *Proper Names.* Trans. Michael B. Smith. Stanford, California: Stanford University Press. 1996.

Levinas, Emmanuel. 1998. *Entre Nous: Thinking-of-the-Other.* Trans. Michael B. Smith and Barbara Harshav. New York: Columbia University Press.

Levinas, Emmanuel. 2000. *God, Death, and Time.* Stanford, California: Stanford University Press.

Oshry, Ephraim. 1980. *Responses to the Holocaust.* New York: Judaica Press.

Schwartz, Yoel, and Yitzack Goldstein. 1995. *SHOAH: A Jewish Perspective on Tragedy in the Context of the Holocaust.* New York: Mesorah.

Recording the Testimonies of Sinti Holocaust Survivors

Gabrielle Tyrnauer

The importance of oral history as a tool for recording the memories of genocide survivors has been repeatedly demonstrated by the Holocaust oral history archives that have sprung up in various parts of the world over the past few decades.

In a speech given to the first colloquium of the Oral History Association in 1966, Alan Nevins, "the father of oral history," traced this form of history to Samuel Johnson, who called for the recording (on paper of course) of the living memories of the survivors of the Great Rebellion as early as 1773. The American writer James Agee pioneered an interview project during the Great Depression (also in the form of written notes), but it was not until the invention of the tape recorder that the history of oral history really began.[1]

From the beginning it was a controversial form of history, which was not acceptable to many academic historians. They questioned the accuracy of memories recorded many years after the event and the biases of participants. But for other scholars, particularly anthropologists, it was seen as a natural extension into the past of a methodology fundamental to their discipline.

The Oral History of Traumatic Events

This is oral history of a very special sort, more sensitive and requiring more training for the interviewers. It has been conducted with survivors of disasters and violence of all kinds. Like other types of oral history, it aims to preserve memories for future generations, collective as well as individual.

Oral history of this type is particularly controversial. Beside the questions of historical accuracy and subjectivity, psychologists and social workers warn of the dangers of reopening old wounds in those interviewed, reviving their

forgotten nightmares. Even members of communities involved often question the utility of this intrusive form of research in helping the group move
on into the future, beyond the traumas of its history. These objections have
frequently been voiced in the context of Holocaust oral history. But the
importance of such testimonies for the survivor who needs to speak of experiences that have been long repressed or ignored by the outside world out-
weighs the pain of remembering.

Oral history is an important weapon in the battle that is under way
against denial and historical revisionism, the attempt to dismiss the historical truth of the Holocaust even while the survivors are alive to tell their stories. Had oral history been in use at the time of the Armenian genocide, perhaps the infamous rhetorical question of Hitler as he was preparing the Final
Solution a scant two decades later "Who now remembers the Armenians?"
would not have been uttered.

Most members of the Jewish community have come to accept the legitimacy and urgency of survivor testimonies. But survivors of the other World
War II genocide, the Sinti and Roma, commonly known as "Gypsies"[2], are
just beginning to come to terms with history. They have been a people without a written language or recorded history of their own. The story of their
appearance in Europe, their centuries-long persecution and the genocide,
has been told in fragments by outsiders. Now a small number among them
are beginning to fight for control over their collective memory. Survivor oral
history, they realize, is one way they can come closer to this goal. As many
of the survivors and younger political activists now recognize, the task
becomes more urgent with every passing year.

In this paper, I will describe my own efforts to record, on audio- and
videotape, the experiences of German Sinti survivors of the Holocaust.

The Accidental Journey

Very little was known about the Gypsy genocide when I began my
research; there was almost no literature on the subject in English.[3] The project began as a kind of accidental journey, a place I stumbled into while looking for something else-and never left. It was a place at once strange and fearfully familiar where my own family's history connected with my research and
drove me into the inner landscape of the Holocaust.

The journey began in 1981, when I was spending the year as a Fellow of
Harvard's Center for European Studies. I received a German government grant
(*Deutscher Akademischer Austauschdienst*) for a study of social change among
German "Gypsies", a subject which, in the preceding few years, I had studied
in the U.S., among the Roma of Washington State and Massachusetts. I

wanted to compare my findings with some European data. I chose Germany because I could speak German and because, as a child of World War II refugees, that country had always held a somewhat morbid attraction for me.

When I arrived at the Frankfurt airport in the spring of 1981, I began the task of preparing for my field work. As my Roma acquaintances in the U.S. had lost their contacts with Europe several generations earlier, I had collected the names of a few academics and museum people who had some knowledge about the subject and contacted them before my departure. One of them invited me to spend my first few days in Frankfurt with her. There I learned much about the current situation of the Sinti, the German Gypsies, and began to network.

Shortly before my departure I had learned that the World Romani Union, the Gypsies' international organization, had scheduled its third international congress in Göttingen, West Germany that May. It seemed like a good place to begin my research.

Göttingen, 1981

I arrived in the medieval university city, eager to plunge into my field work. The Congress was held in the town hall. The setting, the participants and the musical entertainment that went on long into the night could not have been more colorful. But the principal reason for this meeting was not celebration; it was mobilization.

The *Gesellschaft für bedrohte Völker*, a German civil rights organization, had helped to organize the Congress. The mayor gave a reception and many city officials participated. There were some famous guests and speakers, such as Simon Wiesenthal, the renowned "Nazi hunter" from Vienna, and Heinz Galinski, the Berliner who headed the German Jewish community. They were warm supporters of the Romani cause, for reasons that had much to do with their own lives and causes.

The sense of solidarity with Jewish Holocaust survivors expressed at the Congress was extraordinary. They called them *Leidensgenossen* (comrades in suffering). I understood why two prominent Jewish survivors were keynote speakers; also why an Israeli citizen, Miriam Novitch, from the Warsaw ghetto fighters' *kibbutz* (Lohamei Hagetaot) was a delegate, speaker and honored guest. In the months that followed, I was to see this sense of solidarity expressed in many ways. Some Sinti, including their leader Romani Rose, wore a Star of David around their necks. One Gypsy survivor told me in an interview: "If Israel is attacked and has to fight another war, I will send my sons there to fight." Others expressed a longing for a homeland which would, like Israel, provide them with protection and refuge in their diaspora.

I was familiar with the term "Roma", then coming into vogue in many countries to replace the pejorative "Gypsy" or *Zigeuner*. But everywhere at the conference I saw banners with the word "Sinti" as well as "Roma." I had read of Sinti and Lowari and Gitani as subgroups of the nomads who had wandered from Northern India to Europe in the late Middle Ages. However, the two names emblazoned on the banners in Göttingen – Sinti and Roma – were not ethnic or linguistic descriptions, but expressions of political consciousness. They suggested at once rivalry and solidarity. The German Sinti, among the best organized of "Gypsy" groups in Europe, would take second place to none. They would not be subsumed under the name "Roma".

In Göttingen, I came to understand that the glue of this Romani Union was not the cultural similarities or common language of its constituent groups, nor even their long common history of migration and nomadism, but their pariah status in every European country through which they passed, their shared oppression, climaxing in the Nazi genocide. Between a quarter and half a million European Gypsies-approximately one fourth of those living in pre-war Europe – had been murdered by the Nazis simply for the crime of existing.[4]

The ideology on which Nazi Gypsy policy was based derived in part from traditional prejudices, in part from the then current "scientific" theories of eugenics and "racial hygiene". Gypsies, like Jews, were targeted for elimination from national life in Nazi Germany and its conquered territories. Men, women, and children were identified by bureaucrats and "racial scientists", rounded up by the police, incarcerated, and deported in cattle cars to concentration camps throughout the Third Reich, where they were exterminated in massive numbers by slave labor, hunger and disease, bullets and gas. Sometimes they were classified as "asocial", sometimes as "racially inferior", often as both. It made little difference whether they lived as "primitive" nomads or well-assimilated citizens.

The final day of the conference was devoted to oral testimony of Rom and Sinti genocide survivors. Many had never publically spoken of their tragedies. Now they were persuaded by their families, their leaders, their own consciences that the time had come.

It was at this international congress that I decided what my task in Germany would be: to gather as much testimony from these survivors in the form of oral history as they and time would permit.

I made my decision as I was speaking to a survivor of a fascist massacre in Yugoslavia, many of whose relatives had died in the gas chambers of Auschwitz. I had been introduced to him as an American journalist, not an anthropologist, though both identities applied at the time. I did not realize until later what a fortunate thing that was for my rapport with these people.

"Harry," the man to whom I was speaking, was a German Sinto, a Prussian whose forebears were for centuries wandering circus artists and puppeteers. He thought that as a journalist, I could be of help to their cause, as were a number of sympathetic German media people. Copies of a recent article I had written about American Gypsies had been circulated at the conference along with other literature.

When the man asked me where I would be staying, I named the village where my friend from student days lived and he exclaimed that it was close to his own village and immediately invited me to visit him and his family after the end of the conference. I gladly accepted and knew that my field work had truly begun.

I was introduced to the leader of the German Sinti, a charismatic young man named Romani Rose. I heard that he was the child of a Sinto Auschwitz survivor and a German mother; and that "Romani Rose" was his real name, not a "nom de guerre". By the end of the conference, he had been elected vice-president of the international organization. I was to meet with him often during the year that followed, but this first meeting was the most memorable.

I was introduced to him also as an American journalist. He looked at me intensely. There was a moment of silence. Then he asked me in flawless German with a slight regional accent: "Sind Sie jüdisch?" ("Are you Jewish?") He posed the question like a challenge. I was taken aback. I had never been asked such a direct question in Germany and my thoughts were whirling as I groped for an appropriate answer that would at once be honest and express resentment at the intrusiveness. I dismissed all elaborations and simply replied "Ja", unable to guess where the question would lead. Only then did he stretch out his hand and with a voice firm as his handshake said, "Dann sind Sie unter uns willkommen" ("Then you are welcome among us").

The Field Work

The Göttingen congress served as my initiation, it provided me with my passport for the next year. With the help of my first friend in the community, "Harry", the puppeteer I had met in Göttingen, and his wife "Juliana", 20 years his junior-conceived in Chelmno and born the day the war ended-I was able to enter home after home.

I interviewed the survivors and their families with an unobtrusive audio-cassette recorder. They spoke of their lives before the Nazis came to power, of the increasing restrictions during the early years of the National Socialist regime, and of the darkness that overcame them as war approached. They spoke of life in hiding, escapes and recapture; of deportations and concentration camps all over Europe, but especially of Auschwitz, in which almost every family had lost some members. Some of them were the sole survivors of large families. Some had been sterilized. This was the most difficult experience for them to recount. One couple would only speak of it separately, most not at all. Next came other violations of cultural tabus, such as the German command to undress in front of family members, particularly male elders and children. Memories of these forced violations were as painful as torture or the death of loved ones.

The Gypsies, like the Jews, were identified, segregated from the surrounding population and deported East to areas of concentration, euphemistically designated as "resettlement". Their possessions were confiscated, they were transported in trucks and cattle cars, first to regional transit camps, then to concentration camps throughout German-occupied Europe. As new territories were annexed to the German Reich, their Gypsy inhabitants became stateless and thus could be deported with few formalities.

"I was picked up at my workplace in Düsseldorf," Moses A. said. "I did not know where I would go. My cousin was in the *Wehrmacht*. I thought that would protect me, so I went to see him. But soon he and his whole family were in Auschwitz." There were many reports of Gypsies in *Wehrmacht* uniforms saluting the guards as they entered the gates of Auschwitz.

Most Gypsy survivors report their initial arrest and deportation in terms that reflected shock and anomie. While nomadic Roma were more accustomed to periodic police razzias, even for them, these roundups had a different flavor. The police were often accompanied by the ever present racial scientists.

But the greater shock came to the more sedentary Sinti. A common theme of many of the Sinti interviewees was "aber wir waren gar nicht vorgestraft" ("we were not previously convicted"). Philomena Franz, one of the few Sinti survivors who wrote about their experiences, describes her reaction when she was arrested in 1943 at the factory where she had worked for three years: "It came like a blow with a hammer-to the middle of my face" (Franz 1985, 38). Like other sedentary Sinti, she did not believe that Auschwitz (of which she had heard) had anything to do with her. After all, her brother was in the *Wehrmacht*, wounded in the service of the *Führer*. She had been examined by the racial scientists who had determined "that I am a pure blooded Indian [...]. What did these people understand as Aryan? Whatever they wanted" (Franz 1985, 38).

This statement reflects the paradox of Nazi policy and practice with respect to Gypsies who – according to the writings of earlier German scholars – were the European ethnic group closest to the mythical racial Aryans. Yet through centuries of interaction, German society had labelled them as undesirables, "asocials".

From the early 1940s – following a special meeting organized by Reinhardt Heydrich in 1939 – Poland became the final destination of Gypsies, as of Jews. The plan formulated at the Heydrich meeting applied to all Gypsies in Greater Germany, estimated by the racial scientist enumerators, to be approximately 30,000. In 1940 the first 3,000 were sent to Poland (Kenrick and Puxon 1972, 139).

The special sections of Jewish ghettos reserved for Gypsies were usually fenced off areas designed to isolate them from the rest of the ghetto population. In the Lodz ghetto, for example, 5,000 Gypsies were interned between 1941 and 1942. The typhus epidemic which decimated them led to the further deportation of the remnants to the extermination centers at Chelmno and Treblinka. The Gypsy section of the Lodz ghetto was then closed. Gypsies were also concentrated in special sections of other Polish ghettos, including Warsaw, Radom, Cracow, and Chelm.

The office in charge of the deportation to ghettos of both Jews and Gypsies was IVB4, headed by Adolf Eichmann. Responsibility was shared by the *Kriminalpolizei* (criminal police) under Colonel Arthur Nebe.

In reply to a telegram from Nebe requesting information as to where to send the Gypsies in his custody in Berlin, Eichmann wired on 16 October 1939: "With regard to the deportation of Gypsies, the first transport (of Jews) from Vienna is announced for Friday October 30th. Three to four trucks of Gypsies can be attached to this transport [...]" (Kenrick and Puxon 1972, 77). This was the method which Eichmann recommended for the entire Gypsy deportation and which was, to a large extent, implemented, sometimes with trucks, at other times with cattle cars.

In preparation for the transports to Poland, the Gypsies were placed in regional holding camps. Some of these, like Lackenbach, in the Austrian Burgenland, was set up with the cooperation of the governing councils of various communities in the area.

The ultimate destination of all apprehended Gypsies in Germany after Himmler's infamous Auschwitz decree of 16 December 1942 was the "family camp" at Auschwitz-Birkenau, generally referred to as the *Zigeunerlager* (Gypsy camp). Some 20,000 Gypsies from all parts of Europe were registered there and several thousand more were believed to have been sent directly to the gas chambers.

As in the ghettos, the Gypsy camp, which adjoined the crematoria at Birkenau, was fenced off and isolated from the rest of the camp. But most Jewish survivors of Auschwitz-Birkenau who were in the camp that summer night of 1944 when the entire Gypsy camp was liquidated were aware of what had taken place. Some, whose barracks were located nearby, recalled hearing the screams long into the night.

The Video Project

In the early 1990s, I became associated with "Living Testimonies", a McGill University Holocaust oral history project. I received a contract from Yale University's Fortunoff Videoarchive for Holocaust Testimonies to do 20 hours of interviews with German Sinti survivors. It was to be the first Gypsy testimony in any North American Holocaust archive. Beside Yale, two Canadian Universities, McGill and Concordia, contributed to the project.

In the summer of 1992 I went to Europe to prepare the way for the later arrival of my cameraman and now independent producer, William Kerrigan. He spoke no German, had little knowledge of the subject but was skilled and enthusiastic.

In the weeks preceding his arrival, I found many of my earlier contacts, particularly the family of "Harry" and "Juliana", with whom I had remained in touch during the years since my first field trip. Once again they became my guides and provided me entrees for this more difficult undertaking, which involved the greater formality of cameras, lights, and the presence of another outsider. I believe it would not have been possible without my previous work and the cooperation of key informants who had become my friends.

The cameraman and I worked as a team, each with our areas of expertise. We did two, sometimes three interviews a day in two encampments. By this time Germany had been reunified and many Sinti conducted their business of buying and selling in the border towns of the former GDR. On our final day in the field, we squeezed in an extra interview with "Harry" by my taking over his role of chauffeur to "Juliana" in her *hausieren* (selling from house to house) rounds. Her work, as that of most other Sinti women, was the principal source of the family income. While I drove her around, Bill assumed my role as interviewer – though he knew no German and "Harry" only a few words of English – in addition to his own role as cameraman. This was accomplished when I wrote the same questions in German for "Harry", in English for Bill. It was a good interview!

The two encampments in which we interviewed were near the city of Hof, almost on the Czech border. In most cases, the interviewees were closely related people living in different worlds. "Harry" and "Juliana" lived in the smaller, more traditional type of encampment. Their group, or *Kumpania*, had made an arrangement with a farmer for the use of a corner of one of his fields. The sanitary facilities were deplorable: one bathroom for some 15 families, with an improvised outdoor water tap. Although they lived in large modern trailers, they could not use their individual bathrooms on account of cultural tabus. All cooking and washing of dishes took place outdoors, usually under a canopy attached to their trailers. There was much music making and drinking and celebration. The women went *hausieren* as they always had in neighboring villages. Some of the men were involved in other independent occupations, such as the buying and selling of antiques and musical instruments.

The other, larger encampment was about 10 kilometers away, in a well-kept camping area presided over by a fundamentalist Protestant minister. The sanitary facilities were good, there was no drinking of alcohol and there were revival camp meetings to which outsiders came and members of the group provided musical accompaniment.

The evangelical missionary movement had made considerable inroads among Sinti and Roma in Germany and elsewhere in Europe. Sometimes it had split families along ideological and economic lines. The superior facilities enjoyed by the evangelical group were obviously due to the presence of the pastor and his family living among them in a trailer of their own. Through him, they had access to many goods and services unavailable to the more traditional Sinti. Fortunately, he was sympathetic to our project and helpful in pointing out families with survivors in the camp and persuading those who were reluctant to be interviewed. They interspersed their Holocaust testimony with little homilies on forgiveness and religious testimonials to the powers of the Deity and their pastor.

Due to the nature of the medium, the video interviews were more structured than most of those I had done on audiotape, which often included long digressions and rambling. In those early interviews, especially, when I knew I was on uncharted ground, I tried to get as much information as possible in any way possible; rapport was most important. Often I switched off the machine at the interviewee's request, usually when he or she began to speak about very personal matters or those related to cultural tabus. Then I would record my observations in the traditional written field notes. The videotaped interviews, on the other hand, were carefully planned both technically and in terms of time and content. We had only ten days to film in Germany.

The videotapes have been partially transcribed and translated into English with the help of the Center for Holocaust Studies at the University of Vermont. A small grant from the Jewish Community Foundation of Montreal helped with further transcriptions. About a quarter of the tapes still remain untranscribed. Translations were begun at the University of Vermont. Funding for these tasks was difficult to find and came in slow increments.

Copies of the videotapes have been deposited in archives of two American universities (Yale University and the University of Vermont) and two Canadian ones (McGill and Concordia).

The Politics of Collective Memory

The discrepancy between the frequently expressed approval of this work of memory by Holocaust scholars, who generally acknowledge its importance to Holocaust history, and the unavailability of funds for carrying it out is a reminder that memory and memorializing are also expressions of power. The powerless remain without access to resources. Their cries of anguish remain unheard and are soon forgotten. The crimes against them go unpunished. No one was prosecuted at Nuremberg for crimes against Gypsies. Although individual German Sinti have attempted to prosecute Germans they believed responsible for crimes against them, there were no convictions until 1992, when former SS Auschwitz guard Ernst-August Koenig was sentenced to life imprisonment for three individual killings but absolved of the crime of genocide.[5] When Sinti survivors in Germany applied for reparations in the 1950s, the West German Supreme Court ruled that their deportation was a measure of crime prevention.[6] Yet the crimes against them were real, though the victims long remained silent and invisible. They had no homeland, they were – and still are – unwanted everywhere; they had no spokesmen in the parliaments of nations.

There were a few exceptions in Europe, the most notable in Tito's Yugoslavia, where the Gypsies had a flag, a representative in the Macedonian Parliament, schools, and cultural activities. In fact, it was rumoured that Tito himself was a Rom.

For a time there was a movement to establish a Romanistan – a Gypsy national homeland in India or elsewhere. This idea has long since been abandoned. Romanistan, they now say, is a place in the heart.

There were other memorials too, resulting not from a change of heart in the oppressors and bystanders but from the politicization and organization of the victims who had learned the lessons of political pressure and where it can be most effectively applied. There are now monuments in several concentration camps including Auschwitz, Buchenwald, and Ravensbrück. There is the impressive Sinti and Roma cultural center and exhibit in Heidelberg, home of Romani Rose. Unlike other museums devoted to

Gypsies, the permanent exhibit does not primarily focus on the culture of the colorful nomads who for centuries had peopled European landscape and artistic imagination (an approach which often reinforces existing stereotypes). It is a moving Holocaust exhibit, designed to educate and correct the omissions and distortions of a history created by outsiders.

As a result of demonstrations and political pressure by American Romanis and their non-Gypsy supporters, an educated and assimilated Hungarian-American Rom from Minneapolis in the music business, William Duna, was seated on the U.S. Holocaust Memorial Council as the single Gypsy representative; a Romani college professor, Ian Hancock, was appointed consultant and the present author was contracted to produce a report on the fate of Gypsies during the Holocaust. A Gypsy exhibit (considered inadequate by many Romani leaders) was included in the Washington museum that the Council created – the U.S. Holocaust Memorial Museum.

The international Romani Union has consultative status at the U.N. The Council of Europe has examined its grievances and eventually made humane treatment of its Gypsy minority an entrance requirement for new former East bloc applicants. International human rights organizations such as Helsinki Watch have monitored the treatment of Gypsies in various countries where they form a sizeable minority.[7] The U.N. High Commissioner for Refugees commissioned a report on the situation of Roma in central and eastern Europe (Braham 1993).

The new constitutions of the former East bloc countries guarantee them freedom, equality and sometimes nationality. But Europe-wide polls better portray the popular mind. "Gypsies" come out of them as the most despised minority. The liberal Czech president Vaclav Havel has expressed solidarity with them and described prejudice and discrimination against them as "the breeding ground which produced the Holocaust" and compared his bigoted fellow citizens to "the thousands of inconspicuous, non-murdering anti-Semites who helped send their fellow citizens to the gas chambers" (Helsinki Watch, 1992).

Yet, despite this high level of support, a few years later the Roma of the Czech Republic were fleeing to Canada and other western lands in desperate search of asylum from the hatred of those fellow citizens. Refugees were streaming out of Rumania, Hungary, and other central and east European "new democracies", where the situation of the Gypsy minority has deteriorated dramatically since the fall of Communism. The socialist governments in central and eastern Europe, many now feel, protected them from the hatred of the majority. Many of my German Sinti informants said, "We should rebuild the Berlin wall to keep the skinheads out."

The uninterrupted continuity of old hatreds and the rise of new ones can also be documented by oral history as well as by the polls. The slide from prejudice to hatred, from discrimination to persecution, from persecution to genocide has been seen to happen again and again. None can document these changes like the survivors of earlier genocides.

It is the moral obligation of the communities to which these survivors belong to share their resources with those who are newly endangered, or have not yet had the opportunity to tell their tragic story. The process has already been launched as Holocaust archives reach out to their Romani fellow sufferers under the Nazis: Armenian communities sponsor comparative genocide conferences and publications. This activity, combined with old and new war crimes trials still taking place, may be the largest steps towards the prevention of genocide in this new century. The establishment of an international war crimes tribunal has given new hopes for the victims of "crimes against humanity." But the work has barely begun and, for survivors of the World War II genocides, there is little time left.

Documentation of these crimes through oral history, a method dependent on the technology of audio- and video-recording, has come too late for many, such as most survivors of the Armenian genocide. For survivors of the Holocaust it appeared on the scene only a few years after the events which were to be recorded, though the recording of Jewish testimonies did not begin until decades later. For the Gypsies, however, changes in technology made little difference. They were a people without written history, because they lacked the power and will and resources to record it. With few exceptions, it was the *gaje* or non-Gypsies who recorded what little there is and wrote the few publications on the subject. And interestingly enough, many of these were themselves Jewish Holocaust survivors or refugees.[8]

Aside from this moral imperative, the eye-witness testimonies of "Gypsy" survivors are of great historical importance. They will help to fill blank spaces in Holocaust history, supplementing and confirming Jewish testimony, providing information to combat the spreading poison of Holocaust denial. The Romani survivors can provide vivid details of the regimes in Auschwitz and other concentration camps, the activities of SS functionaries, the medical experiments, etc.

The interest of Romani leaders-particularly German ones – in combating Holocaust denial – has long been evident. "Harry" once provided me with a large stack right wing and neo-Nazi German newspapers, each of which contained one or more pejorative articles about the Gypsies.

The closed character of Gypsy society and the great fear that its members have of government officials, police, bureaucrats, and scholars, at whose hands they have experienced so much suffering, makes this oral history the more difficult and the more urgent.

The choice of interviewers is a sensitive matter. Many survivors recalled clearly how teams of scholars from a variety of biological and social disciplines came to them in their homes and encampments, even to the detention and concentration camps to measure their skulls and ask them about their relatives. Some of the Nazi researchers even spoke their language. Never again would they trust curious German scholars.

I was often told by my informants that it was only because I was a *Leidensgenossin* that made it possible for them to speak to me. If I asked too many questions, my friend "Harry" would begin to call me *Lolitchai* (literally, the red-headed one), which was the Sinti nickname for Eva Justin, one of the most notorious of the racial "scientists", who recommended mass sterilization for the Gypsies. "Harry" and "Juliana's" dog was named "Lolitchai".

Several German universities had "Gypsy projects" in the early 1980s. They were primarily studying the social service agencies' attempts at integration of Gypsies into West German national life or special problems and needs of this minority. They studied them as an ethnic group with a language, folklore, and traditions but without a past. One of these projects even made a collective decision *not* to study Romanes, the language of their informants, a decision virtually without precedent in the history of anthropology. The shadow of the *unbewältigte Vergangenheit*, the "unmastered past", fell heavily on all their endeavors.

Conclusion

As we embark on a new century, a new millennium, the burdens of the past are still with us and will remain so as long as there are living survivors of the Holocaust who are haunted by the traumatic events of that era. These memories should be recorded, while time permits. The massive effort and support coming from the Shoah Foundation and the U.S. Holocaust Memorial Museum greatly accelerated this process for the Jewish survivors; where is the Romani equivalent? Now that the leaders of "Gypsy" communities in many countries are receptive to the idea of such documentation, where are the comparable resources to make it possible?

Ideally, this research should be conducted and funded by an international foundation, or an agency like the United Nations with the cooperation of Romani national and international organizations. The interviewers should work in interdisciplinary teams that include social scientists, oral historians, and psychologists. Interviewers must be trained in the techniques of oral history of traumatic events and must be knowledgeable about their subject.

There should be members of the group being interviewed among them.

Analysis of the data can be postponed, but gathering it can not. It is well past the eleventh hour.

Notes

I would like to thank my husband and colleague, Charles Stastny, but for whose love and determination, under the most difficult of circumstances, this essay would never have been written.

[1]The first oral history program was established by Nevins at Columbia University in the late 1940s when the audiotape recorder was still in its infancy. The tape recorder grew to be an essential tool to oral history. More recently it has been supplemented and often replaced by the video recorder. This project has utilized both.

[2]This term – like American "Indians" – is based on a geographical misapprehension: Gypsies did not come from Egypt. Neither did they belong to the Greek heretical sect, the Atsiganio, which provided another name for them in many other European languages: e.g. *Zigeuner* in German, *Tsigane* in French, etc. While the term in all these languages has become charged with derogatory associations, no other word that covers the many subgroups – all of which have names for themselves – has replaced it. Among the educated and politicized, "Rom" has been used as a more acceptable substitute, but this also has problems. In international circles "Romani" is favored (as in "Romani Union") but this is the term traditionally applied to English Gypsies. So, by default, the term "Gypsy" is still widely used by the people themselves and others, and will be used here, but always in mental, if not physical, quotation marks. Sometimes it will be used interchangeably with "Romani".

[3]Hilberg was a pioneer among early Holocaust scholars in recognizing the destruction of the Gypsies as an integral part of Holocaust history. He has 18 entries for Gypsies in the index and gives the genocide of the Gypsies as the first example of the expansion of the Nazi destructive machinery and process that systematically engulfed Jews, Gypsies, and other groups. The structure of the destructive process – *definition, concentration,* and *annihilation* – was applied to Gypsies as to Jews by the German bureaucracy of murder.

[4]The figure is based on estimates of Kenrick and Puxon (1972), recently revised downward by Kenrick. Some scholars and Romani activists claim the true figures are much higher. Official spokespersons for the German government also accepted these figures. But Lewy criticizes this figure because "No sources of breakdown by country have been provided for this estimate which makes it of questionable value." At the same time, he admits that "no exact count will ever by available" (2000, 222).

[5]The prosecutor in this trial of an Auschwitz SS guard dropped the charge of participation in genocide on the grounds that no order for carrying out such a program against Gypsies had been proven.

[6]In 1956 the Federal Supreme Court ruled that the deportation of Gypsies before 16 December 1942 – the date of Himmler's Auschwitz decree consigning all Gypsies to Auschwitz – was not racially motivated but on grounds of national security (Kenrick and Puxon 1972).

[7]Helsinki Watch has produced monographs on the Roma of the Czech Republic, Hungary, Rumania and Bulgaria.

[8]For further bibliographic references see Tyrnauer (1991).

Literature Cited

Braham, Mark. 1993. *The Untouchables. A Survey of the Roma People of Central and Eastern Europe*. Geneva: Office of the United Nations High Commissioner of Refugees.

Franz, Philomena. 1987. *Zwischen Liebe und Hass*. Freiburg: Herder.

Helsinki Watch. 1992. *Struggling for Ethnic Identity: Czechoslovakia's Endangered Gypsies*. New York: Human Rights Watch.

Hilberg, Raul. 1961. *The Destruction of the European Jews*. Chicago: Quadrangle Books.

Kenrick, Donald, and Grattan Puxon. 1972. *The Destiny of Europe's Gypsies*. New York: Basic Books.

Lewy, Guenter. 2000. *The Nazi Persecution of the Gypsies*. New York: Oxford.

Tyrnauer, Gabrielle. 1991. *Holocaust: A Bibliography and Introductory Essay*. Montreal: Institute for Genocide Studies.

Tyrnauer, Gabrielle. 1981-1992. Unpublished transcriptions of audio- and video-taped oral history interviews with Sinti survivors of the Holocaust.

About the Contributors

Howard Ball is Professor of Political Science at the University of Vermont. His fields of study include civil rights, constitutional law, the U.S. Supreme Court, and the international laws of war and war crimes. He has published numerous books in these areas, including his biography of Thurgood Marshall, entitled *A Defiant Life* (1999). He has also published dozens of articles in law reviews, political science, and public administration journals.

Robert Bernheim is a former high school teacher of eleven years in Maine and Vermont. He is currently completing his Ph.D. degree in German History at McGill University in Montréal. Working under the direction of Professor Peter Hoffmann, his dissertation is entitled *The Seventh German Army Command and the Commissar Order: 22 June 1941 - 31 January 1942.*

Jonathan Huener is Assistant Professor of History at the University of Vermont, where he teaches courses on German history, the Holocaust, and modern European history. His book *German Deeds, Polish Soil, Jewish Shoah: Auschwitz Memory and the Politics of Commemoration* addresses the meaning, symbolism, and political instrumentalization of the Auschwitz site in the postwar era, and is forthcoming with Ohio University Press.

Carroll McC. Lewin is Associate Professor of Anthropology at the University of Vermont. She received her B.A. from Oberlin College in 1965 and Ph.D. from Brandeis University in 1971. Professor Lewin's extensive research in Holocaust Studies has focused on the activities of the Jewish Councils (*Judenräte*) and on the intersection of memory and narrative in accounts on the Holocaust.

Yehudi Lindeman is Associate Professor of English at McGill University in Montréal. He is the founder and past director of Living Testimonies, the Holocaust Video Archive at McGill. Professor Lindeman has published widely on Renaissance poetry and translation. One of his books is a critical edition with translation of the neo-Latin playwright Macropedius.

Wolfgang Mieder is Professor of German and Folklore and chairperson of the Department of German and Russian at the University of Vermont. With David Scrase he co-edited *The Holocaust: Introductory Essays* (1996) and *The Holocaust: Personal Accounts* (2001). Among his books are *Proverbs Are Never Out of Season: Popular Wisdom in the Modern Age* (1993) and *The Politics of Proverbs: From Traditional Wisdom to Proverbial Stereotypes* (1997).

Francis R. Nicosia is Professor of History at Saint Michael's College in Vermont. He is author of *The Third Reich and the Palestine Question* (2000), co-author with Donald Niewyk of *The Columbia Guide to the Holocaust* (2000), and co-editor with Lawrence Stokes of *Germans Against Nazism: Non-Conformity, Opposition, and Resistance in the Third Reich* (1990). He is also the author of numerous articles on the history of Nazi Germany and the Holocaust.

Robert D. Rachlin is president and senior director of the law firm of Downs Rachlin & Martin PLLC in Burlington, Vermont. He received his A.B. from Yale University and J. D. from the University of Chicago Law School. He was State's Attorney of Caledonia County (Vermont) from 1961-1964. He is chair of the Advisory Board of the University of Vermont Center for Holocaust Studies.

David Scrase is Professor of German in the Department of German and Russian and Director of the Center for Holocaust Studies at the University of Vermont. He has written on and translated contemporary German literature and is especially interested in the Holocaust and post-war German writing. With Wolfgang Mieder he co-edited *The Holocaust: Introductory Essays* (1996) and *The Holocaust: Personal Accounts* (2001).

David Shiman is Professor of Education and Director of the Center for World Education in the College of Education and Social Services at the University of Vermont. He teaches courses in the sociology of education, comparative education, and global and multicultural education. His publications include: *The Prejudice Book: Activities for the Classroom Teacher* (1994), *Economic and Social Justice: A Human Rights Perspective* (1999), and *Teaching Human Rights* (1999).

Richard Sugarman is Associate Professor of Religion at the University of Vermont. He teaches courses on Philosophy and Contemporary Jewish Thought, including a seminar on moral and religious perspectives on the Holocaust. He is the author of *Rancor Against Time: The Phenomenology of Ressentiment* (1976), and he has translated and commented on the philosophy of Emmanuel Levinas.

Gabrielle Tyrnauer is an anthropologist by training and the Co-Director of the Refugee Research Project at McGill University at Montréal in Canada. She has also served as the Associate Director of Living Testimonies, a project for videotaping oral histories of Jewish and Gypsy Holocaust survivors. Her major research interest is concentrated on the fate of Gypsies during the Holocaust.